Controlling W
the easy

Books Available

By the same authors:

BP525	Controlling Windows XP the easy way*
BP522	Microsoft Works Suite 2002 explained
BP514	Windows XP explained*
BP513	Internet Explorer 6 and Outlook Express 6 explained*
BP512	Microsoft Access 2002 explained
BP511	Microsoft Excel 2002 explained
BP510	Microsoft Word 2002 explained
BP509	Microsoft Office XP explained
BP505	Microsoft Works Suite 2001 explained
BP498	Using Visual Basic
BP493	Windows Me explained*
BP491	Windows 2000 explained*
BP487	Quicken 2000 UK explained*
BP488	Internet Explorer 5 explained*
BP486	Using Linux the easy way*
BP478	Microsoft Works 2000 explained
BP474	Microsoft Access 2000 explained
BP473	Microsoft Excel 2000 explained
BP472	Microsoft Word 2000 explained
BP471	Microsoft Office 2000 explained
BP465	Lotus SmartSuite Millennium explained
BP456	Windows 98 explained*
BP448	Lotus SmartSuite 97 explained
BP433	Your own Web site on the Internet
BP429	MS-Excel 97 explained
BP428	MS-Word 97 explained
BP426	MS-Office 97 explained
BP420	E-mail on the Internet*
BP409	MS Office 95 one step at a time
BP408	Access 95 one step at a time
BP407	Excel 95 explained
BP406	MS Word 95 explained
BP388	Why not personalise your PC
BP341	MS-DOS explained
BP284	Programming in QuickBASIC
BP259	A Concise Introduction to UNIX*
BP258	Learning to Program in C

If you would like to purchase a Companion Disc for any of the listed books by the same authors, apart from the ones marked with an asterisk, containing the file/program listings which appear in them, then fill in the form at the back of the book and send it to Phil Oliver at the stipulated address.

Controlling Windows XP the easy way

by

N. Kantaris
and
P.R.M. Oliver

Bernard Babani (publishing) Ltd
The Grampians
Shepherds Bush Road
London W6 7NF
England

www.babanibooks.com

Please Note

Although every care has been taken with the production of this book to ensure that any projects, designs, modifications and/or programs, etc., contained herewith, operate in a correct and safe manner and also that any components specified are normally available in Great Britain, the Publishers and Author(s) do not accept responsibility in any way for the failure (including fault in design) of any project, design, modification or program to work correctly or to cause damage to any equipment that it may be connected to or used in conjunction with, or in respect of any other damage or injury that may be so caused, nor do the Publishers accept responsibility in any way for the failure to obtain specified components.

Notice is also given that if equipment that is still under warranty is modified in any way or used or connected with home-built equipment then that warranty may be void.

First Published - June 2002

British Library Cataloguing in Publication Data:

A catalogue record for this book is available from the British Library

ISBN 0 85934 525 4

Cover Design by Gregor Arthur
Printed and Bound in Great Britain by Cox & Wyman Ltd, Reading

About this Book

Controlling Windows XP the easy way was written to help both the beginner and those moving from older versions of Windows to the Windows XP Professional or Home edition (the latter being a cut-down version of the former). The material in the book is presented in the new Tasks pane approach adopted by Microsoft in Windows XP which leads to a much easier way of understanding and using the various Windows features which we are sure will benefit both newcomers and veterans of the Windows environment alike.

Although Windows XP can be made to appear similar to previous versions of Windows, which might appeal to veterans of the Windows environment, doing so can bypass a lot of the new features built into this latest version. As in previous versions of Windows, this version includes all the usual built-in accessories such as a text editor, a word processor, a paint program, a drawing facility, and many other features multimedia (including Media Player 8), networking, electronic communications (Outlook Express for e-mail and Internet Explorer for browsing the Web). However, all these accessories are covered already in detail in another book by us entitled *Windows XP explained* (BP514). If e-mail and browsing the Web are you passion, then may we suggest our book *Internet Explorer 6 and Outlook Express 6 explained* (BP513), both published by Bernard Babani (publishing) Ltd.

In this book, after a general overview of the package and an introduction on the common Windows XP interface (included here for the sake of completeness), we mainly concentrate on the controlling features of Windows XP as they appear in the new **Category View** of the **Control Panel**. Additional topics associated with this control are also covered. In general, we discuss such topics as: New features in Windows XP; Appearance and Themes; Printers and other Hardware; Internet and Network Connections; User Accounts; Add or Remove Programs; Date, Time, Language, and Regional Options; Sound and Audio Devices; Accessibility Options; and Performance and Maintenance.

Like the rest of our computer books, this book was written with the busy person in mind - you don't need to read many hundreds of large format pages to find out most of what there is to know about the subject, when fewer pages can get you going quite adequately! Also, an attempt has been made not to use too much 'jargon', but with this subject, some is inevitable, so a fairly detailed but relevant glossary of terms is included, which should be used with the text of this book where necessary.

It is hoped that with the help of this book, you will be able to get the most out of your computer, when using Windows XP, in terms of efficiency and productivity, and that you will be able to do it in the shortest, most effective and enjoyable way. Have fun!

About the Authors

Noel Kantaris graduated in Electrical Engineering at Bristol University and after spending three years in the Electronics Industry in London, took up a Tutorship in Physics at the University of Queensland. Research interests in Ionospheric Physics, led to the degrees of M.E. in Electronics and Ph.D. in Physics. On return to the UK, he took up a Post-Doctoral Research Fellowship in Radio Physics at the University of Leicester, and then a lecturing position in Electrical Engineering at the Camborne School of Mines, Cornwall, (part of Exeter University), where he was also the CSM Computing Manager. At present he is IT Director of FFC Ltd.

Phil Oliver graduated in Mining Engineering at Camborne School of Mines and has specialised in most aspects of surface mining technology, with a particular emphasis on computer related techniques. He has worked in Guyana, Canada, several Middle Eastern and Asian countries, South Africa and the United Kingdom, on such diverse projects as: the planning and management of bauxite, iron, gold and coal mines; rock excavation contracting in the UK; international mining equipment sales and international mine consulting. He then took up a lecturing position at Camborne School of Mines (part of Exeter University) in Surface Mining and Management. He has since retired from full-time lecturing, to spend more time writing, consulting and developing Web sites for clients.

Acknowledgements

We would like to thank friends and colleagues, for their helpful tips and suggestions which assisted us in the writing of this book.

Trademarks

HP and LaserJet are registered trademarks of Hewlett Packard Corporation.

IBM is a registered trademark of International Business Machines, Inc.

Intel is a registered trademark of Intel Corporation.

Microsoft, **MS-DOS**, **Windows**, **Windows NT**, **Windows Me**, and **Windows XP**, are either registered trademarks or trademarks of Microsoft Corporation.

PostScript is a registered trademark of Adobe Systems Incorporated.

All other brand and product names used in the book are recognised as trademarks, or registered trademarks, of their respective companies.

Contents

1

Windows XP Overview

Windows XP (XP for eXPerience) comes in two versions; the Home edition (less expensive) as a direct upgrade to Windows 98/Me for home users and the Professional edition (more expensive but with additional functionality) for Windows 2000 or business users. Of course, provided you are running Windows 98/Me or Windows 2000, you can upgrade to either version of Windows XP.

At first glance, Windows XP looks slightly different to previous versions of Windows. The changes to the desktop, ***start*** menu and the **Control Panel** are only too obvious, while other concepts are borrowed from Windows Me or Windows 2000. Windows XP has many improvements incorporated into it which fall into several general categories. These are:

- Added features that make Windows XP load faster than any previous version of Windows, run more reliably, and the ability to return to a previous working version of the Operating System (similar to that under Windows Me) if a newly installed program causes errors in your system.
- Improved Wizards (similar to those under Windows Me) let you set up home networks a lot easier and gives you the ability to share Internet connections.
- Improved support for digital cameras, video recorders, and multimedia with an improved version of the **Windows Media Player** (now version 8).
- Improved features and tools in **Internet Explorer 6** allow faster performance, and better Web communication from e-mail (using version 6 of **Outlook Express**) to instant messaging to video conferencing using the **MSN Explorer** - a simple program that combines the functions of Hotmail, Internet Explorer, Windows Messenger, and Windows Media Player.

The most apparent change in Windows XP is the adoption of the Tasks pane which allows easy manipulation of files and folders, and the ability to carry out a host of other operations, such as printing, scanning, faxing, downloading or publishing information on the Web, much easier and quicker than in previous versions of Windows. In Windows XP the content of a Tasks pane changes to accommodate what you are doing at the time, so you don't have to dig deep into the Windows menus to find out what you want to do as in previous versions of the Operating System.

Microsoft has designed the Tasks pane approach to make it easier for newcomers to the Windows environment and it is this approach that we adopt and explain in this book. Whether you are new to Windows or an experienced user of a previous version of Windows, we hope you will find this book useful in explaining and using the Tasks pane approach which should result in a more efficient way of using Windows XP.

Although we have used Windows XP Professional Edition to write this book, it is equally valid for the Windows XP Home Edition, as the Professional Edition offers all the capabilities of the Home Edition plus additional features designed to meet the needs of the business community. These enhancements provide more options for networking computers with added security and simplified management.

Windows XP Professional also includes features for power users, such as enhanced file security, remote access to your computer's desktop and a personal Web server. However, most home PC users will find that Windows XP Home Edition contains all the facilities they will ever need or want. Which version you choose will ultimately be your choice with the price differential being a factor to be taken into account.

In what follows, we assume that Windows XP has been installed on your computer and is up and running. If you need information on such important topics as how to upgrade, what system preparation to make before installing Windows XP, what the hardware requirements are, or which file system to select, then may we suggest you refer to our other book *Windows XP explained* (BP 514) also published by Bernard Babani (publishing) Ltd.

Starting Windows XP

Switching on your PC automatically loads Windows XP (or displays the dual-boot option, if you have another Operating System on your hard disc).

The Windows Desktop

Below we show the Windows XP working screen, called the 'Desktop', with one item on the bottom right of it identified as the **Recycle Bin**. In addition, the ***start*** button at the bottom left corner of the Windows screen has been left-clicked to display the two-column ***start*** menu. By default the left column provides shortcuts to **Internet Explorer**, **Outlook Express** and the six applications that have been used most often.

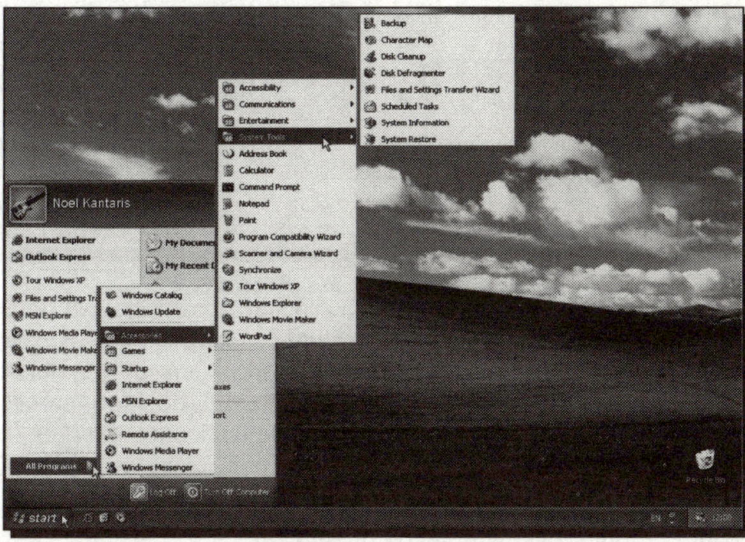

Fig. 1.1 The Windows XP Start Cascade Menu.

On the top of the right-hand column there are shortcuts to such folders as **My Documents**, **My Pictures**, **My Music** and **My Computer**, while on the bottom of the column there are shortcuts to **Control Panel**, **Printers and Faxes**, **Help and Support** and **Search** facility.

Hovering with the mouse pointer over the **All Programs** button, displays the first column of the cascade menu where all Windows applications are to be found. In the screen dump in Fig. 1.1 on the previous page we show the System Tools options which are part of the Windows Accessories.

At the top of the ***start*** menu the name of the current user is displayed with a picture against it. Left-clicking this picture opens the User Accounts screen shown in Fig. 1.2.

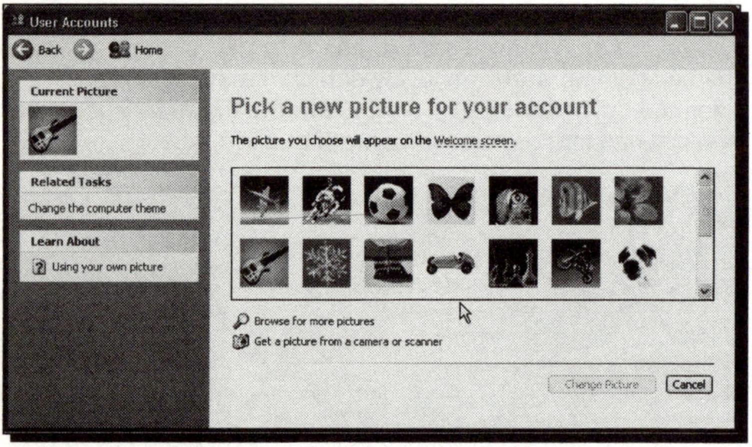

Fig. 1.2 The User Accounts Dialogue Box.

From here you can choose a different picture for the current user either from the ones supplied or from one of your own. You can also change the Computer's theme, desktop, screen savers, etc. Most of these facilities will be discussed later on.

As we mentioned earlier, new to Windows XP is the ability of the first of its two-column menus to adapt to the way you use your computer - an adaptation of what was first introduced with Windows Me. It keeps track of what features and programs you use the most and adds them to the list on the left column. For example, if you use the **Notepad** by selecting from the Accessories sub-menu, next time you click the ***start*** button you will see this application pinned to the bottom of the first column of the ***start*** menu. This saves time as you don't have to scroll through menu lists to find the application you want to use.

To remove an application from the first column of the ***start*** menu, right-click it and select **Remove from this List**. This removes the name of the application from the list, not the application itself from your hard disc. Try it.

Parts of a Window

It is worth spending some time looking at the various parts that make up the Windows screen - we use the word 'Windows' to refer to the whole environment, while the word 'windows' refers to application or document windows. Below we show **My Computer** which is opened by clicking on the ***start*** button and then clicking its shortcut entry on the top-right column of the displayed menu. To see what appears below, left-click the **View** menu command and select **List** from the displayed sub-menu.

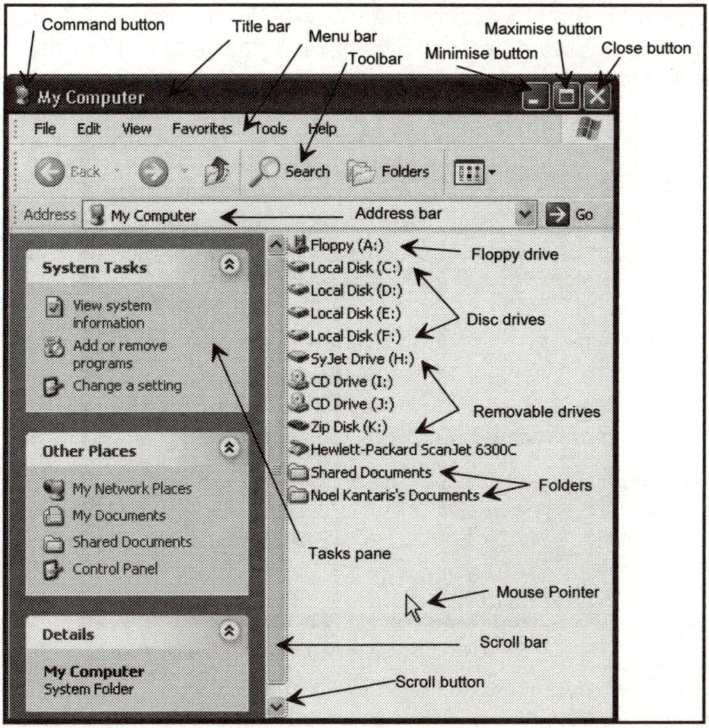

Fig. 1.3 The My Computer Screen.

Application windows contain running applications, while document windows appear with applications that can open more than one document, but share the application window's menu. Each application, and some documents you choose to work with, open and use separate windows to run in. Although every window has some common elements, not all windows use all of these elements.

An application window is easily opened by either double-clicking its icon on the Desktop, or clicking its name on one of the cascaded menus resulting from clicking the ***start*** button. When a program is running, an icon is placed on the Taskbar, which allows you to switch between running programs by simply left-clicking them on the Taskbar.

Although multiple application or document windows can be displayed simultaneously, only one is the active window and displays on the top of any other non-active windows. Title bars of non-active windows appear with a lighter shade than that of the active one, as shown in Fig. 1.4 below.

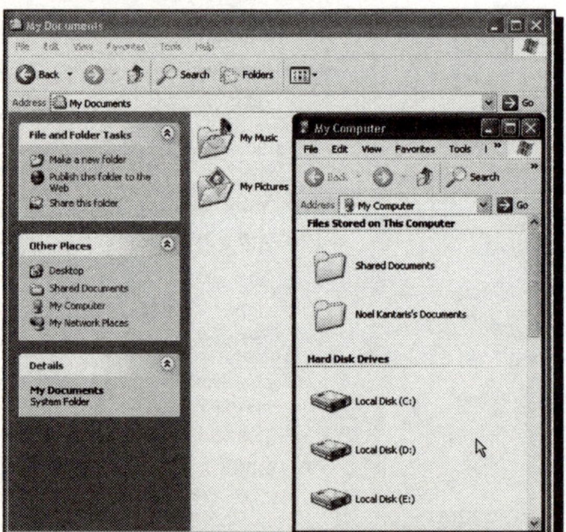

Fig. 1.4 Simultaneous Display of Running Applications.

For the screen above, we have opened the two applications shown, but used the **View**, **Tiles** menu command.

The typical window is subdivided into several areas which have the following functions:

Area	***Function***
Command button	Clicking on the program icon (see upper-left corner of the My Computer window in Fig. 1.3), displays the pull-down Control menu which can be used to control the program window. It includes commands for restoring, moving, sizing, minimising, maximising, and closing the window. 
Title bar	The bar at the top of a window which displays the application name and the name of the current document.
Minimise button	The button you point to and click to store an application as an icon on the Taskbar. Clicking on such an icon will restore the window. 
Maximise button	The button you point to and click to fill the screen with the active window. When that happens, the Maximise button changes to a Restore Down button which can be used to restore the window to its former size.  
Close button	The extreme top right button that you click to close a window. 

Menu bar	The bar below the Title bar which allows you to choose from several menu options. Clicking on a menu item displays the pull-down menu associated with that item. The options listed in the Menu bar depend on the specific application.
Toolbar	A bar of icons that you click to carry out some common actions.
Address bar	Shows the location of the current folder, or the URL (Uniform Resource Locator) of the new page to go to next.
Scroll bars/buttons	The bars/buttons on the extreme right and bottom of each window (or pane within a window) that contain a scroll box/button. Clicking on these bars/buttons allows you to see parts of a document that might not be visible in that size window.
Mouse pointer	The arrow which appears when the pointer is placed over menus, scroll bars, buttons, and folder lists.
Tasks	These change according to the function of the activated application. For example, if you activate My Computer, the Tasks refer to the System; you can view system information, add or remove programs, or change a setting. If you activate My Documents, the Tasks refer to files and folders; you can make a new folder, publish this folder to the Web, or share it with other users.

Other Places	The list shown under this heading also changes according to the function of the activated application. For example, if you activate My Computer, the list refers to activities related to it, such as My Network Places, My Documents, Shared Documents, and Control Panel. If you activate My Documents, the list refers to activities related to it, such as Desktop, Shared Documents My Computer, and My Network Places.
Details	Gives details of the displayed Task.

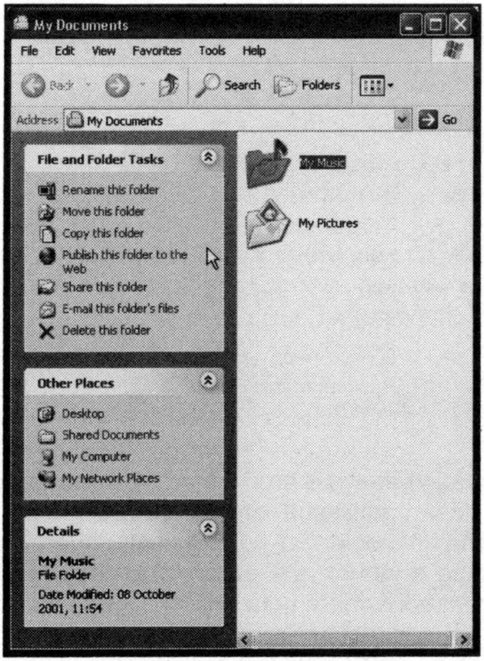

Fig. 1.5 Activity Related Tasks.

Fig. 1.5 shows activity related Tasks. Here we have selected a folder and, as you can see, the Tasks and Other Places lists change to reflect the current activity. For example, you can rename, move, delete, etc., a folder. This allows you to reach easily and quickly related activities that in previous versions of Windows you had to dig deep in menus and sub-menus to find.

The Mouse Pointers

In Windows, as with all other graphical based programs, using a mouse makes many operations both easier and more fun to carry out.

Windows has many different mouse pointers, with the most common illustrated below, which it uses for its various functions. When a program is initially started up probably the first you will see is the hourglass, which turns into an upward pointing hollow arrow. Some of the other shapes, as shown below, depend on the type of work you are doing at the time.

The hourglass which displays when you are waiting while performing a function.

The arrow which appears when the pointer is placed over menus, scrolling bars, and buttons.

The I-beam which appears in normal text areas of the screen.

The large 4-headed arrow which appears after choosing the **Control, Move/Size** command(s) for moving or sizing windows.

The double arrows which appear when over the border of a window, used to drag the side and alter the size of the window.

The Help hand which appears in the help windows, and is used to access 'hypertext' type links.

Windows applications, such as word processors, spreadsheets and databases, can have additional mouse pointers which facilitate the execution of selected commands, such as highlighting text, defining areas for the appearance of charts, etc. Later on, we will discuss in more detail the available mouse pointers in Windows XP when we introduce the 'Printers and Other Hardware' section of the Control Panel.

The Menu Bar Options

Each window's menu bar option has associated with it a pull-down sub-menu. To activate the menu of a window, either press the <Alt> key, which causes the underlining of one letter per menu option and activates (turns to a button) the first option of the menu (in this case **File**). Next, use the right and left arrow keys to activate the other options in the menu, or use the mouse to point to an option. Pressing either the <Enter> key, or the left mouse button, reveals the pull-down sub-menu of the activated option.

The sub-menu of the **View** option of the My Computer window, is shown in Fig. 1.6 below.

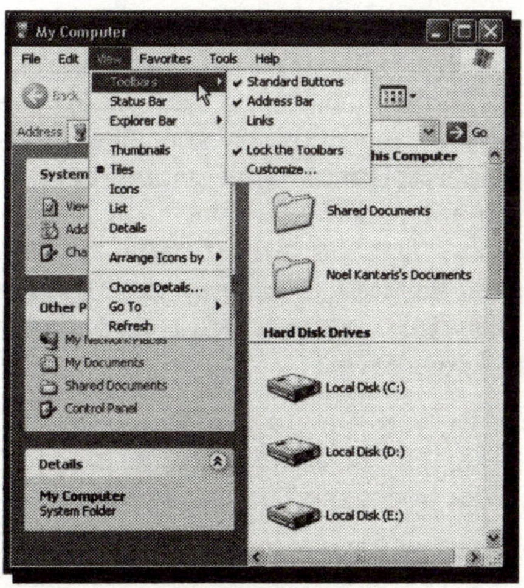

Fig. 1.6 Menu Bar Options.

Menu options can also be activated directly by pressing the <Alt> key, followed by the under-lined letter of the required menu option. Thus pressing **Alt+V**, opens the pull-down sub-menu of **View**. You can use the up and down arrow keys to move the highlighted bar up and down a sub-menu, or the right and left arrow keys to move along the options in the menu bar. Pressing the <Enter> key selects the highlighted option or executes the highlighted command. Pressing the <Esc> key once, closes the pull-down sub-menu, while pressing the <Esc> key for a second time closes the menu system.

Items on the pull-down sub-menu which are marked with an arrow to their right, as shown here, open up additional options when selected, as shown on the My Computer screen dump of Fig. 1.6.

The items on the menu bar of a specific application might be different from the ones shown here. However, almost all Windows XP system applications offer the following options:

File Produces a pull-down menu of mainly file related tasks, which allow you, amongst other options, to **rename**, **move**, **copy**, **publish on the Web**, **e-mail**, **print**, or **close** a file or folder.

Edit Gives access to the most common editing tasks which can be applied on selected items, such as **cut**, **copy** and **paste**, **copy** or **move** such items to a folder, or **select all** files or folders.

View Gives you complete control over what you see on your screen. For example, selecting the **Toolbars**, **Status bar**, or **Explorer bar** options checks these options and allows their display (selecting them once more removes the check mark and toggles them off). Allows you to display files as **thumbnails**, by their **titles**, **icons**, as **lists** or display their **details**, **arrange icons** in various ways and control what detail is displayed.

Favorites Allows you to **add** and **organise** useful URL addresses, customise **links**, or access various pre-set **media** addresses on the Internet.

Tools Allows you to **map** or **disconnect** network drives, and set **folder options**.

Help Activates the **help and support centre**, or opens a window and displays basic system information.

Some applications display a '?' button on the right end of their title bar, as shown here. Clicking this button changes the mouse pointer from its usual inclined arrow shape to the 'What's this?' shape. Pointing with this to an object in the window and clicking, opens a Help topic.

Shortcut Menus

To see a shortcut menu containing the most common commands applicable to an item, point with your mouse at the item and click the right mouse button. For example, right-clicking the **Recycle Bin** icon on the desktop, reveals the options in Fig. 1.7.

Fig. 1.7 Shortcut Menu for the Recycle Bin.

In this case we have the option to **Open** the Recycle Bin which has the same effect as double-clicking its icon, **Explore** its contents, **Empty** it of any files or folders held in it, **Create Shortcut** icon on the desktop, or see its **Properties**.

Right-clicking the desktop itself, displays the shortcut shown in Fig. 1.8. From this menu you can select how to **Arrange Icons** on your desktop, or create a **New** folder or a shortcut icon on the desktop, for your favourite word processor maybe.

Fig. 1.8 Shortcut Menu for the Desktop.

It might be worth your while to right-click a Windows application icon on your desktop, such as that of a word processor, if one was installed on your computer, to find out what the difference is between this shortcut menu and that of the Recycle Bin. For example, you will find that the **My Documents** icon has an additional option to delete it, while the **Recycle Bin** icon does not offer such an option. You will also find out that with a desktop application icon there might be an option to rename the icon, while there is no such option with the Recycle Bin.

Note: Having activated a shortcut menu, you can close it without taking any further action by simply pressing the <Esc> key, or clicking the mouse somewhere else.

Dialogue Boxes

Three periods after a sub-menu option or command, means that a dialogue box will open when the option or command is selected. A dialogue box is used for the insertion of additional information, such as the name of a file.

To see a dialogue box, click ***start*** then the **My Computer** menu option, select **Tools** on the menu bar of the displayed window and **Folder Options** from its sub-menu. This opens the Folder Options dialogue box shown in Fig. 1.9 below with its General tab selected.

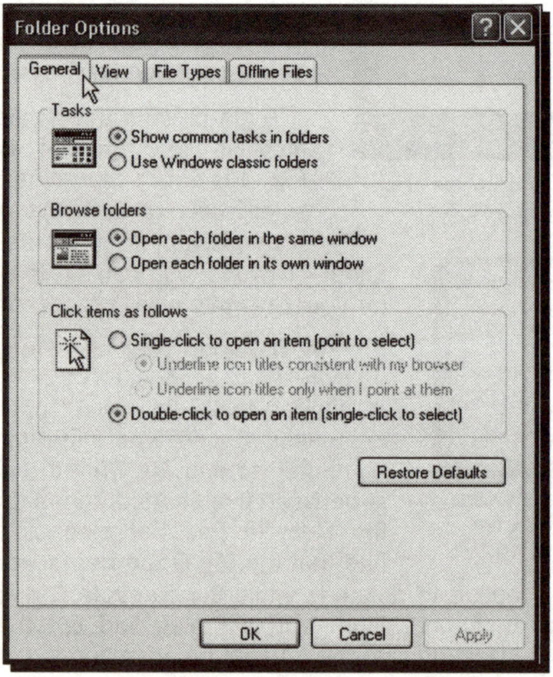

Fig. 1.9 The Folder Options Dialogue Box.

When a dialogue box opens, the <Tab> key can be used to move the dotted rectangle (known as the focus) from one field to another (<Shift+Tab> moves the focus backwards).

Alternatively you can move directly to a desired field by holding the <Alt> key down and pressing the underlined letter in the field name. With the mouse, you simply point and click the left mouse button at the desired field.

Some dialogue boxes (such as the one shown in Fig. 1.9) contain List boxes which show a column of available choices. If there are more choices than can be seen in the area provided, use the scroll bars to reveal them. Such dialogue boxes

may contain Check boxes which offer a list of features you

can switch on or off. Selected options show a tick in the box against the option name. Another type of dialogue box option is the Option button (sometimes called Radio button) with a list of mutually exclusive items. The default choice is marked with a black dot against its name, while unavailable options are dimmed.

Another type of List box may display a column of document files. To select a single file from such a List box, either double-click the file, or use the arrow keys to highlight the file and press <Enter>. Again, if there are more files than can be seen in the area provided, use the scroll bars to reveal them.

Other dialogue boxes may contain groups of options within a field. In such cases, you can use the arrow keys to move from one option to another. Having selected an option or typed in information in a text box, you must press a command button, such as the **OK**, **Cancel** or **Apply** button (unavailable options or command buttons are dimmed), or choose from additional options. To select the **OK** button with the mouse, simply point and left-click, while with the keyboard, you must first press the <Tab> key until the focus moves to the required button, and then press the <Enter> key.

To cancel a dialogue box, either press the **Cancel** button, or the <Esc> key enough times to close the dialogue box and then the menu system.

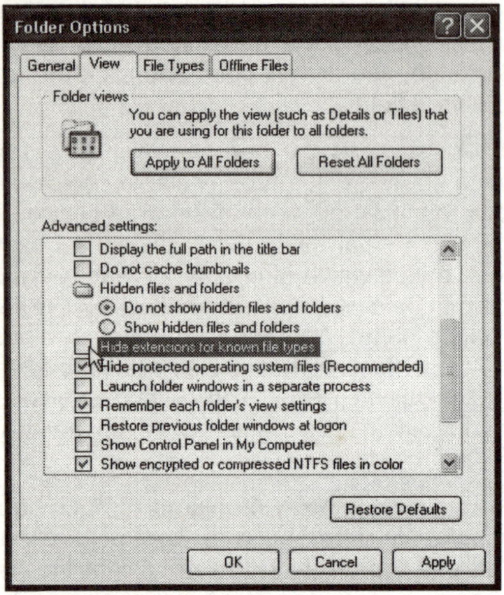

Fig. 1.10 Making Visible the Extensions of Known File Types.

Note: At this stage it might be a good time to change the default settings under the **View** tab of Fig. 1.9 by unchecking the **Hide extensions for known file types** option, as shown in Fig. 1.10.

Doing so could alert you to rogue and potentially lethal e-mail attachments.

Taskbar Buttons

At the bottom of the Desktop screen is the Taskbar. It contains the ***start*** button which, as we have seen, can be used to quickly start a program. Later on we will discuss how we can search for a file, and how to get Help.

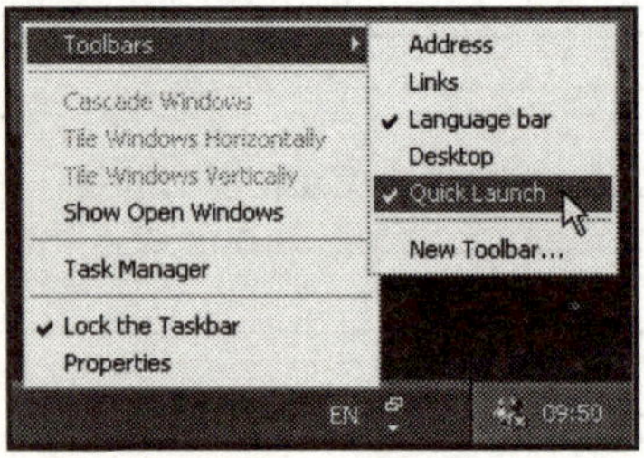

Fig. 1.11 Quick Launch Activation.

Before we go any further, right click an empty part of the Taskbar, point to the **Toolbars** option which displays the sub-menu, shown on the right in Fig. 1.11, and left-click the **Quick Launch** entry. This displays three icons next to the ***start*** button; left-clicking one of these, launches its application (see next page for details).

When you open a program, or a window, a button for it is placed on the Taskbar, as shown in Fig. 1.12 below.

Fig. 1.12 The Windows Taskbar.

You can left-click your mouse on this button to make this the active program, or window, which displays in a darker shade of blue on the Taskbar. So, now you can always see what windows you have open, which is the active one, and quickly switch between them. As more buttons are placed on the Taskbar their size shrinks slightly, but up to a point. After that common entries are grouped together with a number indicating the number of open windows. To see details relating to a grouped button, left-click it to open a list of components, as shown in Fig. 1.13. Try it!

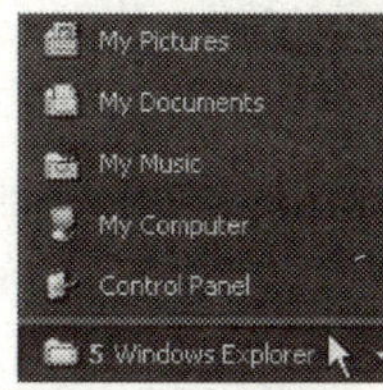

Fig. 1.13 Grouped Taskbar Entries.

Another interesting Taskbar menu option is **Properties** (Fig. 1.11). This allows you to change the Taskbar and ***start*** menu options.

If you have activated the Quick Launch option, there will be three buttons displaying next to the ***start*** button. These, in order of appearance, have the following functions:

 Launch the Internet Explorer Browser.

 Show Desktop.

 Launch Windows Media Player.

Fig. 1.14 Date and Time Properties Dialogue Box.

The Taskbar also shows the current time to the far right, the Windows Messenger, the Options, the Restore and the Language icons. Moving the mouse pointer over the clock will display the date. Double-clicking the clock, opens the Date/Time Properties box, shown in Fig. 1.14, so that you can make changes, if necessary.

Changing the Active Window

To select the active window amongst those displayed on the screen (these will only be displayed on the screen simultaneously if their **Restore Down** button has been left-clicked), point to it and click the left mouse button, or, if the one you want to activate is not visible, click its icon on the Taskbar.

It is a good idea to practise what we are describing here by opening three applications from the ***start*** menu such as **My Computer**, **My Documents**, and **My Pictures**. Do not be afraid if you make mistakes - you will only learn from them!

Moving Windows and Dialogue Boxes

When you have multiple windows or dialogue boxes on the screen, you might want to move a particular one to a different part of the screen. This can be achieved with either the mouse or the keyboard, but not if the window occupies the full screen, for obvious reasons.

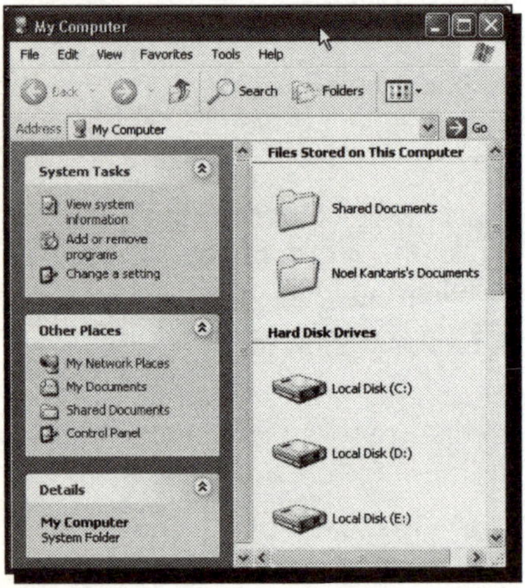

Fig. 1.15 Moving a Window with the Mouse.

To move a window, or a dialogue box, with the mouse, point to the title bar, as shown in Fig. 1.15, and drag it (press the left button and keep it pressed while moving the mouse) until the window is where you want it to be on the screen, then release the mouse button.

Sizing a Window

You can change the size of a window with either the mouse or the keyboard. With the mouse, move the window so that the side you want to change is visible, then move the mouse pointer to the edge of the window or corner so that it changes to a two-headed arrow, then drag the two-headed arrow in the direction you want that side or corner to move.

Minimising and Maximising Windows

Windows can be minimised into Taskbar icons to temporarily free desktop space. This can be done by left-clicking the **Minimise** button (the negative sign in the upper-right corner of the window), shown in Fig. 1.16.

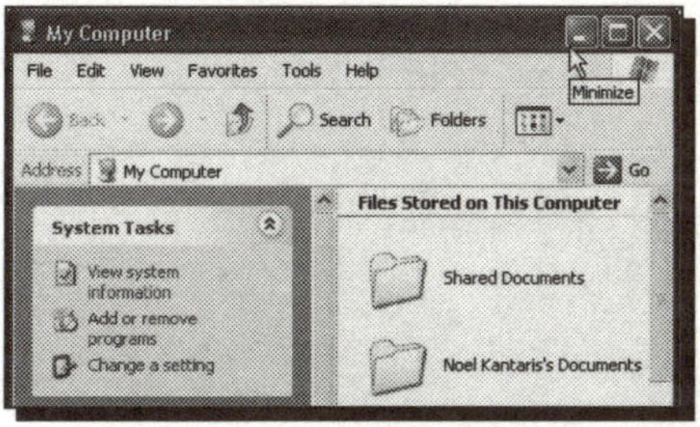

Fig. 1.16 Minimising a Window.

To maximise a window so that it fills the entire screen, left-click the **Maximise** button (the rectangle in the upper-right corner of the window.

An application which has been minimised or maximised can be returned to its original size and position on the screen by either clicking on its Taskbar icon to expand it to a window, or clicking on the **Restore Down** button of the maximised window, to reduce it to its former size.

Closing a Window

A document window can be closed at any time to save screen space and memory. To do this, left-click the **Close** (X) button shown here. If you try to close a window of an application document, such as that of a word processor, in which you have made changes since the last time you saved it, you will get a warning in the form of a dialogue box asking confirmation prior to closing it. This safeguards against loss of information.

Exiting Windows XP

To exit Windows, click the ***start*** button and select the **Turn Off Computer** option, as shown in Fig. 1.17.

Fig. 1.17 The Lower Part of the START Menu.

This opens an additional box, shown in Fig. 1.18 below.

Fig. 1.18 The Turn Off Computer Box.

From here you can either put your computer in a **Stand by** mode, **Turn Off** the computer, or **Restart** it. The **Stand by** mode is used to save power by turning off your monitor and/or hard disc after a specified time interval (we will discuss this in detail later on in the book). Selecting the **Turn Off** option, exits all the open programs, carries out any file saves you require and then tells you when it is safe to switch off your computer. The **Restart** option is used if you want to clear the memory settings and restart Windows XP, or if you have a dual boot system the other operating system.

Note: Unlike previous versions of Windows where this was the only way that you should end a session, with Window XP you can just switch off your computer - the **Turn Off** the computer procedure will then be carried out automatically.

2

The Windows XP Interface

You must have noticed by now that the **My Computer**, **My Documents**, **My Pictures**, and **Recycle Bin** windows, to mention but a few, have a Toolbar with browser-style forwards and backwards arrows similar to the **Internet Explorer** which is bundled with Windows XP. The My Computer window is shown in Fig. 2.1 below.

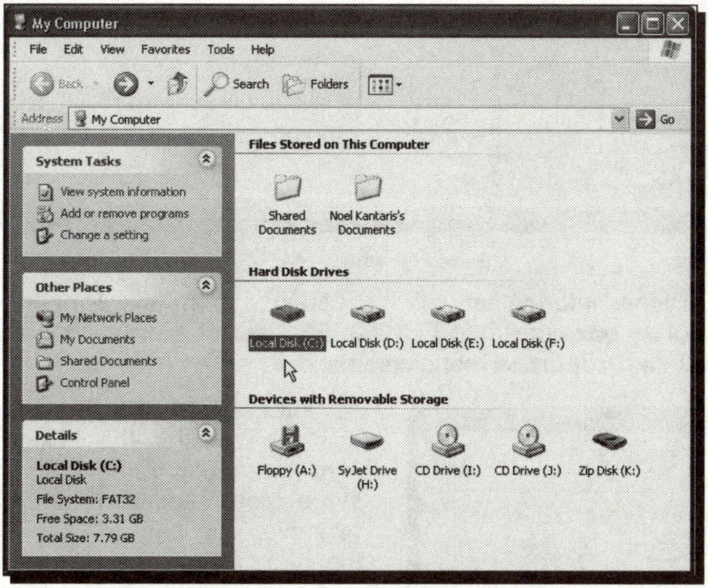

Fig. 2.1 The Toolbar of a Windows Application.

Note that to see the display exactly as it appears in Fig. 2.1, you need to click the down arrow against the **Views** button on the Toolbar and select the **Icons** option from the drop-down menu, as shown above. Try the different display options available to you and see which one you prefer.

For the display in Fig. 2.2, we chose the **Details** option. Highlighting an item, in whichever display option you operate, gives you information about that item.

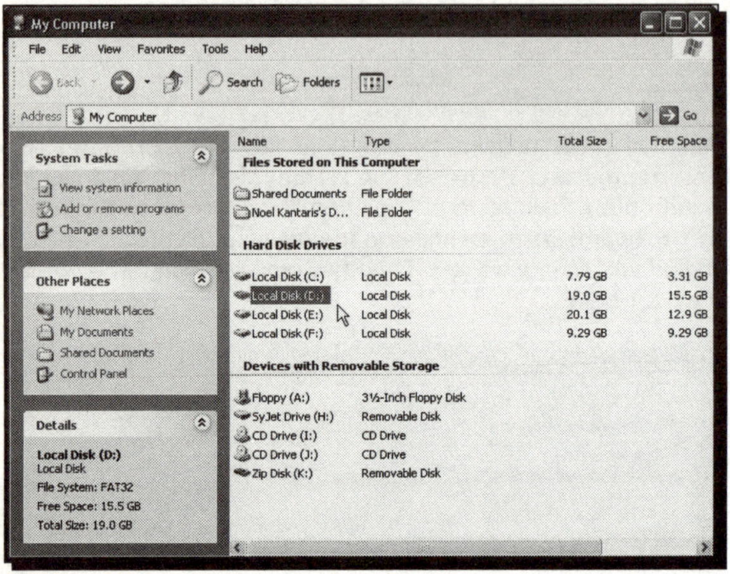

Fig. 2.2 The Details View Option.

Additional information can be obtained from the Properties dialogue box, shown in Fig. 2.3. First select a drive, then use the **File, Properties** menu command.

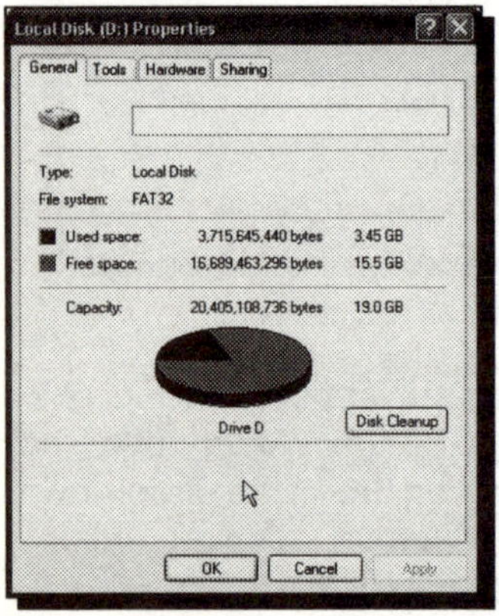

As you can see, the Properties dialogue box for the selected item gives you quite a bit of information relating to it. For example, you can see visually the capacity of the disc. You can also find out whether it can be shared and what maintenance tools are available by clicking the appropriate tab.

Fig. 2.3 The Properties Dialogue Box.

Similar Properties dialogue boxes can be accessed for a folder or a program/document file displayed in **My Computer**. The easiest way is to right-click an item and select **Properties** from the drop-down menu. Do try it for yourself.

The Common Toolbar Buttons

Returning to the common user interface Toolbar, apart from the default buttons appearing on it, there are several others which can be added to invoke extra facilities. To do this, use the **View, Toolbars, Customize** command to display the screen shown in Fig. 2.4 below.

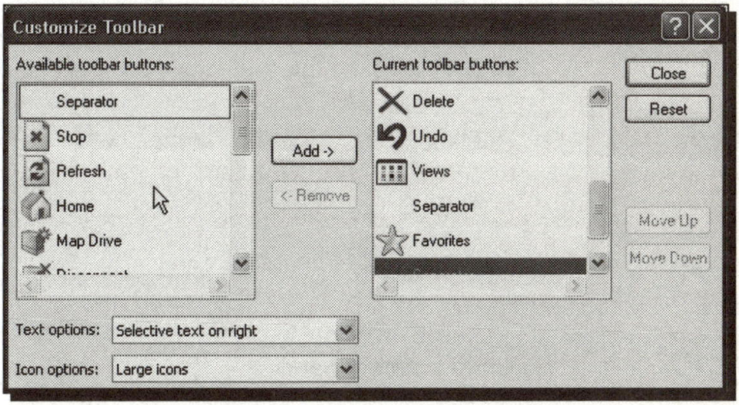

Fig. 2.4 The Customize Toolbar Dialogue Box.

To place an additional button on to the Toolbar, select it in the left pane, and press the **Add** button. Its place on the Toolbar depends on the position of the focus in the right pane. Try adding the **Home** button to the Toolbar at a position to the left of the **Search** button.

One interesting aspect of this common user interface is, that no matter which application you used to add the extra button to its Toolbar, the same button will appear on the Toolbar of all other program applications that use the same common user interface.

The various buttons on the common interface Toolbar have the following functions:

Button ***Function***

Go back to the previous display.

Go Forward to the next display.

Go up one step in the hierarchical tree structure of the filing system.

Search for folders and files, for computers or people or the Internet.

Replace the Tasks pane with a hierarchical tree structure of your filing system.

Delete selected items.

Undo last command.

Select a different view for displaying your files and folders.

Show your favourite links to Web sites on the Internet or to folders on your hard disc.

Obviously there are more buttons you could add to the common interface Toolbar, but if you have done so, you would already know their function, so we will not discuss them here.

Discs

New floppy discs (or hard discs), if not already pre-formatted, must be formatted before they can be used by your computer's operating system. A floppy disc that has been formatted in one type of computer, can only be used in another computer if they are compatible and use the same operating system.

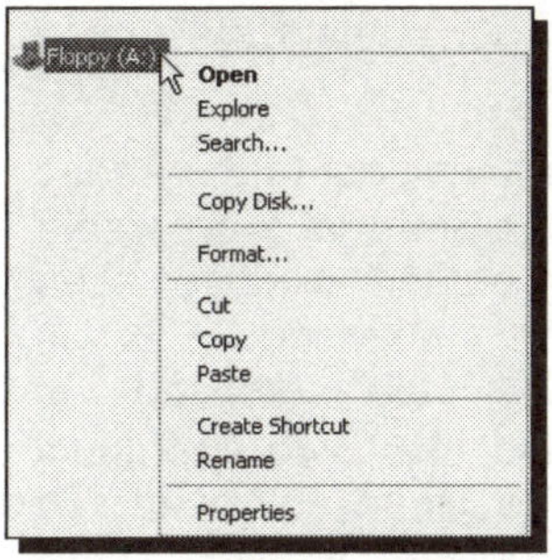

Fig. 2.5 The A: Drive Shortcut Menu.

To format a floppy disc, put it into the correct disc drive, open **My Computer** right-click on the icon for the drive. In our case, this would be the (A:) drive, as shown in Fig. 2.5. From the displayed drop-down menu, select the **Format** option, which opens the dialogue box shown in Fig. 2.6. Choose the required options in this box and press the **Start** button to carry out the formatting.

If you want to name your disc, so that the system will recognise it by that name (in the My Computer windows, for example), enter the name in the **Volume label** text box. Choosing **Quick Format** in the **Format options** section, deletes the File Allocation Table of a previously formatted disc - you cannot use this option on a new disc.

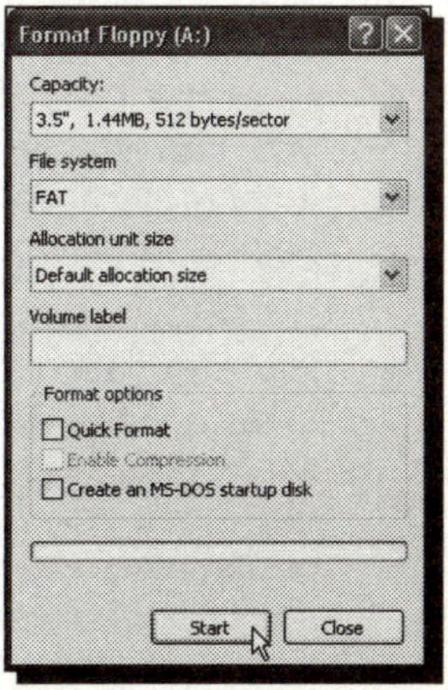

Fig. 2.6 The Format Dialogue Box.

Formatting will destroy any files on the disc, so take care. If you have not created an MS-DOS start-up disc for your system already, you can do so now from this dialogue box.

Note that in the shortcut menu of Fig. 2.5 there is an option for renaming your specified disc drive. You can rename all removable disc drives in Windows XP Home edition, but only some removable disc drives in the Professional edition.

In the Professional edition of Windows XP it is assumed that your computer might be networked and you might be sharing some of the removable disc drives, therefore you cannot change the name of such drives. For example, in our system we have two CD drives; a DVD drive and a recordable CD drive. However, both these drives are shown as CD drives in Fig. 2.2. But which is which? Furthermore, as seen in Fig. 2.7, the shortcut menu of such a CD drive does not contain the option to rename it.

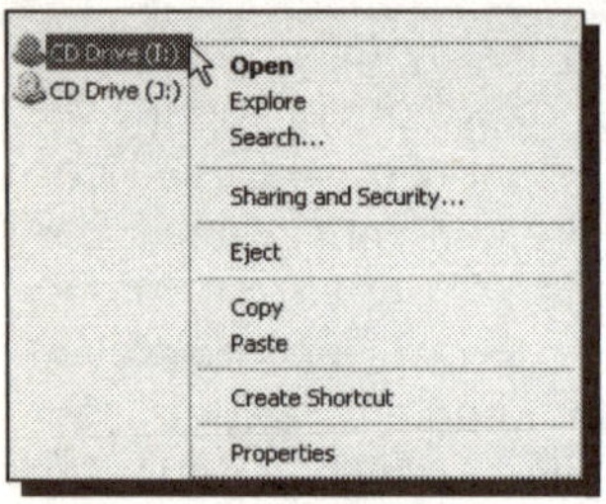

Fig. 2.7 The CD Drive Shortcut Menu.

There is a way out to the above predicament, and that is to create a shortcut on the desktop, then rename the shortcut. This is allowed as the desktop is customisable to suit individual users of the same computer. To create a shortcut to a drive on your desktop, do the following:

- Place a music CD in one of the drives (in our case we used the DVD drive), so that you can identify which drive letter refers to it from the displayed dialogue box shown in Fig. 2.8.

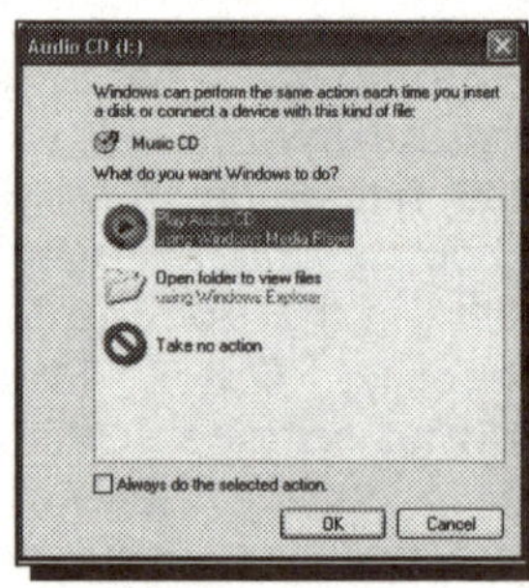

Fig. 2.8 The Format Dialogue Box.

- Highlight the identified CD drive in the **My Computer** screen (see Fig. 2.2) and with the left mouse button depressed, drag it onto the desktop then release the mouse button. This will place a shortcut to the drive in question on the desktop.
- Right-click the desktop shortcut and rename it appropriately as shown here.

- Repeat the process for the other CD drive.

You will now have two distinguishable shortcuts to your CD drives on your desktop.

Folders and Files

Double clicking on a folder, such as the Shared Documents folder, changes the contents of the Tasks pane from those in Fig. 2.2 to the ones shown in Fig. 2.9 below.

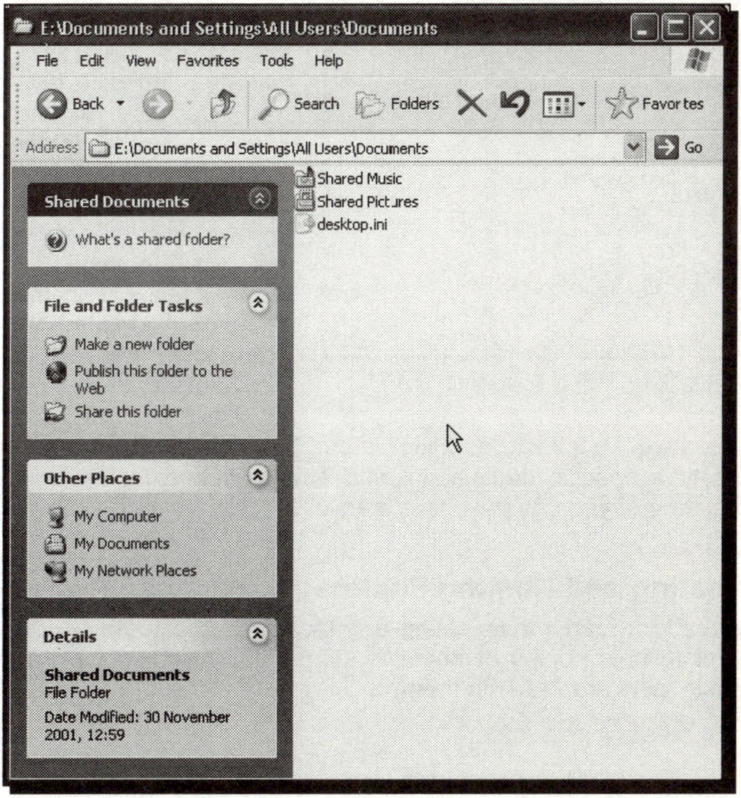

Fig. 2.9 The Contents of the Shared Documents Folder.

A Shared Documents folder complements each user's personal Documents folder. It contains folders which in turn contain files that all logged users on that particular computer (or network) can share. In our case, the Shared Documents folder contains two other folders; a Shared Music and a Shared Pictures folder, each containing appropriate files.

As you can see from the Files and Folders Tasks pane, you can make a new folder in which you could place different kinds of documents, publish a specified folder to the Web, or share a specified folder with other users of your computer or your network.

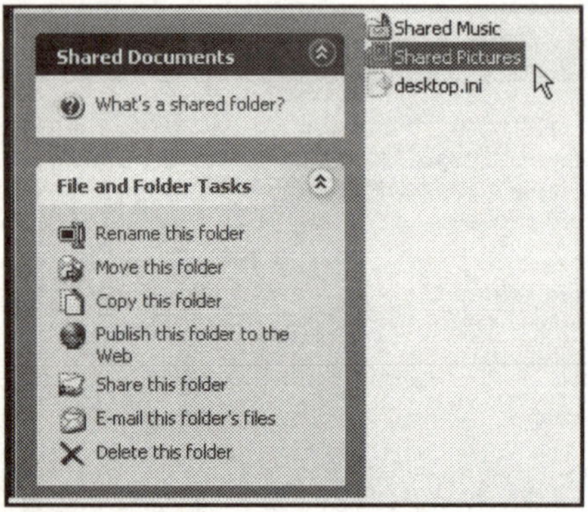

Fig. 2.10 The My Documents Folder.

If you now click a folder to select it, the content of the Tasks panel changes to give you access to the other files and folder commands, as shown in Fig. 2.10. In what follows, we will show you how to create a new folder, say in the Shared Documents folder (we will call it Test Folder), then how to select and copy the contents of your Pictures folder into it, how to send folders and files to a specific destination, and how to delete folders and files, so that you can get some practice.

Creating and Naming Folders

Before you start manipulating any files, we will create a new folder to hold copies of some existing files. It should then be safe to 'play around' with them.

To create a new folder:

- Open **My Computer** and double-click the Shared Documents folder.
- Click the **Make a new folder** option on the Tasks pane, as shown in Fig. 2.11 on the next page, which places a New Folder entry inside the currently active window. At the same time the New Folder entry is highlighted and the **Make a new folder** entry on the Tasks pane changes to **Rename this folder**, as shown in Fig. 2.12 on the next page.

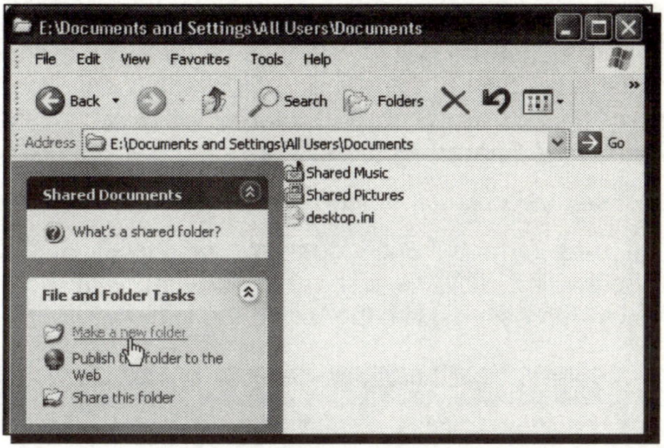

Fig. 2.11 Creating a New Folder.

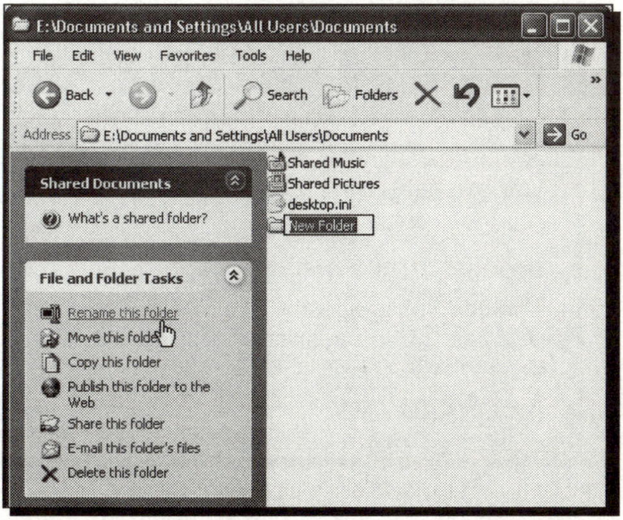

Fig. 2.12 A New Folder Added Inside the Active Window.

- Next, type **Test Folder** into the name slot and click at an empty area of the window. It's as easy as that to create and name a folder. At any time in the future you can rename it by clicking its existing name and typing in the new one. This works for files too.

Selecting Folders and Files

What we demonstrate below with files could also be done with folders, or a mixture of folders and files within any folder. We will select files in the Sample Pictures folder which is to be found within the Shared Pictures folder.

To select several objects, or icons, you have three options:

- If they form a contiguous list, as shown in Fig. 2.13 below, left-click the first in the list, then with the <Shift> key depressed, click the last in the list.

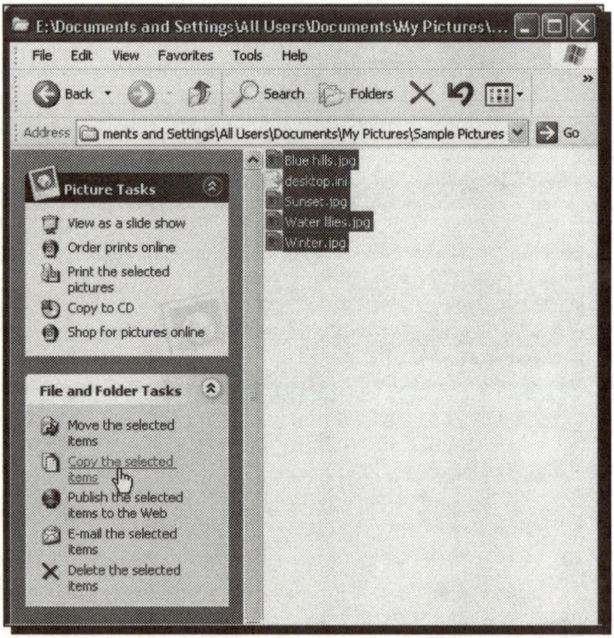

Fig. 2.13 Selecting Items in a Folder.

- To select random objects hold the <Ctrl> key down and left-click them, one by one.
- To select all the items in a window use the **Edit**, **Select All** menu command, or the <Ctrl+A> keystrokes.

To cancel a selection, click in an empty area of the window.

Copying or Moving Folders and Files

When you **copy** a folder or file to somewhere else, the original version of the folder or file is not altered or removed, but when you **move** a folder or file to a new location, the original is actually deleted.

To copy selected items into a target folder, click the **Copy the selected items** entry in the File and Folder Tasks pane, as shown in Fig. 2.13 on the previous page, which opens the Copy Items dialogue box shown in Fig. 2.14 below. All you need to do now is navigate to the Test Folder, highlight it, and click the **Copy** button.

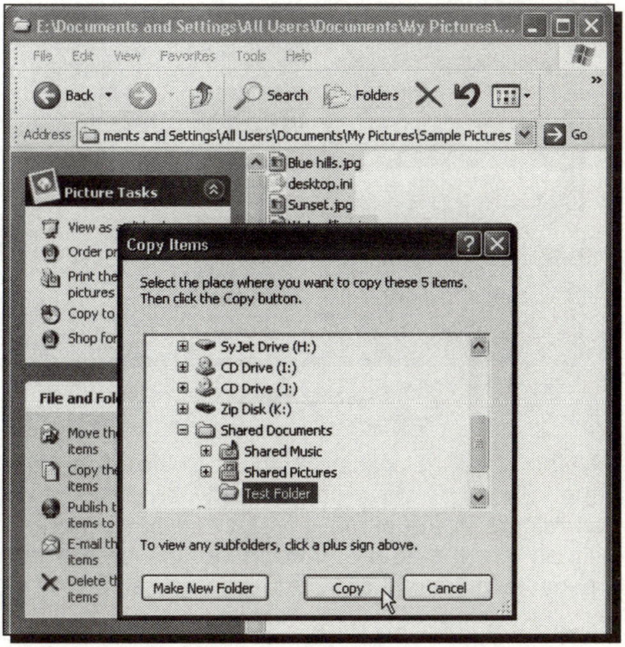

Fig. 2.14 Selecting the Destination Folder.

To move selected items into a target folder click the **Move the selected items** entry in the File and Folder Tasks pane shown in Fig. 2.13.

Double-clicking the Test Folder should now reveal its contents, as shown in Fig. 2.15 below, where we selected to display the contents of the folder in Thumbnails view.

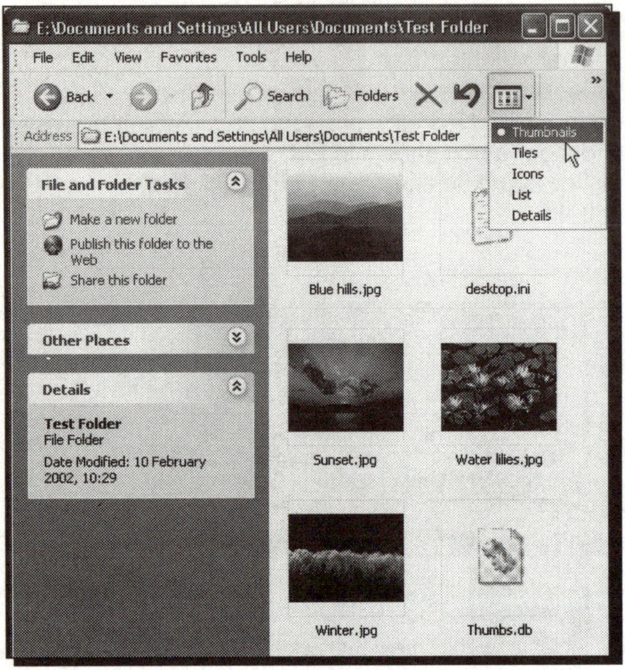

Fig. 2.15 Selecting the Destination Folder.

Note: Although it is possible to use the drag and drop technique to copy or move objects between different drives or between folders in the same drive, it can be confusing to the non-initiated user. It is, therefore, safer to use the described Tasks panel technique to carry out such operations.

However, if you intend to use the drag and drop technique, then may we suggest you drag selected objects with the *right* mouse button depressed to the desired destination. Releasing the mouse button produces a menu which gives you a choice between **Copy Here** and **Move Here**. Clicking one of these, completes the required task.

File Properties

If you want to know more about a particular file, first select it, then either use the **File, Properties** menu command, or right-click the filename and select **Properties** from the drop-down menu to open the Properties dialogue box, as shown in Fig. 2.16. Here, the full properties of the file are listed, including its name, type, location, size, the date when it was created, last modified, etc. You can also change the file's attributes, by making it, say, **Read-only**, to prevent accidental changes to its contents. The Properties dialogue box of some types of files has an extra tab which allows you to preview, or even play, their contents.

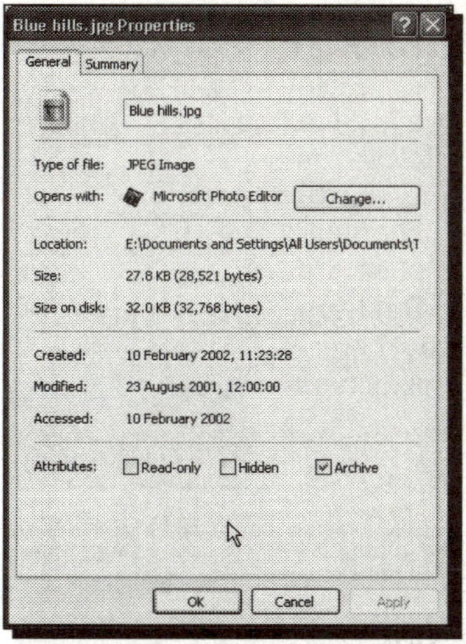

Fig. 2.16 The Properties Dialogue Box.

Creating Shortcuts

With Windows XP, just as with previous versions of Windows, you can put a shortcut to any program, document, or printer on your desktop or in any folder. Shortcuts are quick ways to get to the items you use often; they save you having to dig deep into your system files to access them.

One program we seem to use to process our system files is the Notepad, so we will step you through the process of finding and placing a shortcut to it on the desktop. Double-clicking such a shortcut icon will be easier and quicker than using the ***start***, **All Programs**, **Accessories**, **Notepad** to open the program. However, we must first find the actual executable file of the program which is best done using the ***start*, Search** command. This opens the Search Dialogue box, the left panel of which is shown in Fig. 2.17 on the next page.

Next, click the **All files and folders** entry in the Tasks pane and specify the drive you want to search and the item you are searching for (the E: drive in our case, or whichever drive Windows is installed on your PC), as shown in Fig. 2.18. Soon enough the NOTEPAD.EXE file is found in the Windows XP folder, as shown in Fig. 2.19 below. Select it, right-click it and choose the **Send To**, **Desktop (create shortcut)** entry from the displayed cascade menu.

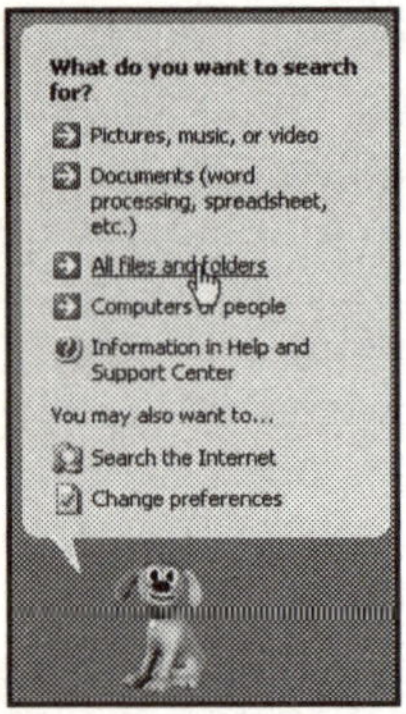

Fig. 2.17 Specifying Type of Search.

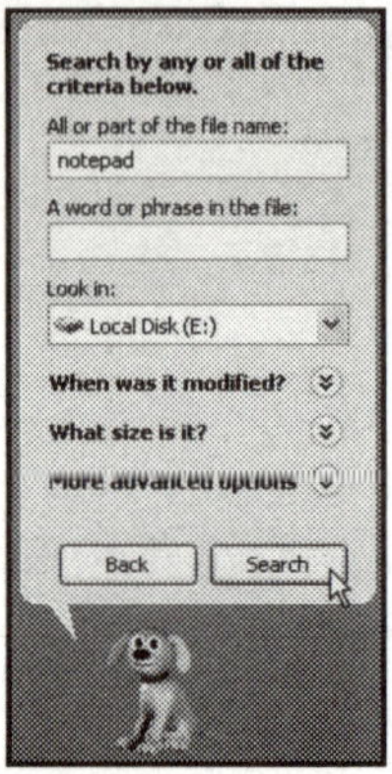

Fig. 2.18 Specifying the Item and Drive for a Search.

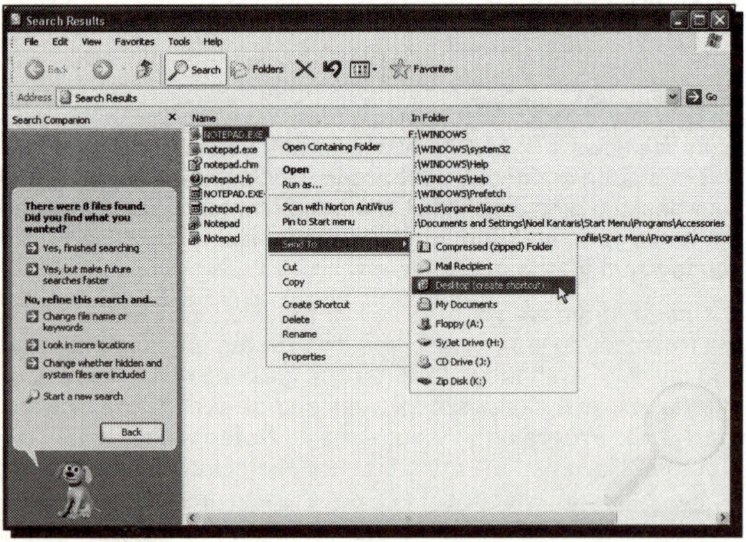

Fig. 2.19 Placing Notepad on the Desktop.

Sending Folders and Files

As we have seen in the previous section, a very useful feature of Windows is the ability to quickly send files and folders to specific destinations.

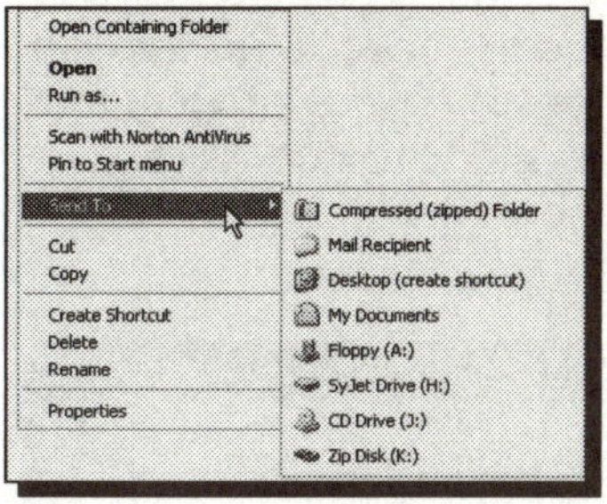

Fig. 2.20 Sending Folders and Files.

Right-clicking selected folders, or files, will open the menu shown in Fig. 2.20. Selecting the **Send To** option opens the list of available destinations. In your case these are bound to be different, for example, SyJet Drive (H:) and Zip Disk (K:) options might not be available to you.

Selecting the **Floppy (A)** option will copy any selected folders and files to a removable disc in the (A:) drive, as shown in Fig. 2.21 by the very decorative animated window that appears while the process is being carried out.

Fig. 2.21 Copying Folders and Files.

It is easy to add more locations to the **Send To** menu, as it is controlled by the contents of the SendTo folder, which is itself in the Windows folder. However, the SendTo folder is hidden by default, so if you use the ***start*, Search** command, you may not find it. To make it visible, start **My Computer**, then use the **Tools, Folder Options** command, click the View tab and finally click the **Show hidden files and folders** option.

To add a destination to the **Send To** menu do the following:

- Click the Documents and Settings folder on the drive where Windows XP is installed.
- Double-click the folder of a specific user.
- Double-click the SendTo folder.

- Use the **File, New, Shortcut** command.
- Follow the instructions on your screen.

It is useful to be able to send text files straight to the Notepad so that you can see, and maybe edit, their contents. To add Notepad to the **Send To** menu, you don't have to go through the above procedure because you already have a shortcut to it on your desktop. Instead, copy this shortcut icon from your desktop to the **SendTo** window, as shown in Fig. 2.22.

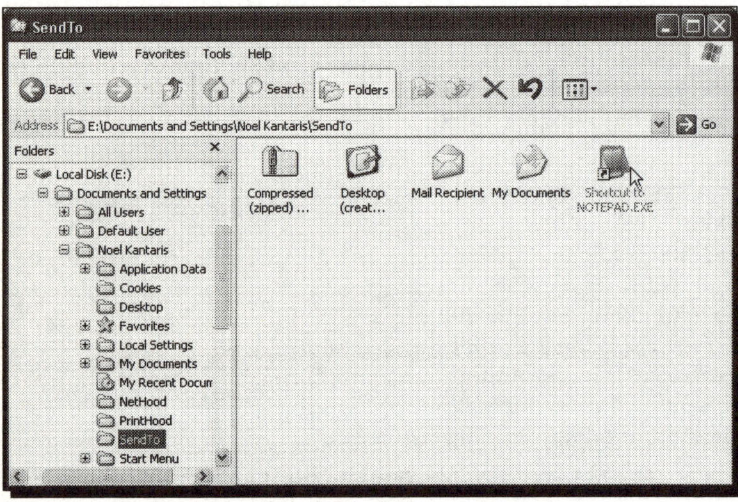

Fig. 2.22 Adding a Shortcut to the SendTo Folder.

When you next open the Send To menu it should have the extra item as shown here in Fig. 2.23. As you can see, we have renamed the shortcut to simply 'Notepad'. We did this by using My Computer, opening the SendTo folder right-clicking the file and selecting the **Rename** command from the shortcut menu.

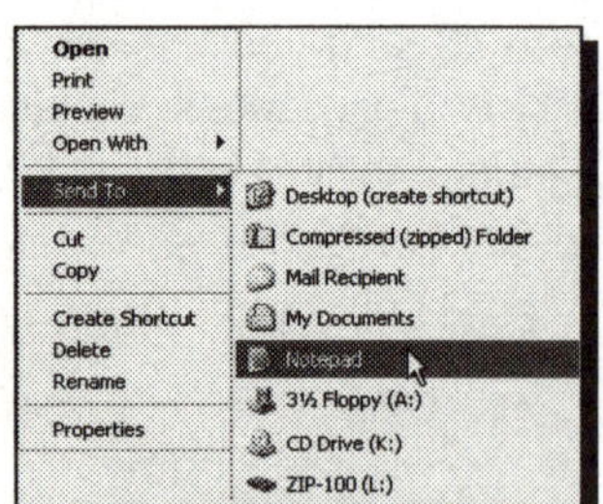

Fig. 2.23 The Modified Send To Menu.

Deleting Folders and Files

The operations described here must only be carried out on the folders or files held in the Test Folder, unless you really want to delete specific items.

- To delete or remove files, first highlight them, and then either select the **Delete the selected items** entry in the Tasks pane, press the <Del> key on the keyboard, or press the **Delete** button on the Toolbar, shown here, or use the **File**, **Delete** command from the window menu bar.

All of these methods open the confirmation box shown in Fig. 2.24 which gives you the chance to abort the operation by selecting **No**.

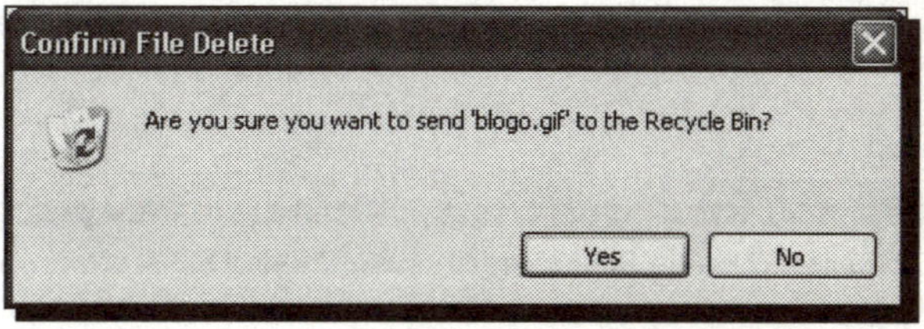

Fig. 2.24 The Delete File Warning Dialogue Box.

To delete folders, follow the same procedure as for files. A similar dialogue box to the one in Fig 2.24 will be displayed. The only difference is that the word 'File' is replaced by the word 'Folder'. To carry on with the deletion in either case, select **Yes**.

Now is the time to first delete two files from our Test Folder (any files will do), then delete the folder itself. Do carry out this suggestion as we need to demonstrate what happens to deleted items when we discuss the Recycle Bin.

The Recycle Bin

As you can see from the message boxes on the previous page, by default all files or folders deleted from a hard disc, are actually placed in a holding folder named the Recycle Bin.

If you open the Recycle Bin, by double-clicking its desktop icon, shown here, you will see that it is just a special folder. It lists all the files, folders, icons and shortcuts that have been deleted from fixed drives since it was last emptied, as shown in Fig. 2.25.

Fig. 2.25 The Recycle Bin Folder Showing Deleted Files and Folder.

Note that Windows keeps a record of the original locations of the deleted files, so that it can restore them if necessary. To see the display as it appears in Fig. 2.25, use the **View** command and select the **Details** option.

To restore or delete specific files or folders from the Recycle Bin, first select them then use the appropriate Tasks pane entry. Choosing **Restore the selected items** will restore the selected files to the folder they were originally in, even if you have deleted that folder; check it out for yourself by restoring one of the files you deleted earlier from the Test Folder. Clicking the **Delete** icon on the Toolbar, removes the selected items from the Recycle Bin. To save disc space, every now and then, open the Recycle Bin and delete unwanted files or folders. To delete all the files and folders held in the Recycle Bin, click the **Empty the Recycle Bin** entry in the Tasks pane.

Using the Help System

To obtain help in Windows XP, click the ***start*** button, then click the **Help and Support** menu option which opens the main Help window, shown in Fig. 2.26 below.

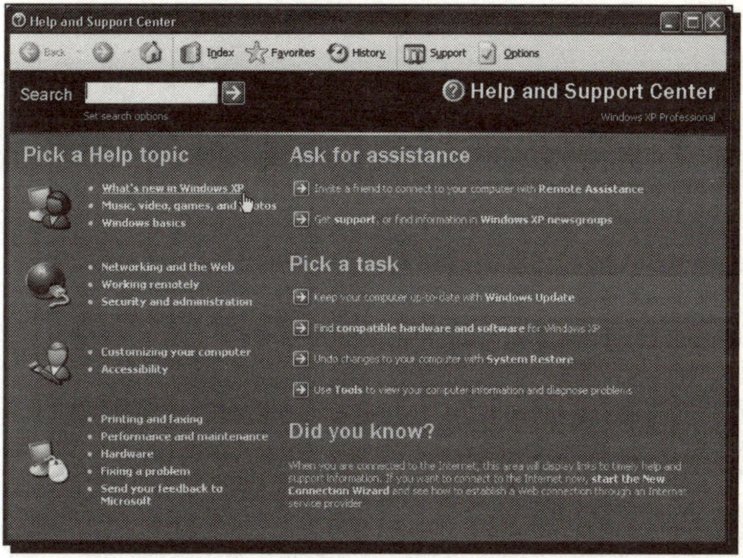

Fig. 2.26 The Windows XP Help and Support Centre.

The **Pick a Help topic** option give you off-line help on various listed topics, while the **Ask for assistance** topics require connection to the Internet, as do the first two options under **Pick a task**. It might be worth your while spending some time here investigating the various options available to you. If you are new to Windows, you might like to have a look at the 'What's new in Windows XP' option.

With all options you get a 'Search' facility, and with all but the 'start a New Connection Wizard' under the **Did you know?** option you are presented with an extraordinary number of hypertext links to various topics. Clicking such a hypertext link, can open up a further list of hypertext links until you home onto the specific subject you are searching for.

The Search facility gives you access to a very powerful individual word search of the Help system, as shown in Fig. 2.27 below. For example, if you wanted to know something about e-mail, type the word *e-mail* in the Search box and click the button to have Windows display almost everything there is to know about e-mail.

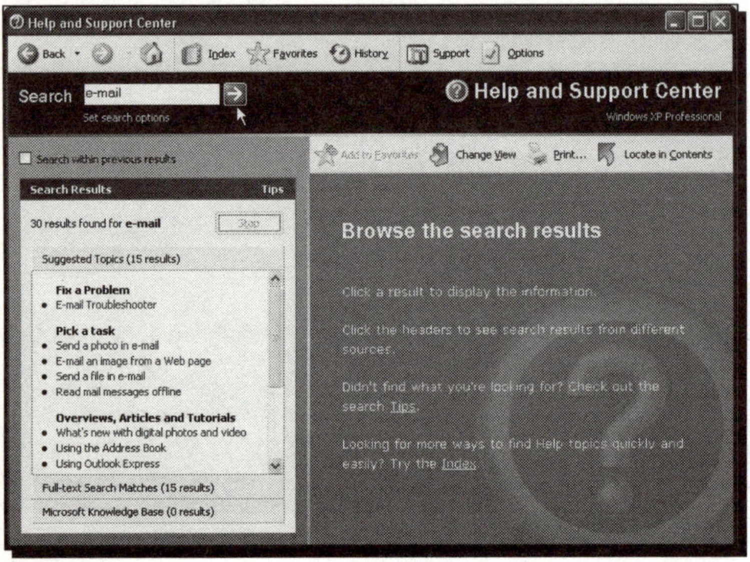

Fig. 2.27 Using the Help Search Facility.

The last item under each Search screen's **Browse the search results** statement is always the **Index** link. Clicking this link, opens up a Help index facility and typing the first few letters of a word in its input box homes onto the available topics in the list. Selecting one and clicking the **Display** button opens its help page on that item. Try it.

Windows XP Features

The My Computer Views

These views in **My Computer** are not new, but are worth discussing as they greatly enhance its functionality. These are to be found mainly in the **View, Explorer Bar** menu options, as shown in Fig. 3.1.

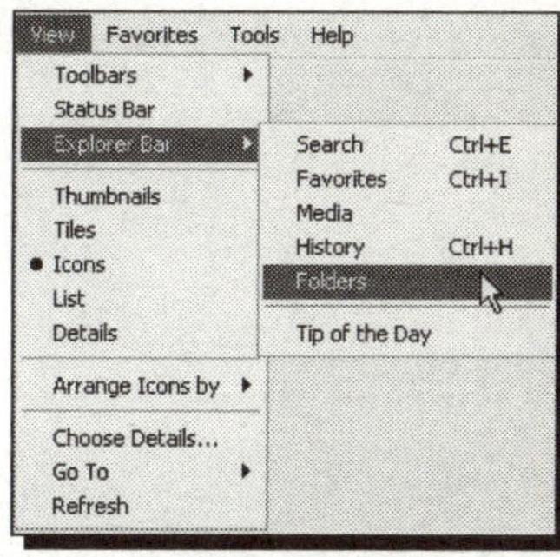

Fig. 3.1 The Explorer Bar Options.

The Search View

Use this to display the **Search** facility in the left pane of a **My Computer** window which is identical in functionality to the ***start*, Search** command.

The Favorites View

Use this to display a list of favourite links in the left pane of **My Computer** window. It allows you to add and organise useful URL addresses, or access various pre-set media addresses on the Internet.

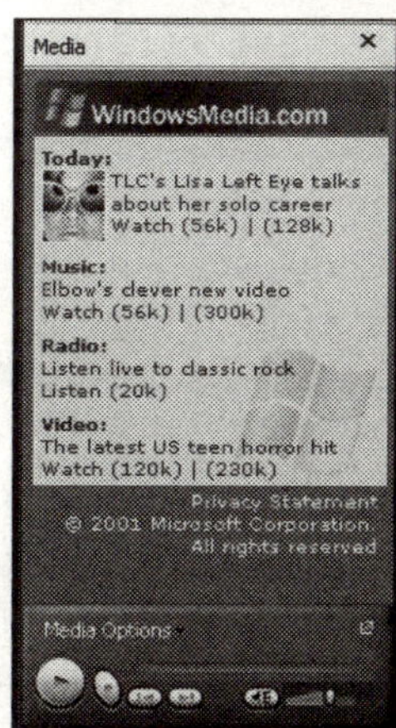

Fig. 3.2 The Media Window.

The Media View

Use this to be connected to the Internet (provided you have this facility) and display the Web site WindowsMedia.com in the left pane of **My Computer**, as shown in Fig. 3.2.

In this window click the Media Options down arrow at the bottom of the screen to select which media you want to connect to. For example, selecting **Radio Guide** displays a full screen in the right pane of **My Computer** window, as shown in Fig. 3.3.

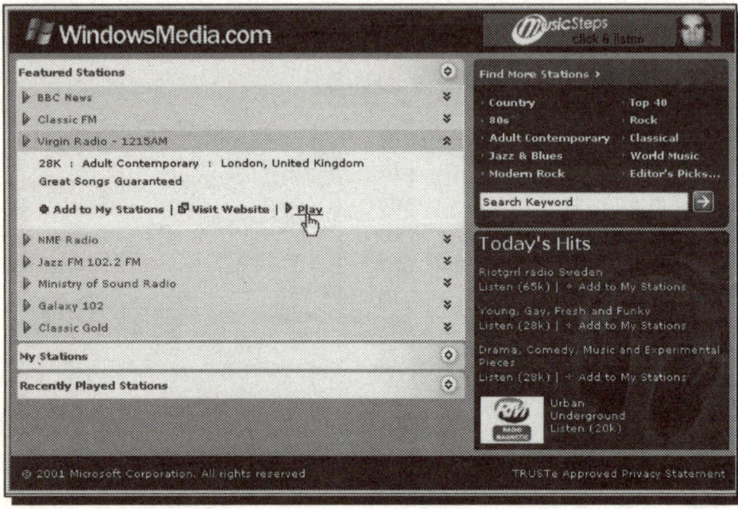

Fig. 3.3 The WindowsMedia.com Web Site.

If you are not connected to the Internet, you can work off-line with files in My Music or My Videos folder, as shown in Fig. 3.4.

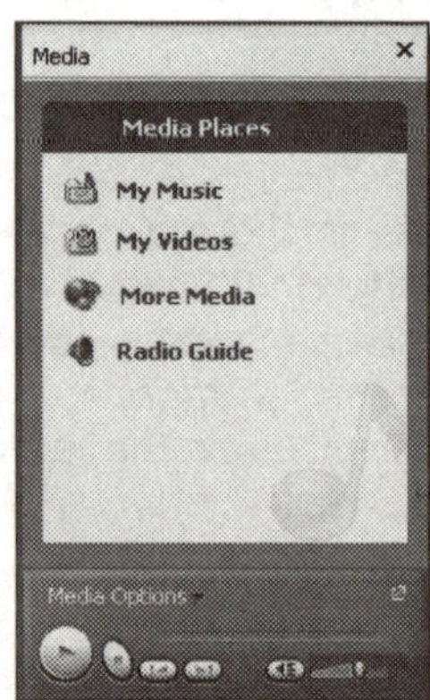

Fig. 3.4 The Media Window.

Selecting one of the radio stations and clicking the **Play** button (pointed to in Fig. 3.3 above) connects you to it and opens up a separate Internet Explorer window and the Media Player to display information about the station and provide a visual accompaniment to the music. For example, selecting Virgin Radio displays the Internet Explorer screen shown in Fig. 3.5 on the next page.

Fig. 3.5 An Internet Explorer Screen of Virgin Radio.

As you can see, there are many choices to be made here, including the ability to buy CDs or look at short promotional videos. Simultaneously, the Microsoft Media Player is opened and after some short delay, the current music being broadcast is played. The delay is due to buffering which is the process of sending a certain amount of information to the computer before the content actually plays.

The History View

Use this to display the **History** facility in the left pane of My Computer window. It allows you to see which 'pages' were visited recently , as shown in Fig. 3.6. It includes files and folders on your system, other computers connected to your system or sites on the Internet. You can select to see today's history or that of other periods as shown at the top of the display.

Fig. 3.6 The History Pane.

The Folders View

Click this to display a hierarchical 'system tree' on the left panel of My Computer window showing all the resources of your computer, as well as those of a network you might be connected to. In your case, the display in Fig. 3.7 will obviously have different contents from ours, as your system is bound to be structured differently.

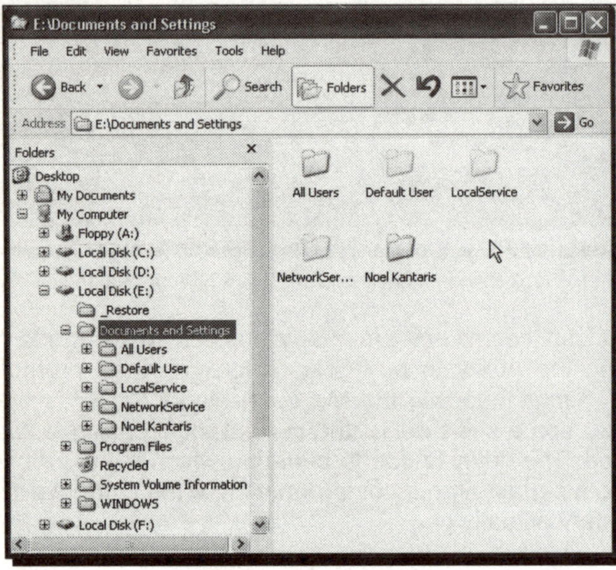

Fig. 3.7 The System Tree.

The system tree lists Objects which contain sub-folders with a plus sign (+). Clicking a (+) sign, opens it up to reveal the sub-folders beneath. When sub-folders are displayed, the (+) sign changes to a minus sign (–), indicating that the parent folder can be collapsed. This is shown in the example above, where the Documents and Settings folder in the E: drive is expanded.

The right-hand, or contents, pane is automatically displayed when you select a folder from the tree. As with most Windows XP system windows, you can change the format of the information shown in the contents pane by clicking the Views button on the Toolbar.

The Picture and Fax Viewer

New to Windows XP is the Picture and Fax Viewer. You can use it to view, rotate, and perform basic tasks with all kinds of image documents, including scanned pictures, downloaded pictures from a digital camera, and fax documents, without opening an image editing program. Such images can be viewed as thumbnails or in a filmstrip, and fax documents can be annotated.

To open the Picture and Fax Viewer, locate the picture you want to view and double-click its filename. This displays your picture in the Viewer, for us the rowing boat shown in Fig. 3.8 below.

Fig. 3.8 The Windows Picture and Fax Viewer.

Note the buttons at the bottom of the screen. You can use these to navigate through your pictures folder, select the viewing size, view the pictures in your folder as a slide show, zoom in or out, rotate the image, and generally carry out certain housekeeping functions, including the opening of the picture in Microsoft Photo Editor so that you can edit it. The precise function of these buttons is described in Fig. 3.9.

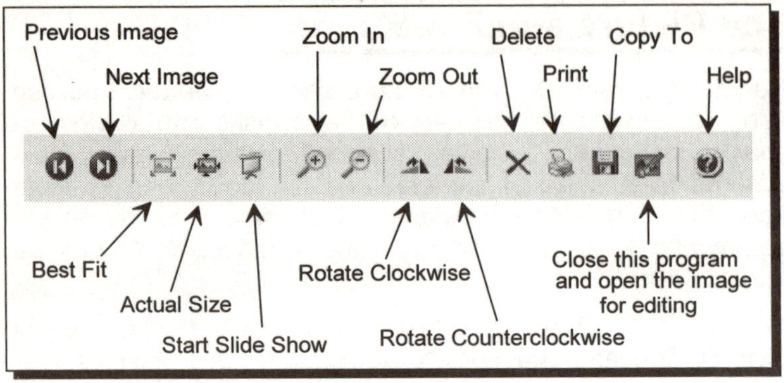

Fig. 3.9 The Windows Picture and Fax Viewer Toolbar.

Clicking the **Close this program and open the image for editing** button on the Windows Picture and Fax Viewer Toolbar, displays the screen in Fig. 3.10 ready for you to edit the selected image.

Fig. 3.10 The Microsoft Photo Editor.

The My Pictures Folder

In Fig. 3.11 below, we demonstrate some of these features by displaying the My Pictures folder in **My Computer** as Thumbnails. The other available viewing facilities are seen in the **View** menu which is also open.

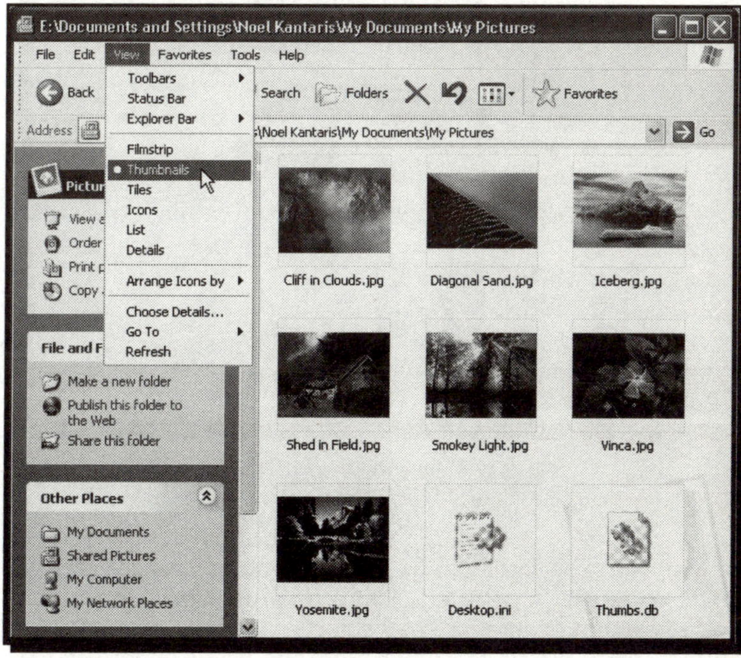

Fig. 3.11 A Pictures Folder Displayed in Thumbnail View.

Icons can be arranged by name, size, type, etc., from the **View** menu, or can be previewed, rotated, set as desktop background, or opened in a variety of imaging programs, from a shortcut (right-click) menu, as shown in Fig. 3.12 on the next page.

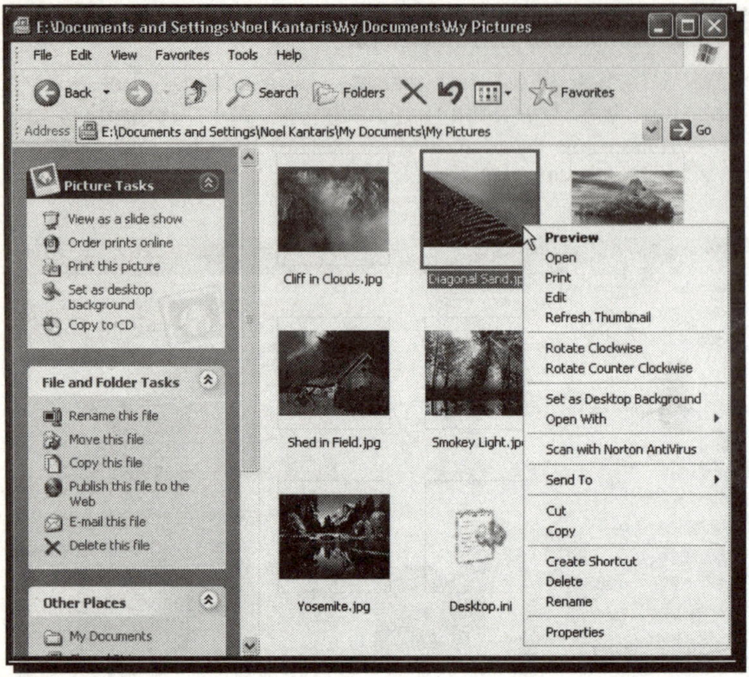

Fig. 3.12 A Picture's Shortcut Menu.

You can also use the Pictures Tasks menu to view pictures as a slide show, set a selected picture as a desktop background, print a selected picture, or copy selected pictures to a CD. You can also carry out all the other functions listed under the File and Folder Tasks.

To see your pictures in another interesting display, use the **View**, **Filmstrip** command. To get the full benefit of this view, you need to increase the size of the displayed window to at least ¾ of the size of your screen. The result should look similar to that in Fig. 3.13 on the next page.

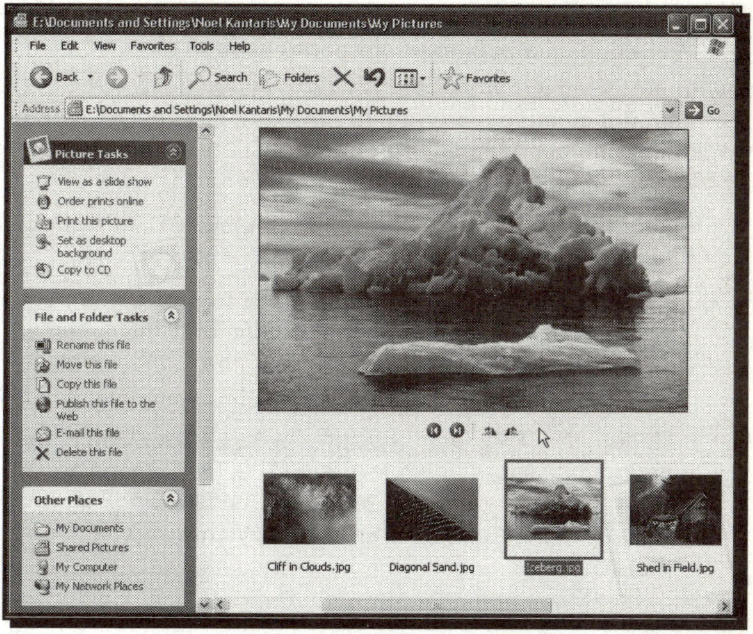

Fig. 3.13 Pictures Displayed in Filmstrip View.

As each picture is selected, an enlarged view of it displays above the filmstrip. The four buttons below the enlarged view can be used to navigate to the previous or the next image, and to rotate the selected picture clockwise or anticlockwise.

Note: If there are several people using the same computer, then each person's My Pictures folder is located in the drive where Windows XP was installed (in our case drive E:) as a sub-folder to the following folders:

E:\Documents and Settings\User name\
My Documents\My Pictures

If the folder is a shared folder then it will be found in:

E:\Documents and Settings\All Users\
Documents\My Pictures

If you have named your computer then its name appears in the address after the Documents and Settings entry.

Copying Files and Folders to a CD

New to Windows XP is the ability to copy files and folders to a CD. You will need a recordable compact disc (CD-R) or a rewritable compact disc (CD-RW) and a CD recorder. To start the process, do the following:

- Insert a blank recordable or rewritable CD in the CD recorder.
- Open **My Computer** and select the files or folders you want to copy to the CD. Make sure that the selected files and folders do not exceed the CD's capacity (normally 650 MB for a standard CD).
- Under the File and Folder Tasks, click **Copy the selected items**, as shown in Fig. 3.14. Depending on what you are copying, the entry under the File and Folder Tasks could change to **Copy this file**, or **Copy this folder**.

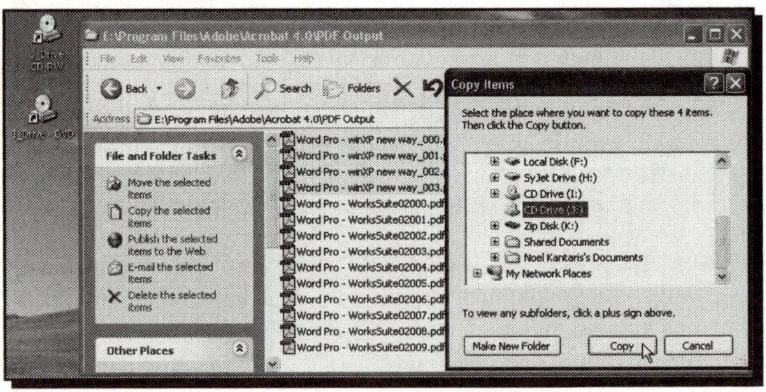

Fig. 3.14 Copying Selected Files to a CD.

- In the displayed Copy Items dialogue box, select the CD-RW drive and click the **Copy** button, as shown above.
- If the files are located in **My Pictures**, then under Picture Tasks, click **Copy to CD** or **Copy all items to CD**, as shown in Fig. 3.15 on the next page.

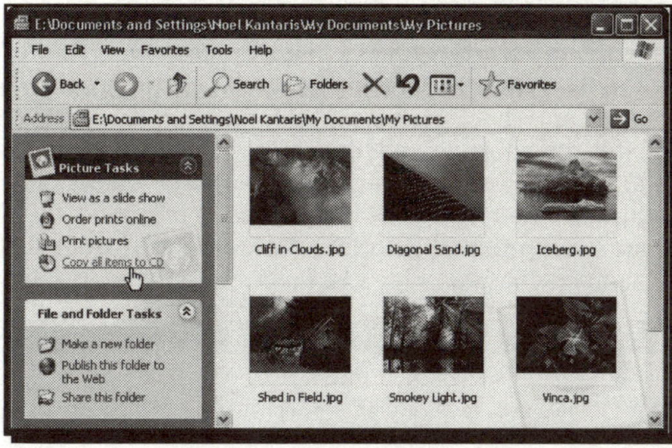

Fig. 3.15 Copying Pictures to a CD.

Either action displays the message shown in Fig. 3.16 on the right end of the Taskbar.

Fig. 3.16 Message on Taskbar.

- To see the files, which are held in a temporary area, before they are copied to the CD, click the message balloon to display a screen similar to that in Fig. 3.17.

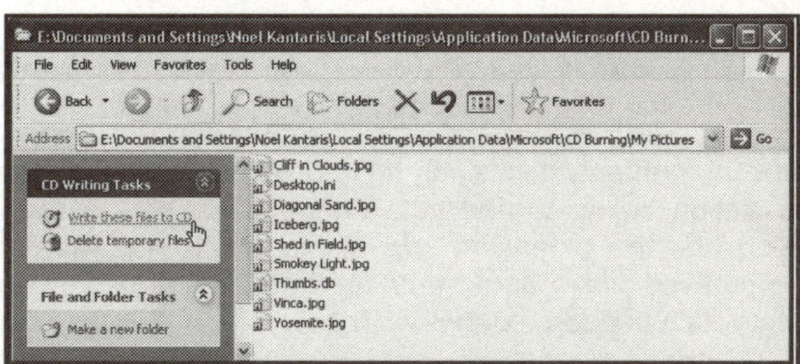

Fig. 3.17 Files in Temporary Area Awaiting to be Burned onto a CD.

Now is the time to perhaps exclude some of these files (by deleting them) before clicking the **Write these files to CD** entry under the CD Writing Tasks panel.

Compressing Files and Folders

Compressing files and folders allows you to greatly increase the storage capacity of your discs with no extra hardware cost. To use this much improved option in Windows XP, select the file(s) and or folder which you want to compress in **My Computer**, then right-click it and choose the **Send To** followed by the **Compressed (zipped) Folder** option from the drop-down menu shown in Fig. 3.18 below.

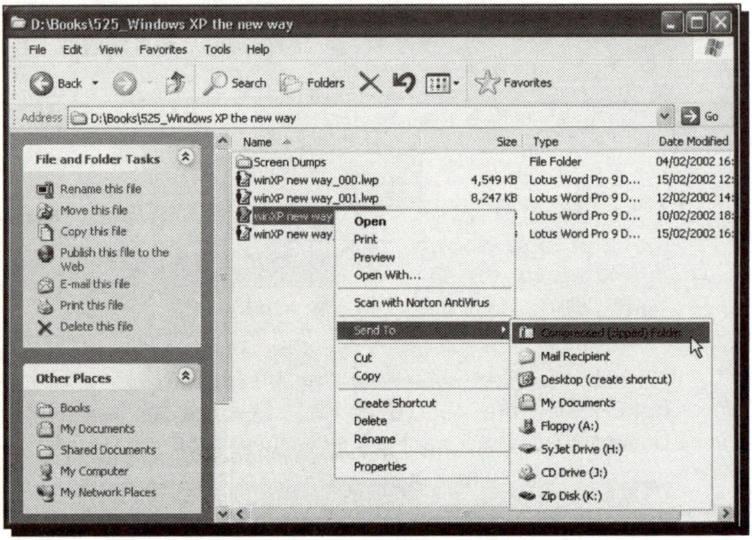

Fig. 3.18 Sending a File to a Zipped Folder.

After momentarily displaying an information box to let you know the action being carried out, Windows creates a new folder which has the extension **.zip** inside which you will find your compressed file. Should you rename this zipped folder, you must retain the **.zip** extension. Try it!

In the screen dump of Fig. 3.19 on the next page, you can see both the uncompressed original file and the renamed zipped folder holding the compressed file inside it which can be seen by double-clicking the zipped folder. As you can see, the compression ratio is very high.

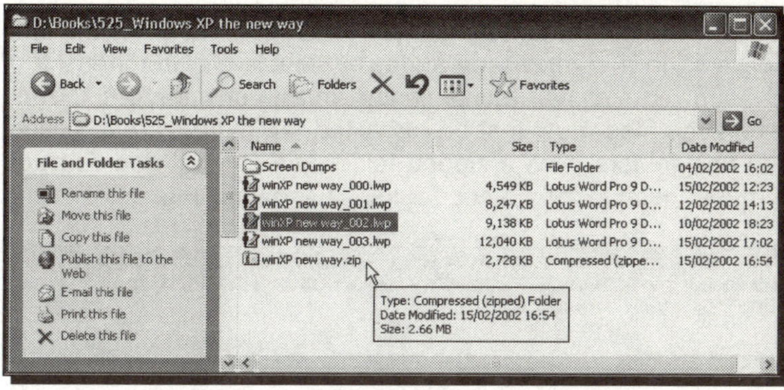

Fig. 3.19 The Original File and the Zipped Folder.

You can send other files and folders into the compressed folder by dragging them onto it. Selected files are then compressed one at time before they are moved into the folder, while the contents of the dragged folders are also compressed.

To find out the size (before and after compression) of an individual file which might be one of many inside a zipped folder, double-click the compressed folder to display its contents, then right-click the required file and select **Properties** from the drop-down menu to display a box similar to the one shown in Fig. 3.20 below.

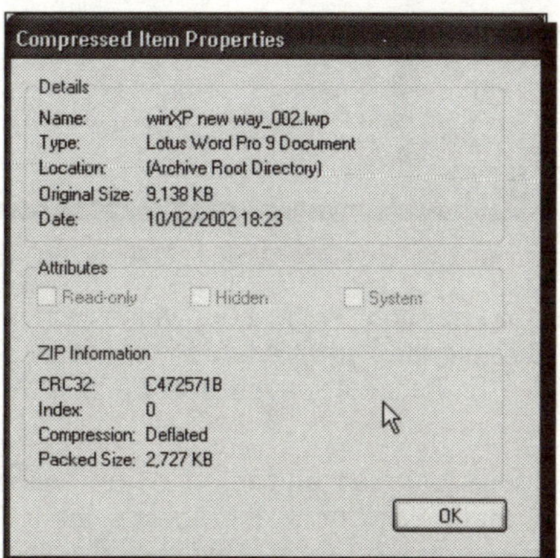

Fig. 3.20 Compressed File Properties.

As we have mentioned earlier, you can open files and programs in a compressed folder by double-clicking them. If a program requires **.dll** (dynamic link library) or data files to run, then those files must first be extracted. To extract compressed files and folders from a zipped folder, simply click the **Extract all files** option in the Folder Tasks, as shown in Fig. 3.21.

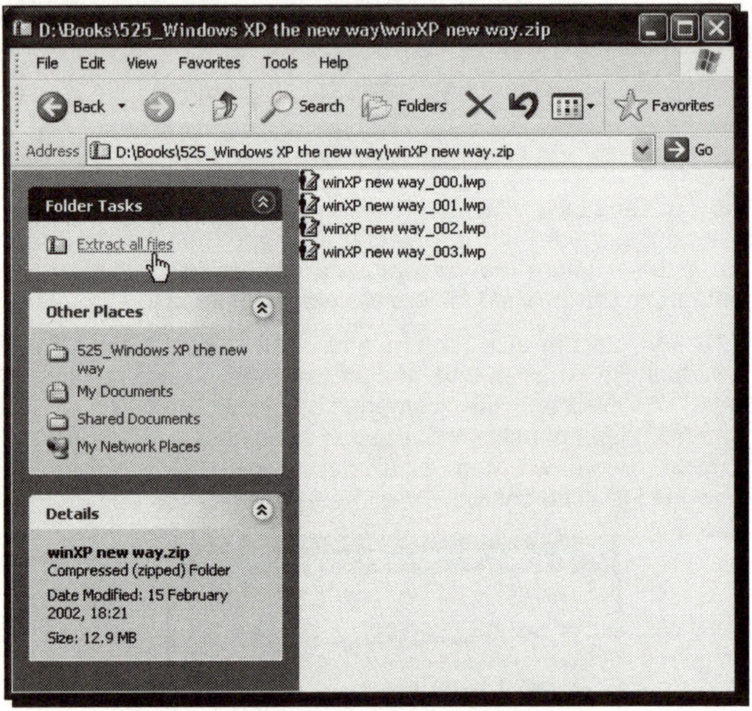

Fig. 3.21 Compressed File Properties.

This starts the Extraction Wizard in which you can specify where you want these files and folders to be extracted to. When you extract a file or folder it leaves a copy of it in the zipped folder.

To remove individual files and folders from within a zipped folder you must first select them, then delete them. To remove all the contents of a zipped folder and the zipped folder itself, delete the zipped folder.

Moving Files and Settings

If you are running Windows XP on a new computer and you want to move your data files and personal settings from your old computer to the new one, without having to go through the same configuration you did with your old computer, then you need to use The Files and Settings Transfer Wizard.

The Wizard can help you easily and quickly move your personal display properties, Taskbar and Folder options, and Internet browser and mail settings from your old computer and place them on the new one. Other folders and files that are also moved are **My Documents**, **My Pictures**, and **Favorites**. The transfer can be carried out either by a direct cable connection between the two computers, via a floppy drive or other removable media, or a network drive.

To start the process, you will need to run the **Files and Settings Transfer Wizard** on both your old and new machine. To do this on your old machine, place the Windows XP distribution CD in its CD-ROM drive and on the first installation screen click the **Perform additional tasks** option to open the screen in Fig. 3.22.

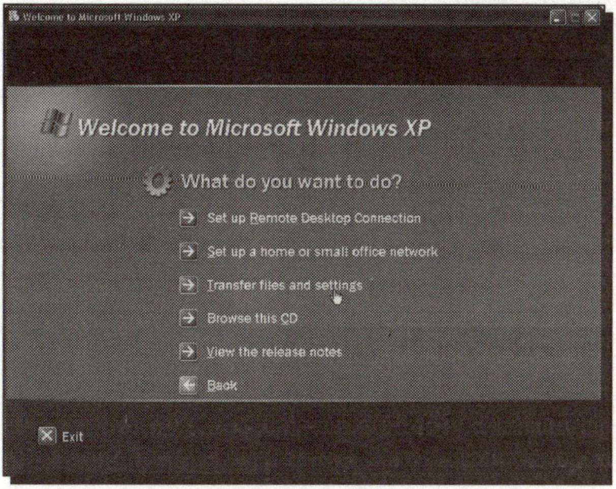

Fig. 3.22 Selecting the Transfer Files and Setting Option from the Windows XP Distribution CD.

On that screen, click the **Transfer files and settings** option to start the Wizard on your old machine.

To open the Files and Settings Transfer Wizard on your new machine, use the ***start***, **All Programs**, **Accessories**, **System Tools** command, then click the **Files and Settings Transfer Wizard** option. This opens the first screen of the Wizard, as shown in Fig. 3.23.

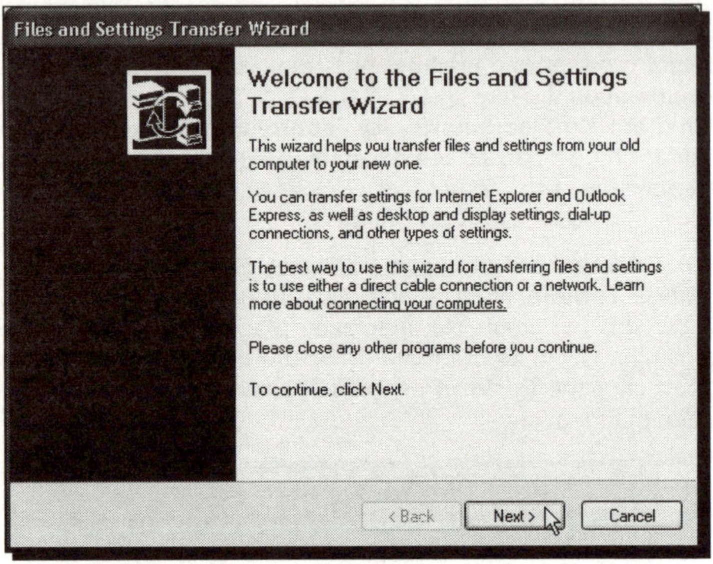

Fig. 3.23 The Files and Settings Transfer Wizard.

In subsequent Wizard screens, on both machines, you are told:

- To state whether this is your new or old computer.
- To state which media you want to use for the creation of a Wizard disc which will contain all your relevant files and settings.
- To specify which files and folders you want to transfer. Don't go overboard with your selection here as it could take a very long time to accomplish the task.
- To go to the new computer with the newly created disc, start the Wizard and complete the transfer.

The Windows XP Control Panel

The Control Panel provides a quick and easy way to change the hardware and software settings of your system. To access it, click the ***start*** button, then click the **Control Panel** entry on the displayed menu to open the default Control Panel window shown in Fig. 3.24 below.

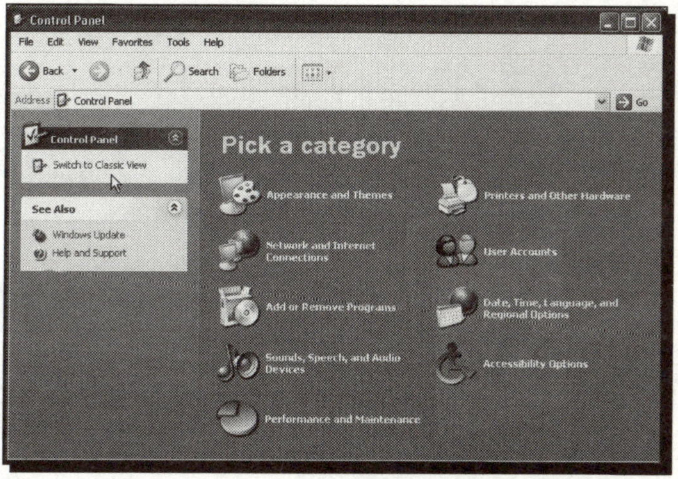

Fig. 3.24 The Control Panel Window in Category View.

New to Windows XP is the ability to group the various Control Panel options by category. Left-clicking the entry **Switch to Classic View** on the left panel (pointed to) provides the display shown in Fig. 3.25 on the next page.

Double-clicking at the Control Panel icons shown in Fig. 3.25 allows you to add new hardware, add or remove programs, change the display type and its resolution, change the printer fonts, and change the keyboard repeat rate. Further, you can change the settings of your mouse, install and configure your printer(s), specify regional settings, such as the formatting of numbers and dates, and access a variety of system administrative tools. If your system is connected to the outside world or supports multimedia, then you can also configure it appropriately.

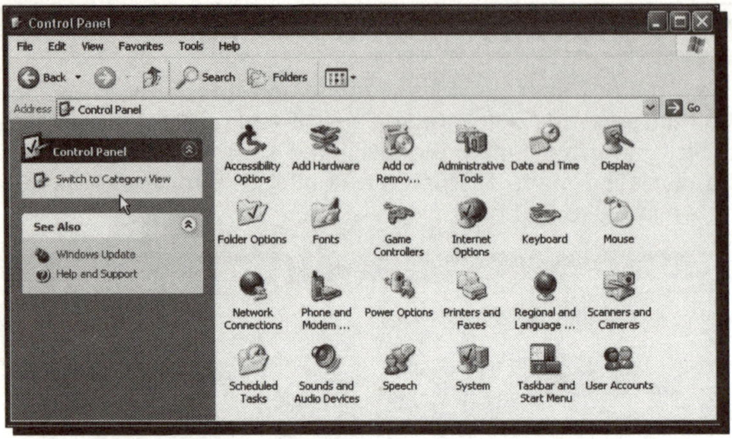

Fig. 3.25 The Control Panel Window in Classic View.

Which view you choose to work with is a matter of preference. We suspect that those of you who have used Windows before will be more familiar with the Classic view of Fig. 3.25. However, those of you new to Windows might prefer the **Category View** (Fig. 3.24) as it appears to be less daunting. Each option within this view displays an additional screen in which you are asked to **Pick a task** or **Pick a Control Panel icon**, as shown in Fig. 3.26.

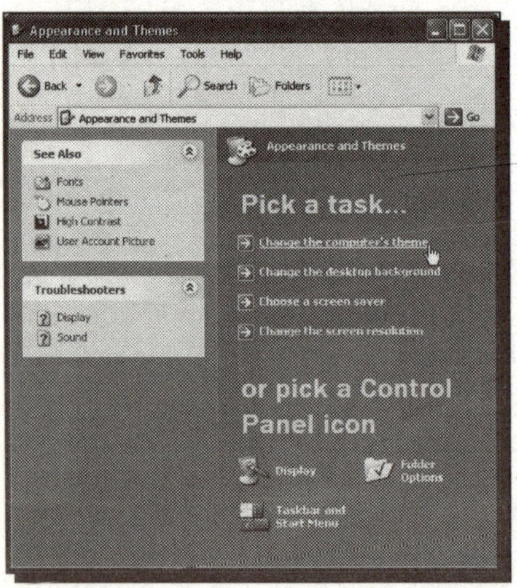

Fig. 3.26 Appearance and Themes Screen.

In the following chapters we will discuss the various options in the Control Panel, each chapter dealing with one Category (Fig. 3.24), but grouping them in subsections as they appear under **or pick a Control Panel icon** in Fig. 3.26.

4

Appearance and Themes

In this chapter we will examine how you can change the appearance and add themes to your PC's display. We begin by using the ***start***, **Control Panel** menu command which displays the screen in Fig. 4.1 below.

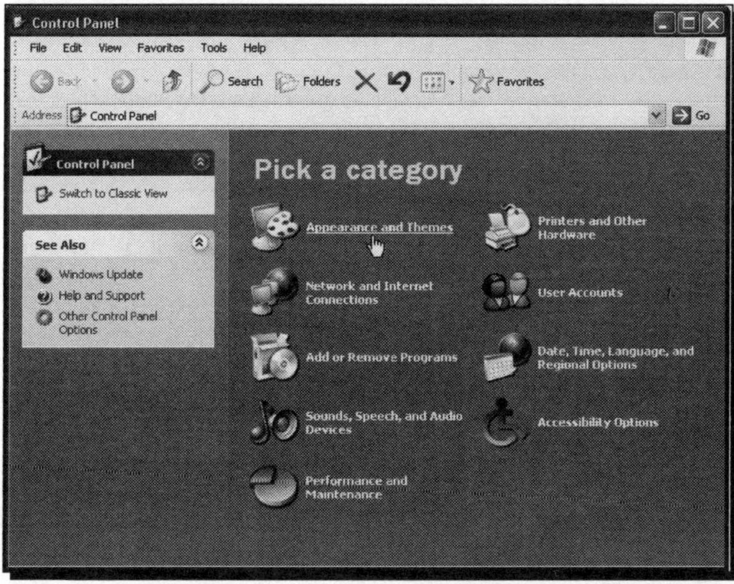

Fig. 4.1 The Control Panel Screen in Category View.

If the **Control Panel** screen displays in Classical View, click the **Switch to Category view** option to be found at the top-left panel of the screen.

Next, click the **Appearance and Themes** link (pointed to) under the **Pick a category** panel to display the screen shown in Fig. 4.2 on the next page.

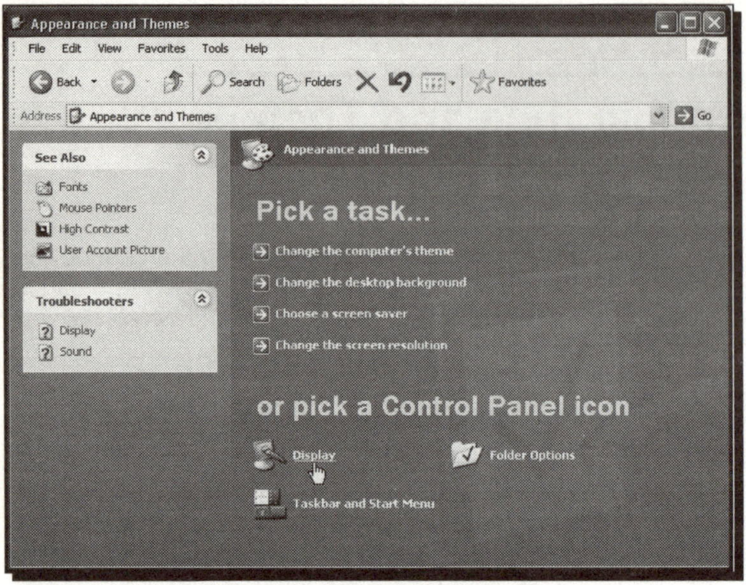

Fig. 4.2 The Appearance and Themes Screen.

Clicking any of the options under the **Pick a task** entry, or the **Display** option under the **or pick a Control Panel icon** entry, opens the same multi-tab dialogue box, as shown in Fig. 4.3. The only difference is that in the former case each selected option displays the appropriate tabbed screen. Having more than one way of finding out what you want to do is the trademark of the 'new look' Windows XP.

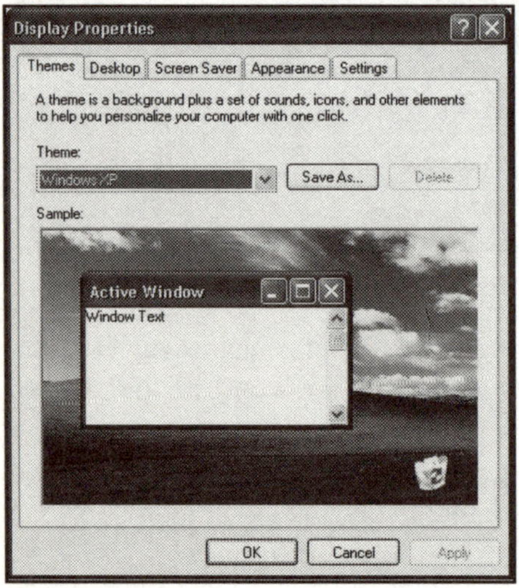

Fig. 4.3 The Display Properties Dialogue Box.

The Display Properties

The display option is used to change the appearance of your desktop by adding a background, employing a screen saver, changing the screen colours and font sizes, and adopting a different screen resolution.

Display Themes

Clicking the down-arrow to the right of the Theme tab sheet (Fig. 4.4), displays a drop-down menu from which you can select a different theme. For example, selecting the Windows Classic theme displays the way your active windows will look from now on if you choose to apply that theme. You can also get different themes from the Internet or browse your hard disc for downloaded **.theme** files.

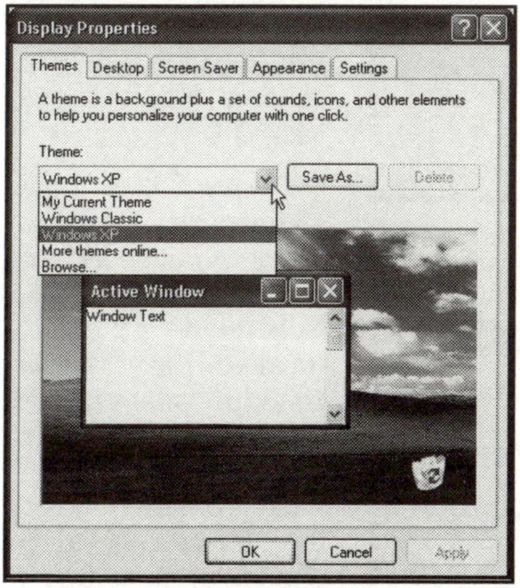

Fig. 4.4 The Themes Dialogue Box.

Desktop Background

Clicking the Desktop tab on the Display Properties dialogue box displays the screen shown in Fig. 4.5 on the next page. You use this screen to change the background of your desktop, which by default was set to 'Bliss'. The first four backgrounds are quite interesting, or you could select 'None'.

On the same display you can choose the **Position** you want to place the background, the default being 'Stretch'; the other two are 'Tile' and 'Center'. You can also select the **Color** to use on your desktop. If you did not choose a background this colour

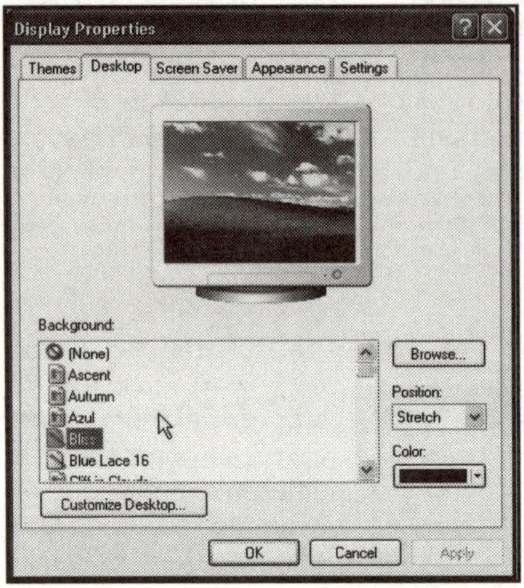

Fig. 4.5 The Desktop Dialogue Box.

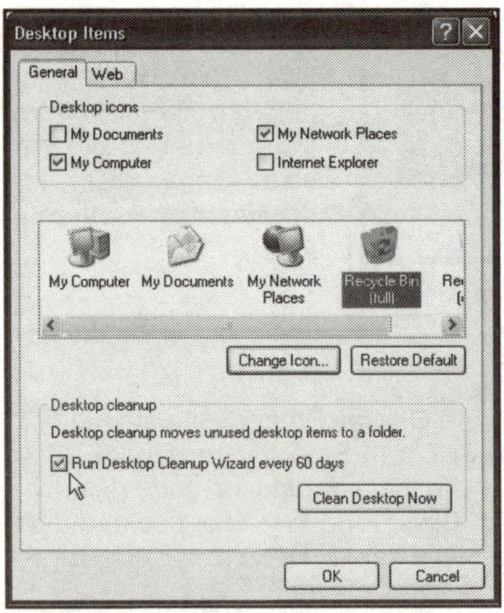

Fig. 4.6 The General Desktop Items Dialogue Box.

will cover the entire screen, while if you choose 'Center' in the **Position** list box, then the selected colour fills the space around the background image. If you make any different selections, you can see at a glance what the result will be by clicking the **Apply** button. Then, to confirm the changes click **OK**.

Finally, click the **Customize Desktop** button to display the screen in Fig. 4.6. Note the default option (pointed to) under **Desktop cleanup** at the bottom of the screen which will move unused desktop icons (including shortcuts) to a folder every 60 days! We suggest you clear this option, but have in mind that you can initiate the cleanup of such items whenever you want.

Other options in this dialogue box allow you to change the icons representing various items. However, be careful here not to end up with an incomprehensible desktop!

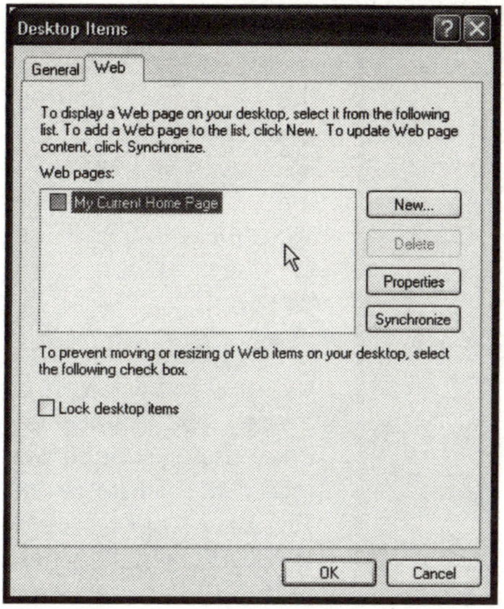

Fig. 4.7 The Web Desktop Items Dialogue Box.

Clicking the Web tab allows you to select from a list (Fig. 4.7) which Web page you would like to appear as the background on your desktop. The number of items on the list will depend on how many Web pages you chose to save on your hard disc. You can **Synchronize** a selected Web page, which means that it will be updated automatically if the original Web page changes.

Screen Savers

By default the screen saver is set to Windows XP, as shown in Fig. 4.8. In this screen you can change the time before the screen saver is activated and whether you want to password protect your PC on resuming normal activity (a good idea if your computer is left unattended in a public place). Also, you can change the picture of the saver by selecting a different one from the drop down list shown in Fig. 4.9 on the next page.

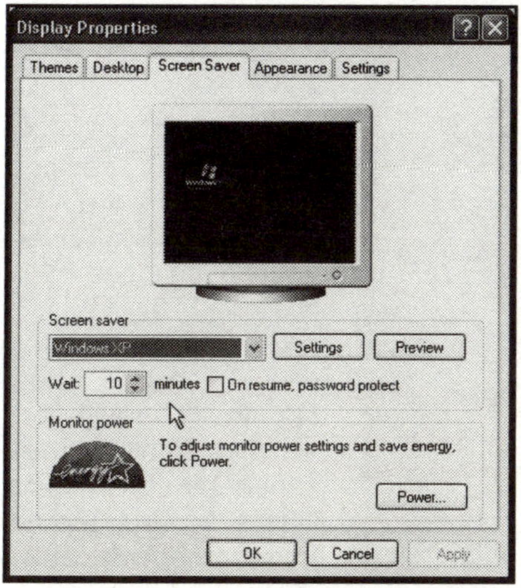

Fig. 4.8 The Screen Saver Dialogue Box.

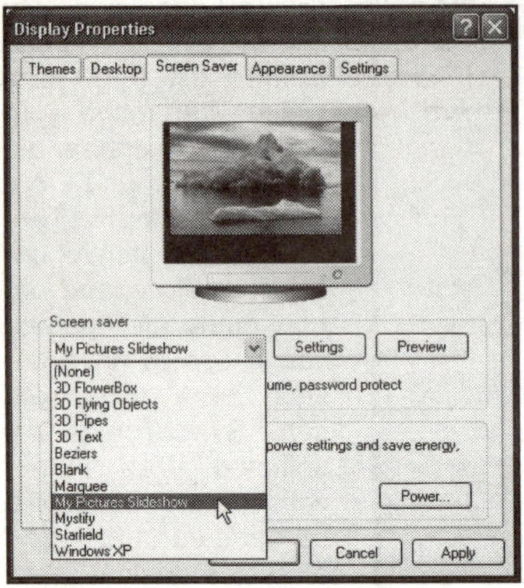

Fig. 4.9 The Screen Saver Dialogue Box.

One interesting option as a screen saver is the My Pictures Slideshow, particularly as you can save in that folder all the pictures you would like to see when not working!

As each selection for a screen saver is made you can see immediately what it will look like. Clicking the **Preview** button will give you a full-screen version. To confirm the changes made, click the **Apply** button followed by the **OK** button.

Most screen savers can be customised by clicking the **Settings** button (see Fig. 4.9). What is available on the displayed dialogue box depends on which screen saver you have selected.

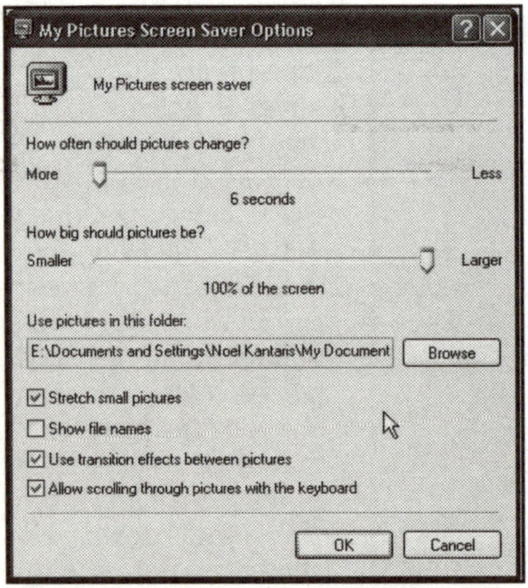

Fig. 4.10 The Screen Saver Options.

In Fig. 4.10, we show the settings options for the My Pictures screen saver. As you can see, it is possible to specify how often the pictures should change, how big they should be, whether small pictures should be stretched to fill the screen, use of transition effects, etc.

Going back to the Display Properties screen in Fig. 4.9, you will also see that there is a **Power** button on it. Clicking this button gives you access to the various power saving schemes available. However, we will not discuss these here, as they will be examined in detail in Chapter 12 under Performance and Maintenance.

Display Appearance

Clicking the Appearance tab on the Display Properties dialogue box opens the screen shown in Fig. 4.11. Here you can select how the windows and buttons appear on your screen (Windows XP style or Classic Windows style), select their colour (default blue, olive, or silver), and choose the font size used (normal, large, or very large).

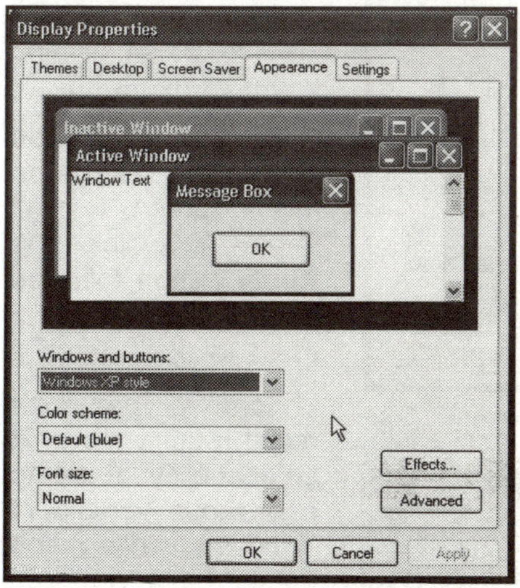

Fig. 4.11 The Appearance Screen.

Finally, have a look at the options on the screens displayed when the **Effects** and **Advanced** buttons are clicked.

On the Effects screen you can choose between two types of transition effect for menu and tool tips, use large icons, show shades under menus, show window contents while dragging, or hide underlined letters for keyboard navigation until you press the <Alt> key.

On the Advanced Appearance screen, you can select different font size and colour for each individual item on a window screen, such as menus, message boxes, scroll bars, etc. If you are one of the people who enjoy spending time customising such things, this is the screen for you!

Display Settings

The last tab on the Display Properties dialogue box opens the screen shown in Fig. 4.12. If your screen is less than 17 inches diagonally, you might find that the settings under **Screen resolution** and **Color quality** are different to ours. We recommend using a resolution of 800 x 600 if you have a 14" or 15" monitor, and a resolution of 1024 x 768 for 17" and larger monitors

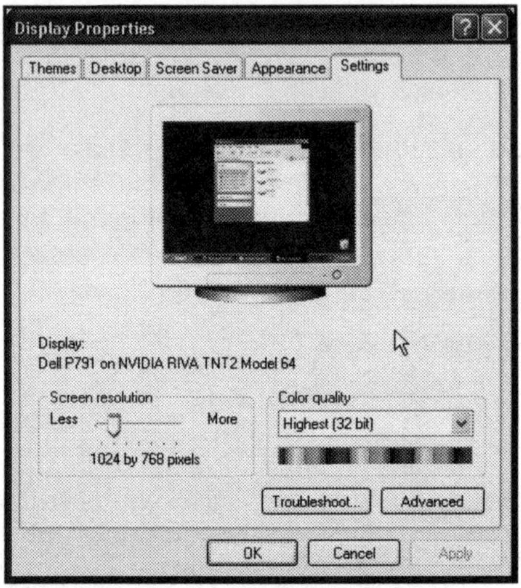

Fig. 4.12 The Settings Screen.

As usual, if you change the settings on this screen, don't forget to click the **Apply** button followed by the **OK** button for these to take effect.

Some programs might require to run in compatibility mode to a previous version of Windows, while some games have to be run in 256 colours. To find out how to do this, click the **Advanced** button on the Settings screen which displays the screen shown in Fig. 4.13. Next, click the link pointed to at the bottom of the screen and follow the instructions in the displayed **Help and Support** screen.

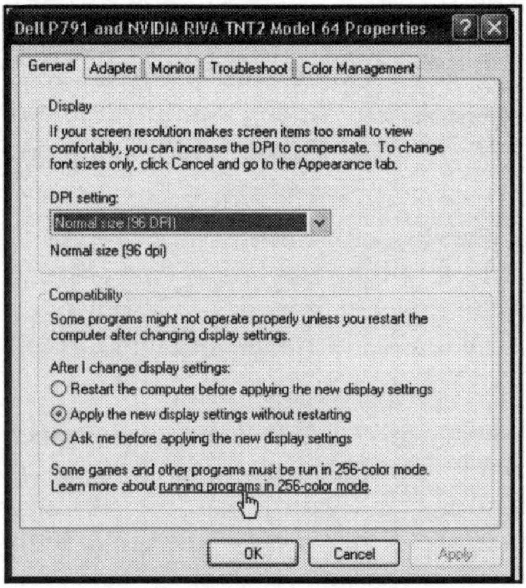

Fig. 4.13 The Advanced Settings Screen.

Folder Options

You use **Folder Options** to specify how your folders should function and how their content is displayed. For example, you can specify that you want your folders to display detailed file information, choose to open items with either a single or a double click, and select to display hyperlinks to common tasks. Also you can change file associations, and make network files available offline.

Begin by using the ***start***, **Control Panel** menu command, then click the **Appearance and Themes** link under the **Pick a category** panel to display the screen shown in Fig. 4.14 below.

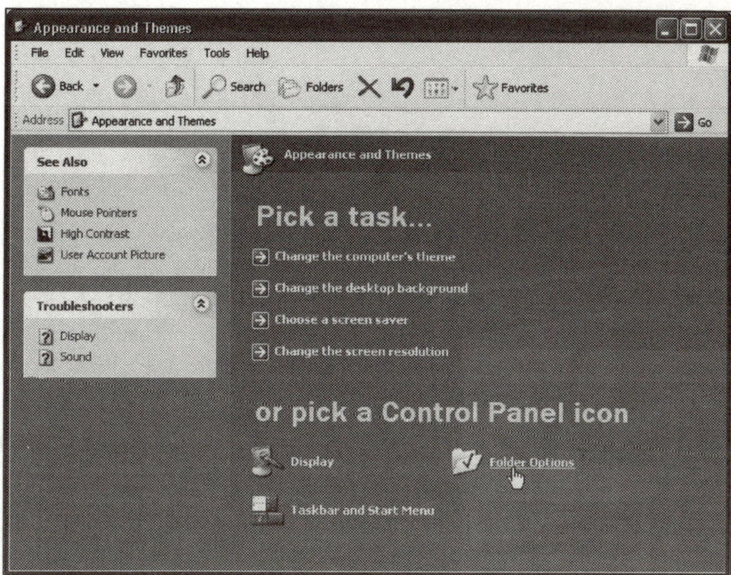

Fig. 4.14 The Appearance and Themes Screen.

Clicking the **Folder Options** link (pointed to) under the **or pick a Control Panel icon** entry, opens a multi-tab dialogue box shown in Fig. 4.15 on the next page.

General Folder Options

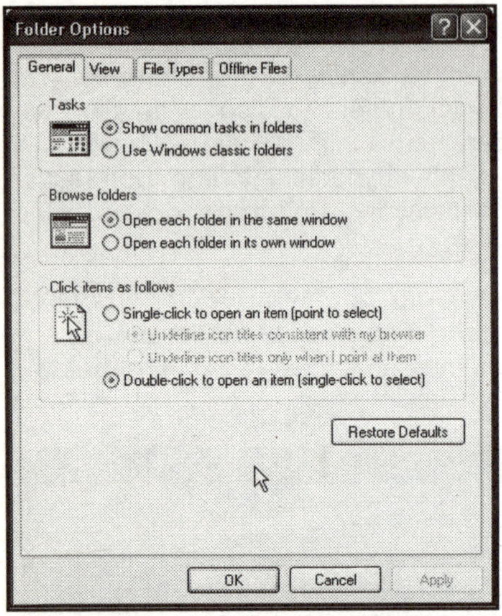

Fig. 4.15 The Themes Dialogue Box.

In the General Folder Options tabbed sheet, you can specify whether common folder **Tasks** are shown in a folder window or not, how folders are opened, and whether a single or a double mouse click should be used to open such folders.

Most of the options available on this tab sheet are very much self-explanatory apart from the first three. These offer you the following possibilities:

Show common tasks in folders - selecting this option displays hyperlinks to common folder tasks and other places, as shown in Fig. 4.16, in the left pane of each window. Hyperlinks to common folder tasks are displayed under the **File and Folder Tasks** pane.

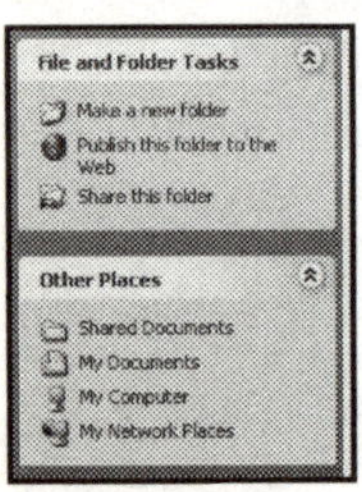

Fig. 4.16 The Tasks Pane.

Use Windows classic folders - selecting this option displays folder contents in the classic Windows manner, which means that the folder window will not show the **Tasks** pane.

Open each folder in the same window - selecting this option displays the contents of each folder in the same window. To go back to the previous displayed folder, click the **Back** button, shown here, on the window's Toolbar.

View Options

It is worth spending some time here going through the available **View** options. For example, you might decide that you would like to be able to see hidden files and folders when using **My Computer**, or that you would like to see the full path of a file in the address bar. The choice is yours!

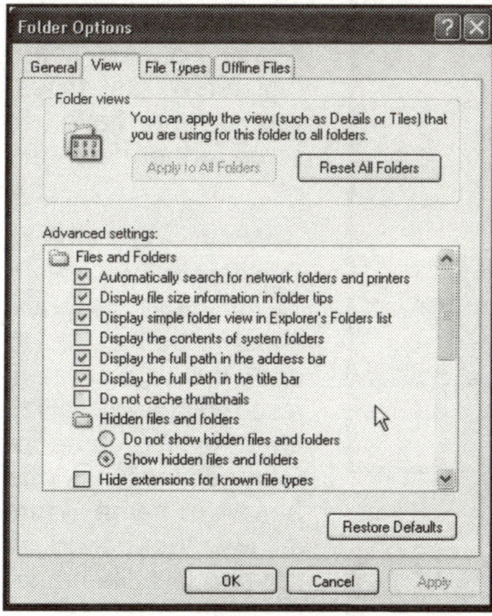

Fig. 4.17 The View Folder Options Dialogue Box.

There is only one default option we would suggest you change, if you haven't already done so, which is to remove the check mark against the **Hide extensions for known file types** option. As we have mentioned already in Chapter 1, doing so could alert you to rogue e-mail attachments.

File Types

Clicking the File Types tab of the Folder Options dialogue box starts searching for registered types of files on your PC, graphically depicted as a search by torch light, as shown in Fig. 4.18. A few seconds later all the registered files types on you computer are listed, as shown in Fig. 4.19 on the next page.

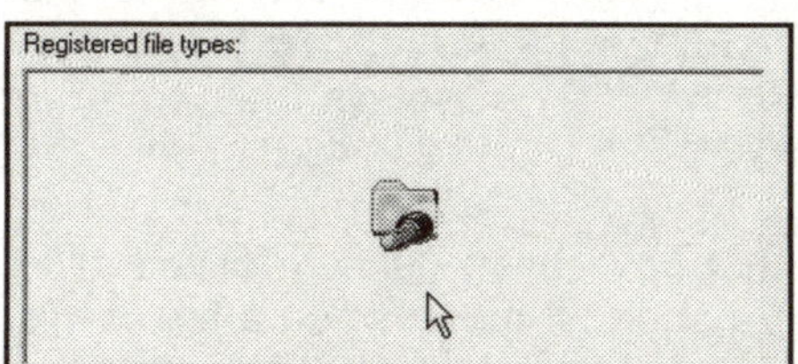

Fig. 4.18 Searching for Registered File Types.

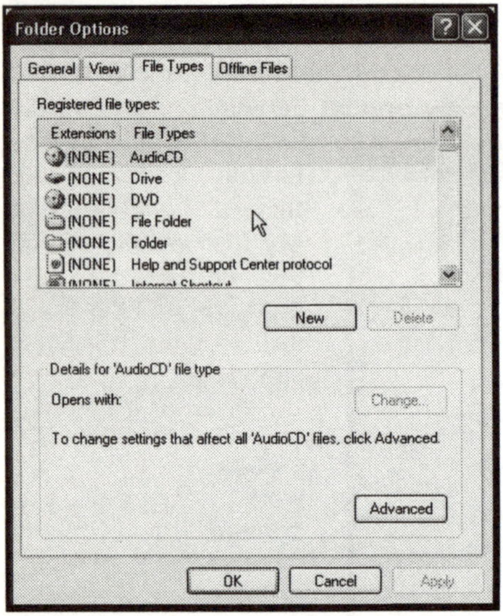

Fig. 4.19 The File Types Dialogue Box.

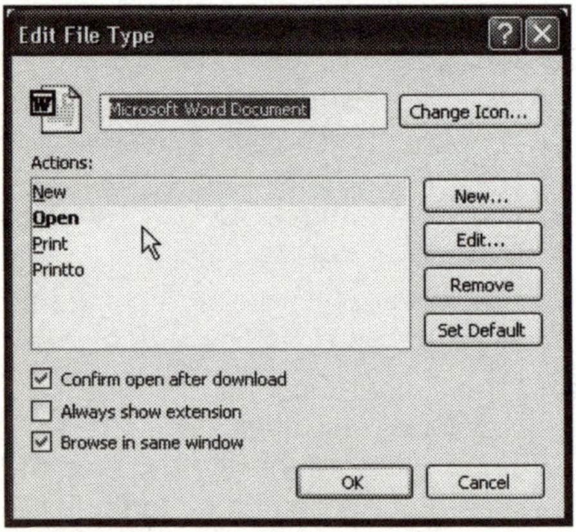

Fig. 4.20 The Edit File Type Dialogue Box.

The displayed list under **Registered file types** shows the file name extensions and their associated file types. To see some registered file types, you might have to scroll further down the list.

When a file type is registered, information about what program should be used to open this type of file is also registered. This is done by the three or four letter extension to a file name that follows the period at the end of a file name, such as **.doc**, **.txt**, or **.html**,.

For example, if you scroll down to the file extension **.doc** you will see that this type of file is associated with Microsoft Word. Selecting this entry and clicking the **Advanced** button displays the screen in Fig. 4.20. In the **Actions** list box appear all the commands that have been defined for this type of file and which appear on a shortcut menu when a file of this type is right-clicked. To add commands to this list, click the **New** button and fill in the displayed dialogue box.

Using Offline Files

Clicking the Offline tab of the Folder Options dialogue box displays the screen shown in Fig. 4.21. By default the Fast User Switching setting is enabled and to be able to use Offline files you must first disable it. To do this, open the **User Accounts** in **Control Panel** and click the **Change the way users log on or off** option under **Pick a task**. This opens a dialogue box in which you can disable the **Fast User Switching** option.

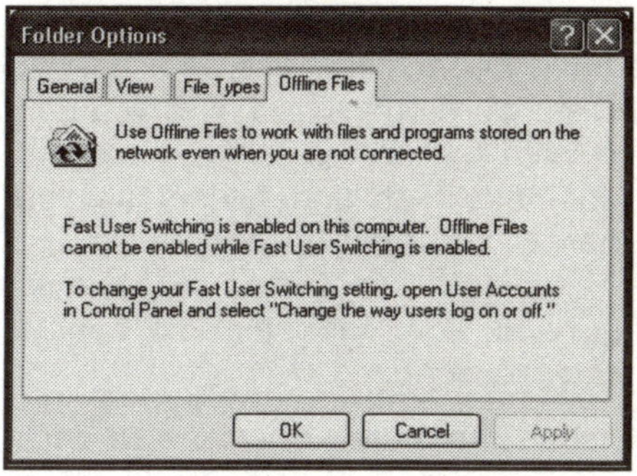

Fig. 4.21 The Offline Files Dialogue Box.

Next, click the Offline Files tab in the Folder Options dialogue box, and select the **Enable Offline Files** check box, as shown in Fig. 4.22. Also, select **Synchronize all offline files before logging off** to get a full synchronisation, or leave it unchecked for a quick synchronisation. A full synchronisation ensures that you have the most current versions of every network file that has been made available off-line, while a quick synchronisation ensures that you have complete versions of all your off-line files, though they may not be the most current versions.

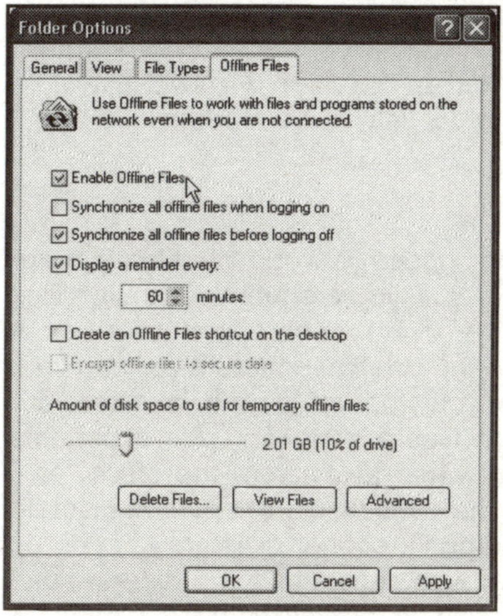

Fig. 4.22 The Enable Offline Files Dialogue Box.

By using Offline Files, you can continue to work with network files and programs even when you are not connected to the network because, say, you have lost your connection to it or undocked your portable computer. In such a case, your view of shared network items that have been made available off-line remains just as it was when you were connected, and you can continue to work with them. With Offline Files, you have the same access permissions to those files and folders as you would have if you were connected to the network. When the status of your connection changes, an Offline Files icon appears in the status area, and an information balloon is displayed near it to notify you of the change.

When your network connection is restored or when you dock your portable computer, any changes that you made while working off-line are updated to the network. If more than one person makes changes to the same file, you are given the option of saving your version of the file to the network, keeping the other version, or saving both.

Your network system administrator can set up shared folders so that either every network file you open in that shared folder is automatically made available off-line, or only those network files you choose are made available off-line. However, unlike shortcuts to files, if a shortcut to a folder is made available off-line, the contents of that folder will not be made available.

Using Briefcase Files

In Windows XP you can also choose to work with files that are stored on your main computer if you frequently transfer files between computers using a direct cable connection or a removable disc. You can use the Briefcase feature to keep your copies of files updated when you work on them away from your main PC. You use Briefcase files if you work with a portable computer, such as a laptop, when away from the office, or if you transport files home in the evening on removable discs to work on your own PC. If you don't, sooner or later, you end up with the situation that the two sets of files become different and you don't know which one to use. In the following few pages, for the sake of completeness, we discuss in detail how you can use Briefcase files.

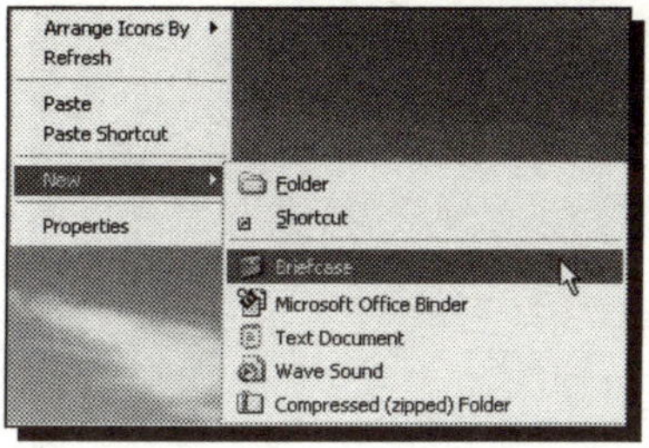

Fig. 4.23 Creating a New Briefcase.

Windows XP does not automatically place the Briefcase icon on your desktop. To activate the tool, right-click on an empty area of your desktop, then select **New, Briefcase** from the cascade menu shown in Fig. 4.23. This selection places the New Briefcase icon on your desktop with its name highlighted ready for you to rename.

To use Briefcase with a portable computer, you connect the portable and desktop computers using a direct cable connection, then drag the files from the folders on your main computer to the Briefcase folder icon on your portable. When you next return to the office, after working on the files, reconnect to your main computer, open the Briefcase and click **Update All** in the Briefcase menu to automatically update the files on your main computer with the modified ones in your Briefcase. Sounds a little complicated, but it's not really.

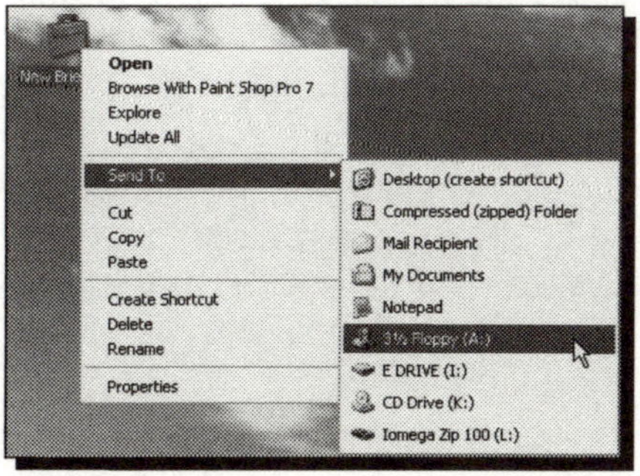

Fig. 4.24 Moving Briefcase to a Floppy.

To use a Briefcase with a floppy, you first copy the Briefcase icon onto the floppy disc (right-click it and select the **Send To** option, as shown in Fig. 4.24), then use My Computer to locate the folder (or file) you want to take home, click the **Copy this folder** (or **file**) option, then click the floppy in the displayed Copy Items dialogue box which then displays the Briefcase on the floppy, as shown in Fig. 4.25 on the next page.

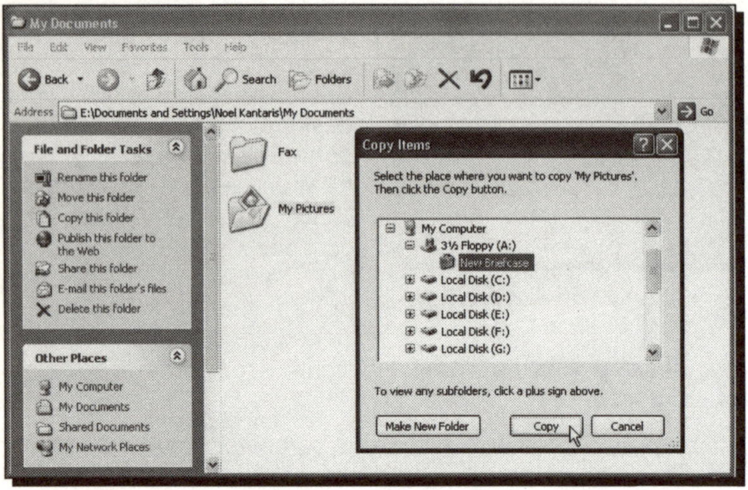

Fig. 4.25 Transferring Files to the Briefcase on the Floppy.

Next, take the floppy home and burn the midnight oil, using the files from the Briefcase. No need to copy them anywhere, but obviously make sure you save your work back to the Briefcase before packing up for the night.

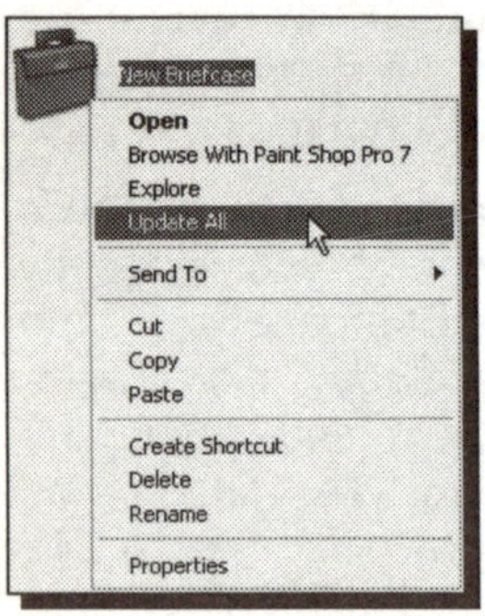

Fig. 4.26 Updating Files.

When back in the office, open your floppy, right-click on the Briefcase icon and select Update All, as shown in Fig. 4.26. Now to the clever bit. The window shown in Fig. 4.27 on the next page will open, listing any files that have been amended.

In our case, there was only one file changed. If you are happy with the suggested course of action in this window, click the Update button.

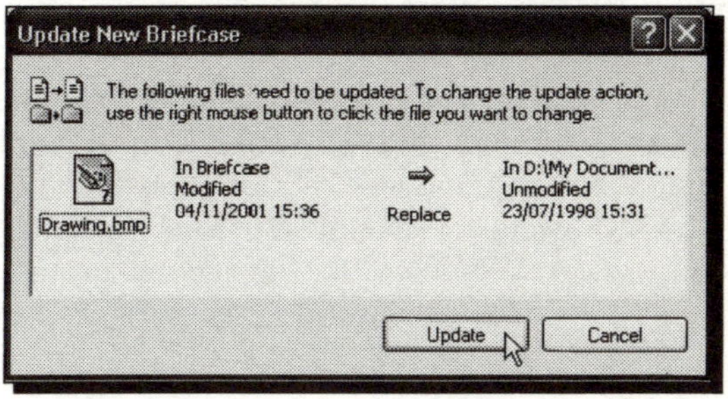

Fig. 4.27 The Update Briefcase Dialogue Box.

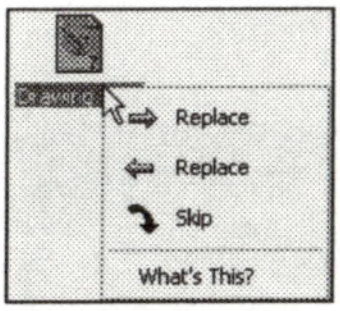

If not, you can right-click a file name and change the action, as shown to the left. The **What's This** option gives you some help, if you need it.

Note: It is essential that you close the Briefcase located on a removable disc, before you actually remove the disc from your PC. This is to ensure that the Briefcase database is updated, otherwise you will be in danger of losing data. If you are careless here, Windows tries to warn you with the message shown in Fig. 4.28 below.

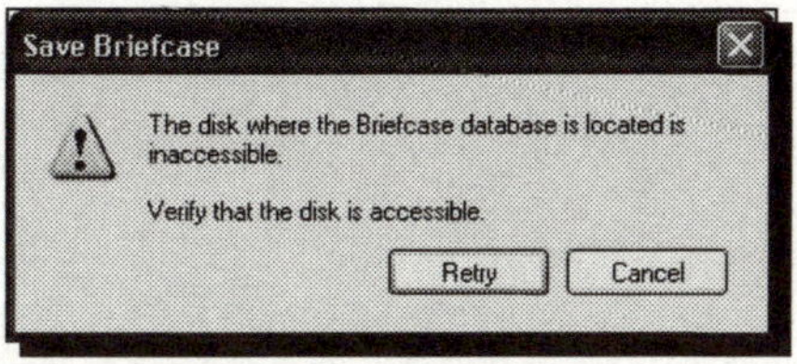

Fig. 4.28 The Save Briefcase Warning Message.

If you still ignore this, you do so at your peril - or rather your data's peril!

Taskbar and Start Menu

The items on the **Taskbar** were set up originally when Windows XP was installed. If the **Quick Launch** icons next to the ***start*** button are not shown on your desktop, then please refer to page 16 under **Taskbar Buttons**, where we also discuss the new to Windows XP ability to group Taskbar entries.

If the Control Panel is not already open, begin by using the ***start***, **Control Panel** menu command, then click the **Appearance and Themes** link (pointed to) under the **Pick a category** panel to display the screen shown in Fig. 4.29 below.

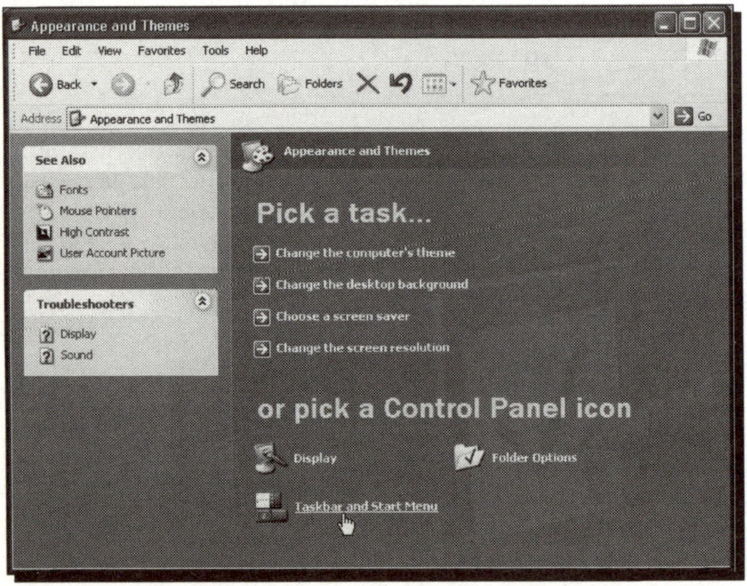

Fig. 4.29 The Appearance and Themes Screen.

Clicking the **Taskbar and Start Menu** link, pointed to, under the **or pick a Control Panel icon** entry, opens a two-tab dialogue box, shown in Fig. 4.30 on the next page.

The Taskbar Properties

In the Taskbar tabbed sheet of the Taskbar and Start Menu Properties dialogue box (Fig. 4.30), you can specify the **Taskbar appearance** and what displays in the **Notification area**. The image under these two main options changes as different choices are made.

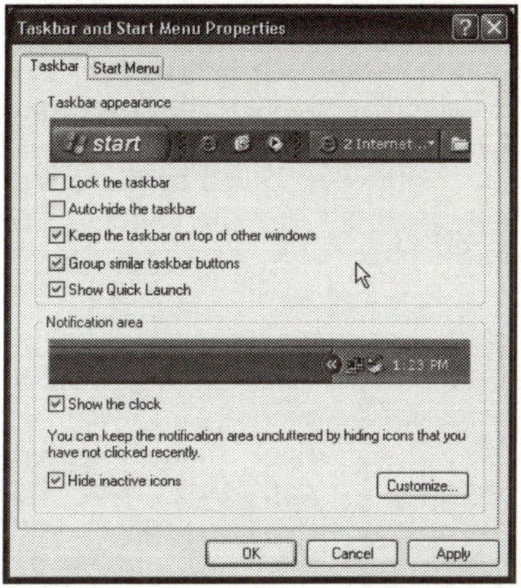

Fig. 4.30 The Taskbar Properties Screen.

The **Customize** button lets you specify the behaviour of an icon in the Taskbar **Notification area**. For each icon displayed, you can choose one of three options. Try it.

The Start Menu Properties

Fig. 4.31 The Start Menu Properties Screen.

The ***start*** menu is compiled during the Windows installation. It is standard, except for the limited addition of the most often used programs to the lower left column of the menu which, however, change with usage. To change this and other properties of this menu click the **Customize** button which displays a further dialogue box, the options on which are self-explanatory.

Adding to the Start Menu

It is very easy to add extra programs or Windows applications to the top left-hand column of the ***start*** menu where they will always be available for use with a single click of the mouse. This can be useful, as this menu opens with one click of the ***start*** button without having to search deep in the **All Programs** cascade menus to find what you want. One such application is the **Character Map** which you might want to use sporadically, but can't be bothered to remember that it is to be found in the **All Programs**, **Accessories**, **System Tools** folder, as shown in Fig. 4.32.

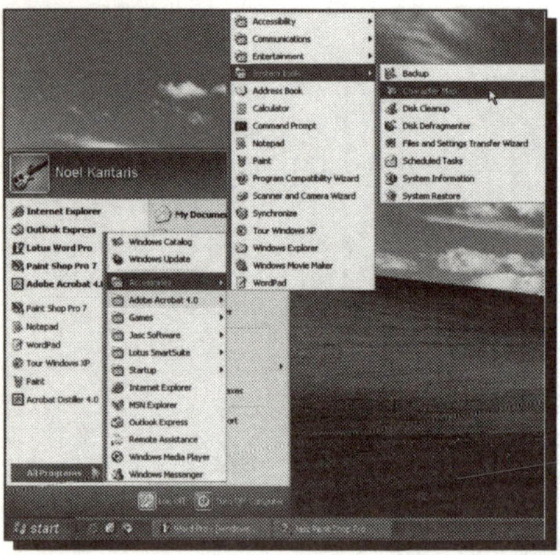

Fig. 4.32 The Location of Character Map.

To do this, you can simply drag the program icon with the right mouse button depressed onto the precise position you want it to appear on the top-left column of the ***start*** menu, as shown in Fig. 4.33 on the next page. When you drag a single icon like this, the drag pointer changes as you move round the screen, to indicate what will happen if you release the mouse button at that location. As shown in Fig. 4.33, the pointer is over the top left column of the ***start*** menu and the black line and open arrow with the 'plus' sign in its bottom right corner shows the position at which the dragged entry will be added.

Over some desktop features, including the right-hand column of the ***start*** menu, the arrow changes to a 'No entry' sign. Releasing the mouse button at the point indicated in Fig. 4.33 adds the required extra entry to the ***start*** menu.

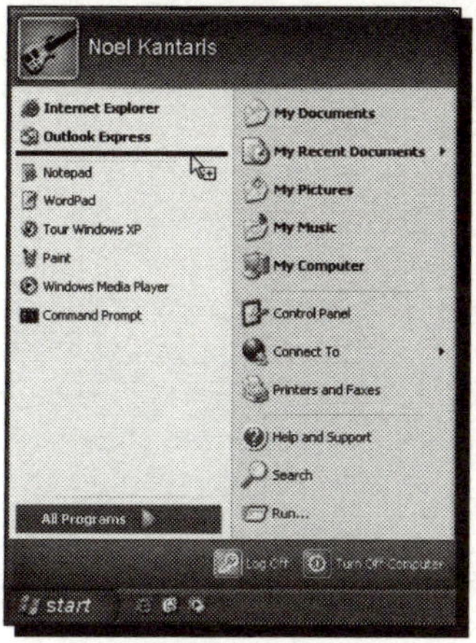

Fig. 4.33 Adding an Entry to the Start Menu.

You can rename the added entry with a more appropriate name by right-clicking the entry and selecting **Rename** from the displayed shortcut menu. If you change your mind, you can remove an entry by right-clicking it and selecting **Remove from This List**.

Within reason, you can add a few more extra items to the ***start*** menu, but if this exceeds seven entries, then there is a corresponding decrease in the number of automatic entries at the bottom of the same column. Apart from the **Character Map**, you could also add your favourite word processing and graphics programs to the list.

Controlling Fonts

Windows XP uses a Font Manager program to control the installed fonts on your system. You can use the Font Manager to:

- Install new fonts.
- View examples of existing fonts.
- Delete fonts.

To open the Font Manager, click the ***start*** button then click the **Control Panel** menu option to reveal the Control Panel window, then click the Appearance and Themes entry to display the screen in Fig. 4.34 on the next page.

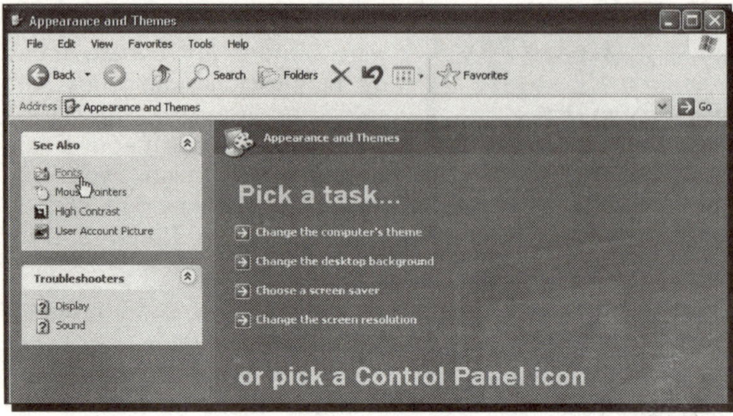

Fig. 4.34 The Control Panel Window.

Next, click the **Fonts** link under the **See Also** Tasks pane to display the Fonts window, shown in Fig. 4.35. To control what you see on the Fonts window, click **View** to display the drop-down menu, shown in Fig. 4.36. We have chosen **Status Bar**, **List** and **Hide Variations.**

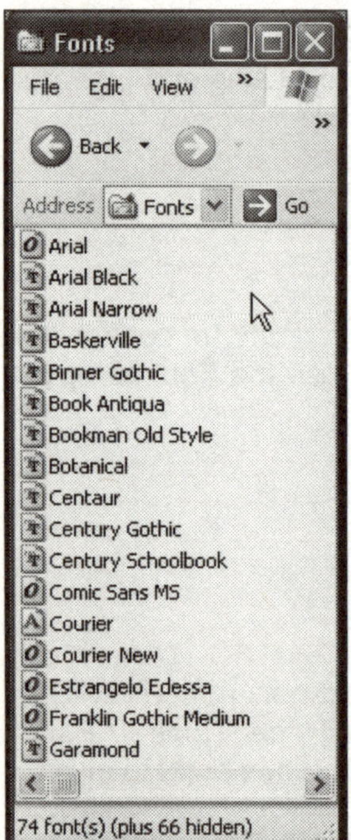

Fig. 4.35 The Fonts Window.

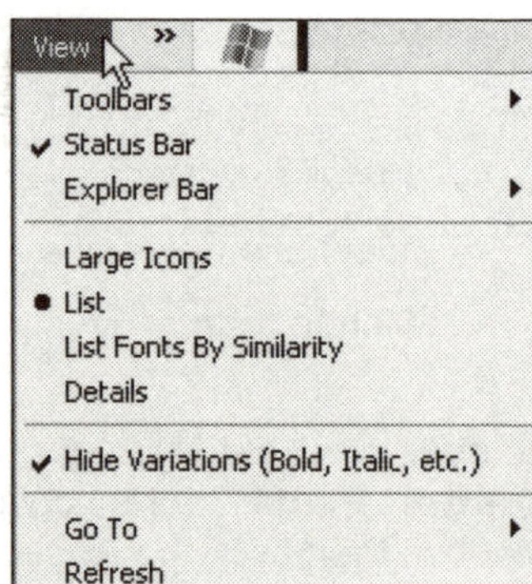

Fig. 4.36 The View Sub-menu.

To see an example of one of the listed fonts, double-click its icon in the Fonts window (Fig. 4.35). Below we show the Symbol (OpenType) font in three different sizes.

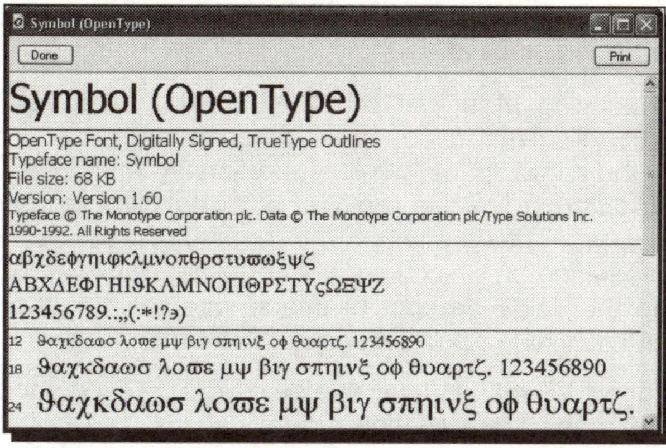

Fig. 4.37 Font Size Sample Window for a Selected Font.

The Symbol font, as you can see, contains an abundance of Greek letters, while the Webdings and Wingdings Fonts contain special graphic objects.

Installing New Fonts

New fonts can be installed by selecting the **File, Install New Font** menu command in the Fonts window, as shown in Fig. 4.38. This opens the Add Fonts dialogue box in which you have to specify the disc, folder and file in which the font you want to install resides.

Unwanted fonts can be removed by first highlighting them in the Fonts window, then using the **File, Delete** command. A warning box is displayed.

Fig. 4.38 Installing New Fonts.

Some Font Basics

Font sizes are measured in 'points' (a point being, approximately 1/72 of an inch), which determine the height of a character. There is another unit of character measurement called the 'pitch' which is the number of characters that can fit horizontally in one inch.

The spacing of a font is either 'fixed' (mono spaced) or 'proportional'. With fixed spacing, each character takes up exactly the same space, while proportionally spaced characters take up different spacing (an 'i' or a 't' take up less space than a 'u' or a 'w'). Thus the length of proportionally spaced text can vary depending on which letters it contains. However, numerals take up the same amount of space whether they have been specified as fixed or proportional.

Windows XP makes available several 'TrueType' fonts which can be used by Windows applications, such as word processors. TrueType are outline fonts that are rendered from line and curve commands. These types of fonts are scalable to any point size, can be rotated, and look exactly the same on the screen as they do when printed.

5

Printers and Other Hardware

In this chapter we will examine how you can change your PC's settings for printers, keyboard, mouse, modem, scanner and camera. We begin by using the **Start**, **Control Panel** menu command which displays the screen in Fig. 5.1 below.

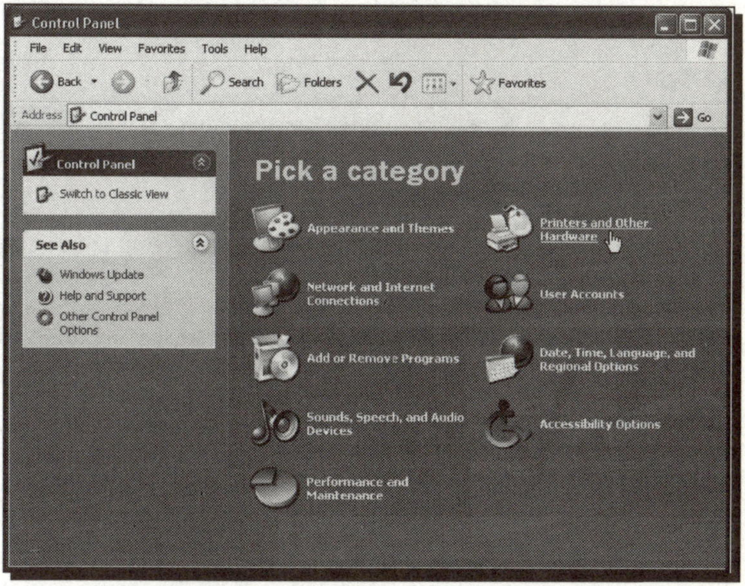

Fig. 5.1 The Control Panel Screen in Category View.

If the **Control Panel** screen displays in Classical View, click the **Switch to Category view** option to be found at the top-left panel of the screen.

Next, click the **Printers and Other Hardware** link under the **Pick a category** panel to display the screen shown in Fig. 5.2 on the next page.

The Game Controllers

Clicking the **Game Controllers** link under the **or pick a Control Panel icon** entry (Fig. 5.2), opens the dialogue box shown in Fig. 5.3.

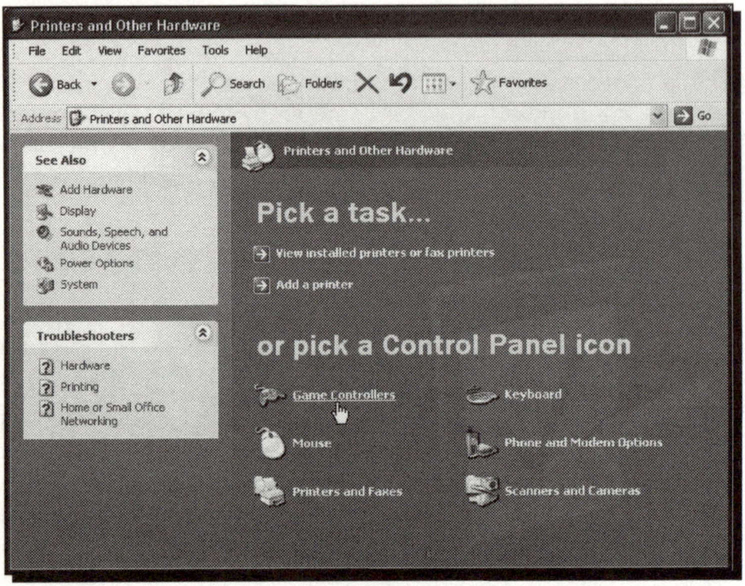

Fig. 5.2 The Printers and Other Hardware Screen.

Normally, if you had any game controllers installed on your computer they will be listed here. If you wanted to test, configure, or re-calibrate a controller you would select it from the list and click the **Properties** button.

Fig. 5.3 The Game Controllers Dialogue Box.

The Games Folder

We will not spend long on this topic, but many people only seem to have a PC to use it for playing games, but maybe not the ones provided with Windows! If that is the case and your games folder was within the My Documents folder, you could use the File and Settings Wizard to transfer them to your new computer. Alternatively, you could reinstall them which might be the best choice.

Our version of Windows XP placed the eleven games shown below in the Games folder of the **All Programs** menu.

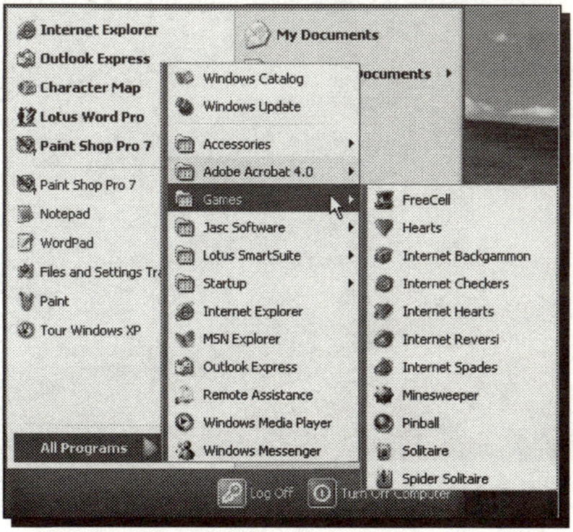

Fig. 5.4 The Games Menus.

Of these, five games require you to connect to the Internet to find opponents of different skill levels, while the other six can be played without additional expense. Classic Hearts can be played over a network against real opponents or against opponents supplied by the computer. FreeCell is a patience based game, while Classic Solitaire, Minesweeper, Spider Solitaire are designed to help with mouse skills. Pinball is a 3D arcade type game with impressive sounds that tests your reactions.

All of these games come with quite good Help sections and we will leave it to you to explore these games at your leisure!

The Keyboard

To adjust or troubleshoot your keyboard, click the **Keyboard** link pointed to in Fig. 5.5.

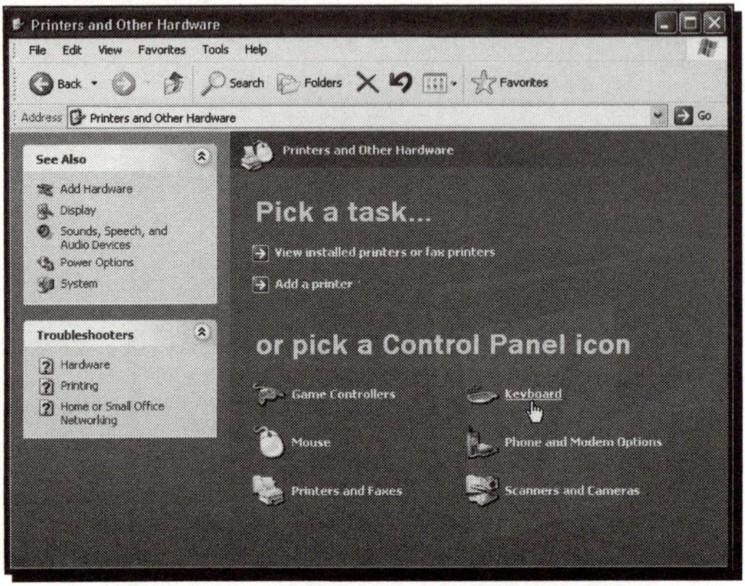

Fig. 5.5 The Printers and Other Hardware Screen.

This opens the Keyboard Properties dialogue box shown in Fig. 5.6 on the next page. You can use this dialogue box to:

- Adjust the amount of time that passes before a character begins to repeat when you hold down a key.
- Adjust the speed at which a character repeats when you hold down a key.
- Adjust the speed at which the insertion pointer blinks.

All these adjustments can be carried out by dragging the appropriate slider.

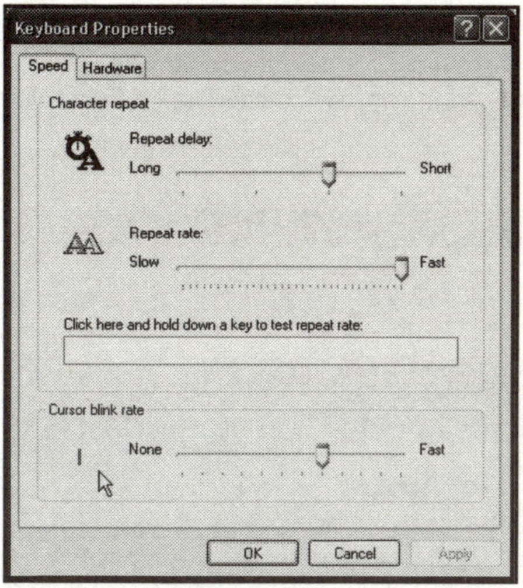

Fig. 5.6 The Speed Keyboard Properties.

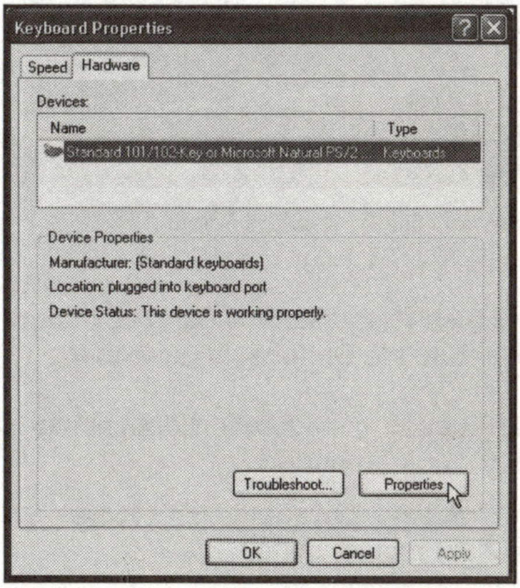

Fig. 5.7 The Hardware Keyboard Properties.

Clicking the Hardware tab on the Keyboard Properties dialogue box, opens the screen shown in Fig. 5.7. Under **Devices**, the name of the keyboard is listed, and under that the name of its manufacturer.

If you want to display more information about a listed device, or change the information relating to a device, select it and click the **Properties** dialogue box. This opens a three-tab dialogue box (not shown here). In the first tabbed screen you can check whether the device works properly, and if not, use the troubleshoot facility. In the second tabbed screen you can get information about the device driver and update it if necessary. Finally, in the third tabbed screen you can select the power management facilities available for the selected device.

The Mouse

To adjust or troubleshoot your mouse, click the **Mouse** link pointed to in Fig. 5.8.

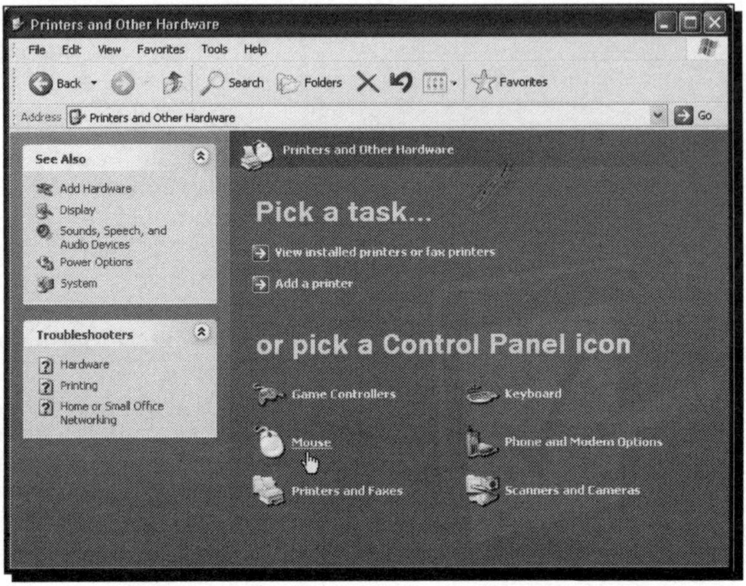

Fig. 5.8 The Printers and Other Hardware Screen.

This opens the multi-tab Mouse Properties dialogue box shown in Fig. 5.9 on the next page. Use the Buttons tab screen to:

- Change the primary button configuration depending on whether you are right- or left-handed.
- Adjust the amount of time between clicks when you double-click the primary mouse button.
- Lock the primary button after a single click, so that you can select or drag items without having to continuously hold down the mouse button. Click again to release ClickLock. To change the time interval before ClickLock takes effect, click the **Settings** button.

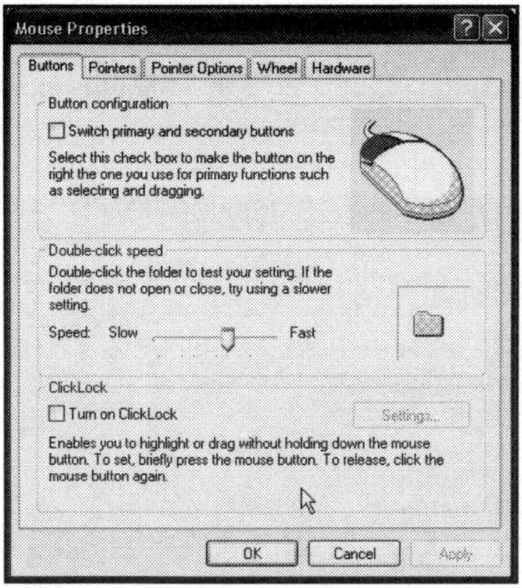

Fig. 5.9 The Mouse Properties Screen.

You can use the Pointers tab sheets on the Mouse Properties dialogue box to see the default set of pointers used by the system to indicate what action is being carried out at any given moment. You can even build your own set of pointers by using the **Browse** button on the sheet to display and choose from the alternative pointers held in the **Cursors** folder.

The Mouse Pointer Options

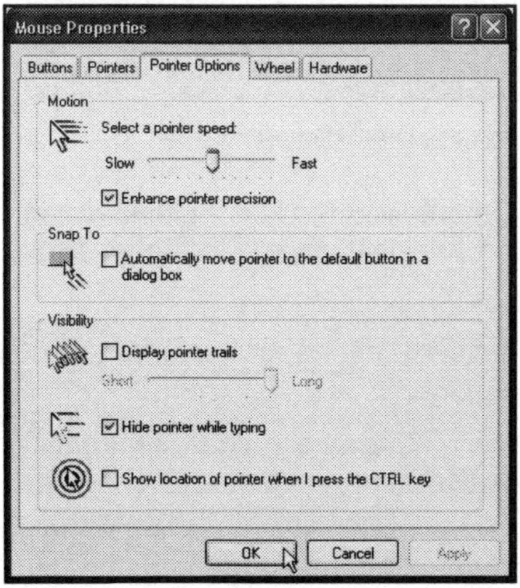

Fig. 5.10 The Mouse Pointer Options Screen.

You use the tab screen shown in Fig. 5.10 to make it more convenient for you to work with the mouse. For example, you can adjust the distance that the pointer moves with respect to the distance covered by the mouse; you can add a trail to the mouse pointer to make it more visible; or you can show the location of the mouse pointer when you press the <Ctrl> key.

Phone and Modem Options

Use the **Phone and Modem Options** link pointed to in Fig. 5.11, to check that they are configured correctly.

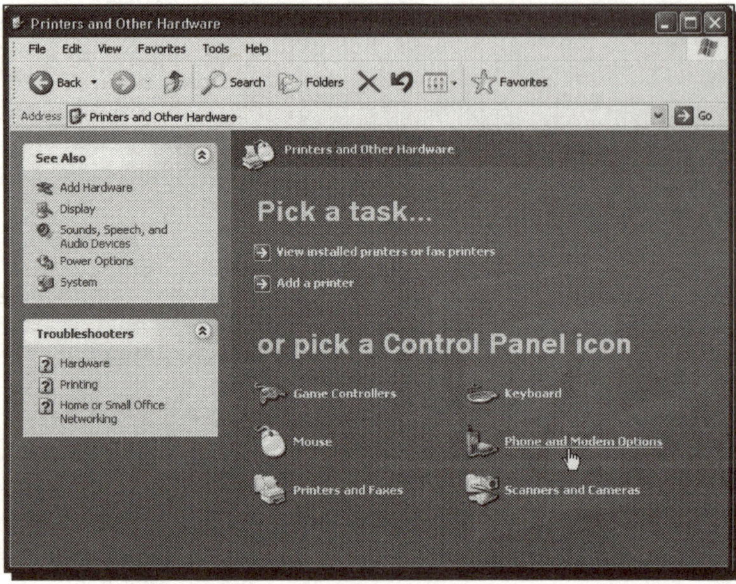

Fig. 5.11 The Printers and Other Hardware Screen.

This opens the three-tab Phone and Modem Options dialogue box shown in Fig. 5.12 on the next page. Use these tabbed sheets to:

- Add new dialling locations to your computer, or edit existing dialling locations.
- Install a new modem or display and change information about a selected modem.
- Display or configure installed telephony providers on your computer, add to the list, or remove from the list.

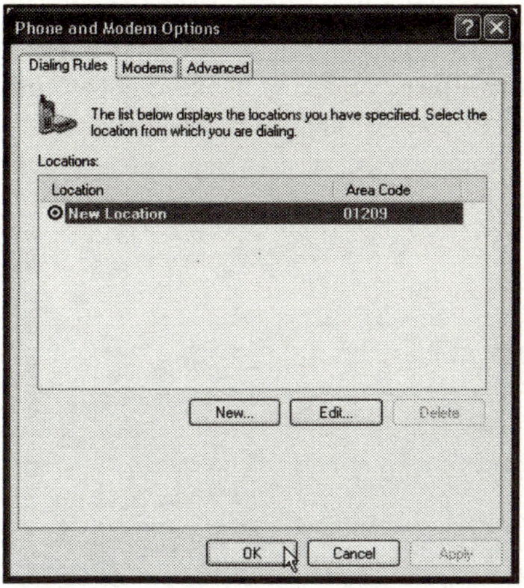

Fig. 5.12 The Phone and Modem Options Screen.

Before using your modem, check to ensure it is correctly configured. To do this, click the Modems tab (Fig. 5.12), then in the displayed dialogue box (Fig. 5.13a), click the **Properties** button, which opens the Properties dialogue box for the installed modem. Next, select the Diagnostics tab and click the **Query Modem** button, as shown in Fig. 5.13b below.

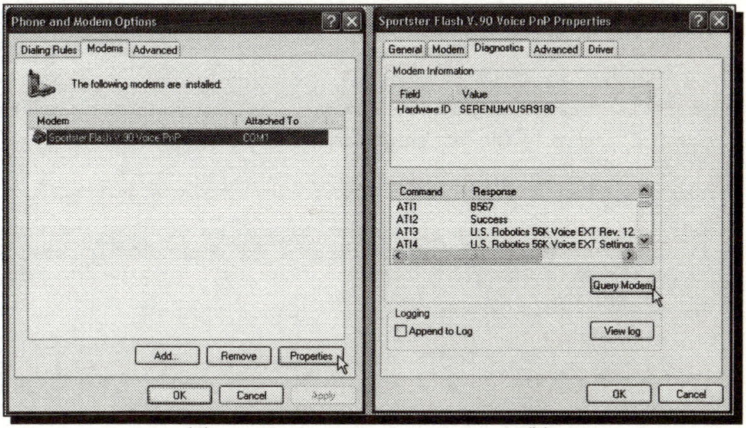

(a) (b)

Fig. 5.13 Performing a Diagnostic Test on your Modem.

In Fig. 5.13b we show the action to be taken and the result of this action. If under 'Response' it displays the word 'success' your modem is working fine.

Printers and Faxes

Click the **Printers and Faxes** link pointed to in Fig. 5.14, to add a printer or a fax printer, or to check their configuration.

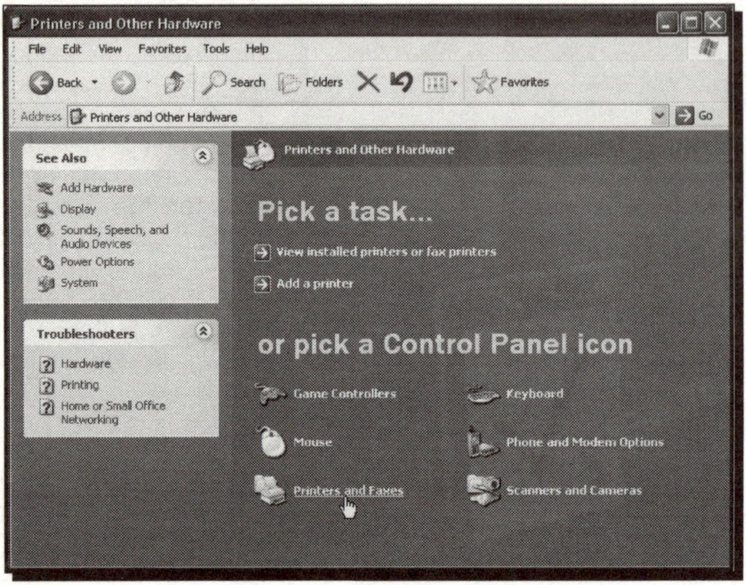

Fig. 5.14 The Printers and Other Hardware Screen.

This opens the Printers and Faxes folder shown in Fig. 5.15.

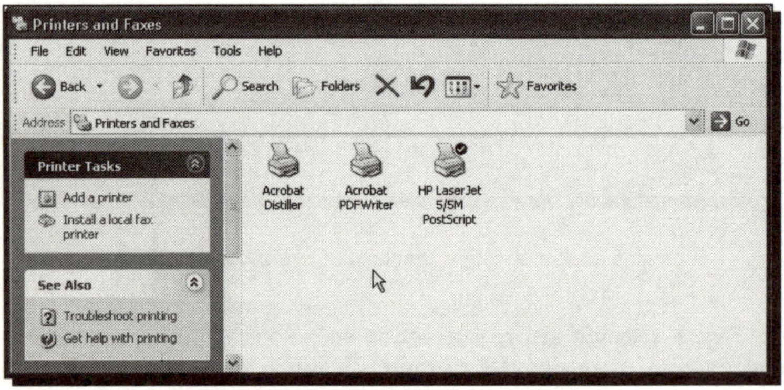

Fig. 5.15 The Printers and Faxes Folder.

Nearly 1,000 different printers are supported by Windows XP so, hopefully, you shouldn't have too much trouble getting yours to work. The printer and printing functions are included in a single Printers and Faxes folder, which you can also open by

clicking its entry, shown to the left, in the ***start*** menu. Our Printers and Faxes folder, shown in Fig. 5.15 on the previous page, has several printers available for use, and a list of **Printer Tasks**. Items in this list provide an easy way of adding new printers, configuring existing ones, and managing all your print jobs.

Windows XP, just like previous versions of Windows, supports the following printer set-up methods:

- Plug and Play printers are automatically detected at installation time, or during the boot-up process. You will be prompted for the necessary driver files if they are not already in the Windows directory, these should be supplied with a new Plug-and-Play printer.
- Point and Print printing enables you to quickly connect to, and use, printers shared on some other networked PCs.
- For other situations, the Add Printer Wizard steps you through the printer installation process, whether the new printer is connected to your PC, or on a network.

Adding a Printer

Installing an additional printer (not connected to your system, but available to you, say, at work) allows you to use the additional fonts available to this printer (we have already discussed fonts at the end of the previous chapter). Below we will step through the procedure of installing such a printer to your system.

To start installation, click the **Add a Printer** entry in the **Printer Tasks** list of the Printers and Faxes window, shown in Fig. 5.15. This opens the Add Printers Wizard, which makes the installation procedure very easy indeed. As with all Wizards, you progress from screen to screen by clicking the **Next** button.

In the second Wizard screen, shown in Fig. 5.16, click the **Local printer attached to this computer** option.

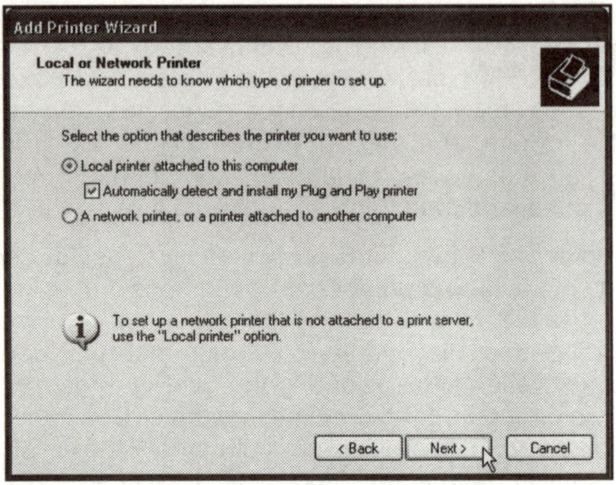

Fig. 5.16 The Second Screen of the Add Printer Wizard.

The first time you activate the Add Printer Wizard, and after pressing the **Next** button on the screen of Fig. 5.16, the Wizard scans your computer for installed plug and play printers and updates its built-in database. If it doesn't find one, it assumes that you want to install a printer manually and asks you to click **Next** to proceed.

On the next Wizard screen choose FILE: as the port you want to use with the printer and select it from the displayed extensive list, as shown in Fig. 5.17. If your printer is not on the list, then either use the disc provided by the manufacturer of your printer, or go to the Internet for an update on the list of printers.

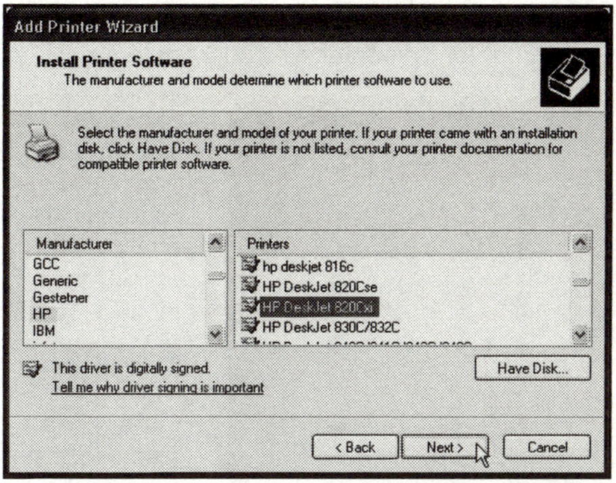

Fig. 5.17 Using the Wizard to Manually Select a Printer.

Documents prepared with this printer selection, can then be printed to file on, say a 3½" floppy disc, and later printed out on the selected printer (even if it is not connected to your computer and does not itself have access to the particular application you are using). Later you can copy that file to the selected printer from its attached PC by issuing the simple command

```
COPY A:\Filename LPT1: /B
```

The /B switch in this command tells the printer to expect a binary file (with embedded printer codes).

Note that the PC which is connected to the additional printer does not even have to operate under Windows for you to print your work, as the command is given at the Command prompt. If the PC does operate under Windows XP, you will need to use the ***start***, **All Programs**, **Accessories**, **Command Prompt** command, then issue the COPY command.

Configuring your Printer

All configuration for a printer is consolidated onto a tabbed property sheet that is accessed from its icon in the Printers and Faxes folder. Right-clicking a printer icon opens the object menu, shown in Fig. 5.18, which gives control of the printer's operation.

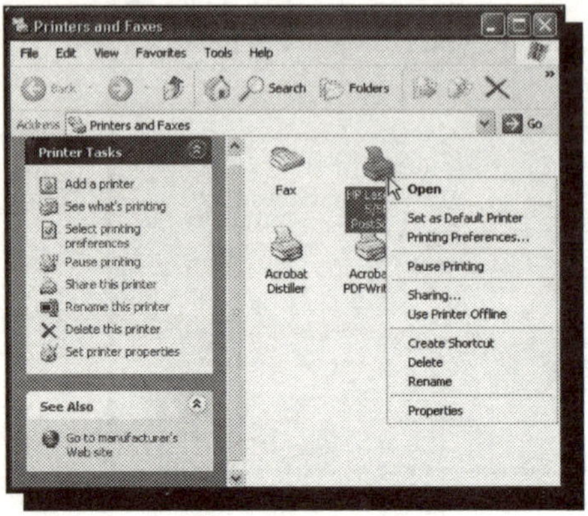

Fig. 5.18 The Object Menu.

As a newly installed printer is automatically set as the default printer, you might want to change this by selecting the printer connected to your PC and clicking the **Set as Default Printer** option on the object menu. If you click the **Properties** option, the window shown in Fig. 5.19 opens and lets you control all the printer's parameters, such as the printer port (or network path), paper and graphics options, built-in fonts, and other device options specific to the printer model. All these settings are fairly self explanatory and as they depend on your printer type, we will let you work them out for yourself.

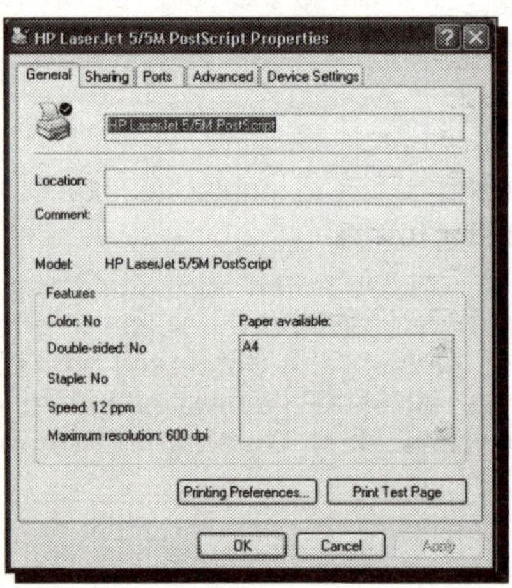

Fig. 5.19 The Printer Properties Window.

Once you have installed and configured your printers in Windows they are then available for all your application programs to use. The correct printer is selected usually in one of the application's **File** menu options.

Managing Print Jobs

If you want to find out what exactly is happening while a document or documents are being sent to your printer, double-click the printer icon, to open its window.

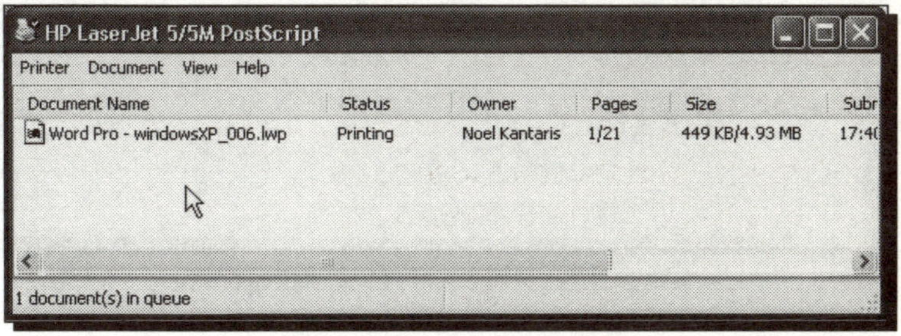

Fig. 5.20 The Print Queue Window.

As shown in Fig. 5.20, this displays detailed information about the contents of any work actually being printed, or of print jobs that are waiting in the queue. This includes the name of the document, its status and 'owner', when it was added to the print queue, the printing progress and when printing was started.

You can control the printing operation from the **Printer** and **Document** menu options of the Print Queue window, from the object menu, or from the **Printer Tasks** list. Selecting **Printer, Pause Printing** will stop the operation until you make the same selection again; it is a toggle menu option. The **Cancel All Documents** option will remove all, or selected, print jobs from the print queue.

Installing a Fax Printer

Windows XP includes its own Fax printer driver. To install it click the Install a local fax printer option in the Printer Tasks box as shown in Fig. 5.21 below.

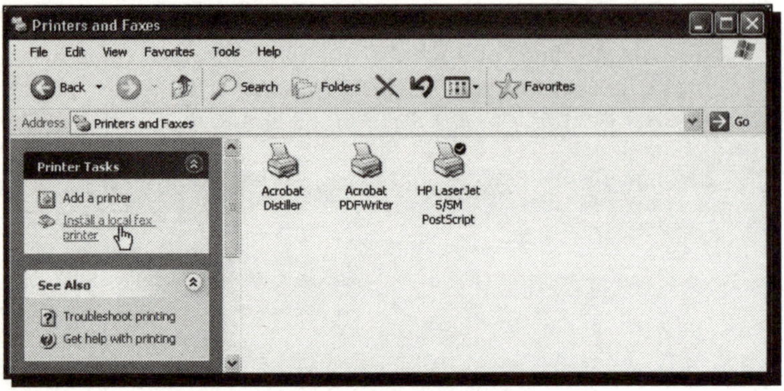

Fig. 5.21 The Printers and Faxes Dialogue box.

This starts the Install Fax Wizard which might ask you to insert the Windows XP distribution CD in the CD-ROM drive so that required files can be copied. Once that is done and you supply the information you want to be included in your faxes, a Fax printer is installed in your Printers and Faxes folder, as shown in Fig. 5.22 below.

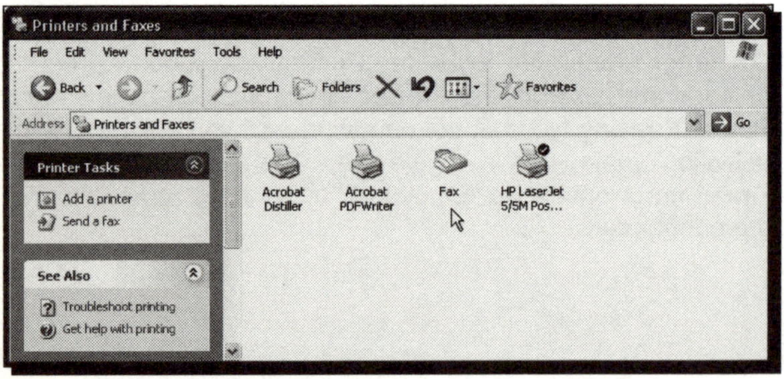

Fig. 5.22 The Printers and Faxes Dialogue box.

The Fax Utility

You can use the Fax utility to fax a text document or graphic image as easily as clicking the **Print** icon on an open document in a Windows-based program. Fax supports scanned graphic images and will automatically convert graphics to the appropriate file format before you send them.

To send and receive faxes all you need is a fax device, such as a fax modem - it must support fax capabilities, not just data standards. As we saw in the previous section, installing a fax printer driver is easy. You will have to go through the described procedure as Windows XP does not install the fax printer driver during Windows Setup. Once this is done, you can send faxes from a local fax device attached to your computer, or with a remote fax device connected to fax resources located on a network.

If you have a fax device installed, click ***start***, then select **All Programs, Accessories, Communications, Fax** to display the available command options shown in Fig. 5.23.

Fig. 5.23 The Fax Menu Options.

Below we give a brief explanation of each fax command option.

Command	***Action***
Fax Console	Displays incoming and outgoing faxes and allows you to view and manage your faxes. Clicking this option displays the screen shown in Fig. 5.24.

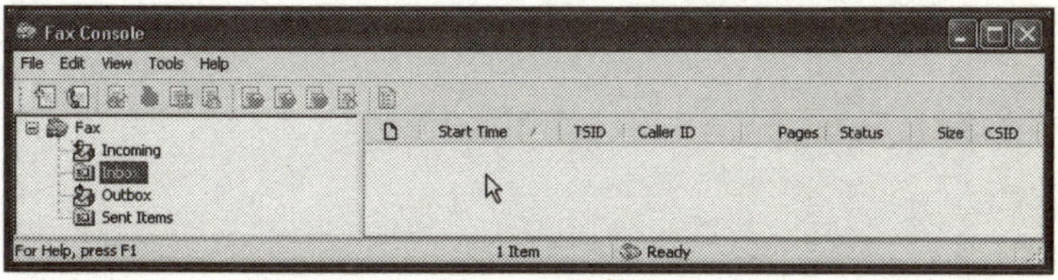

Fig. 5.24 The Fax Console Screen.

The **File** menu options allow you to send a fax (it starts the Send Fax Wizard asking you for the recipient's name and other details - you can use the information held in your Address Book, and specify multiple recipients for the one fax), receive a fax now, view, print, save and mail a fax. While a fax is being sent, you can pause or resume its transmission, restart or delete it. You can also import sent or received faxes into the Fax Console.

The **Edit** menu options allow you to select faxes in various ways for further operations.

The **View** menu options allow you to configure what you see and how you see it on the Fax Console.

The **Tools** menu options allow you to enter sender information, create, open, copy or delete personal cover pages, display the fax printer's status, start the Fax Configuration Wizard, or display the fax properties and monitor screens.

Fax Cover Page Editor Creates and edits cover pages used when sending faxes. The editor allows you to design a template (it also includes drawing facilities), to be used each time you send a fax, as shown in Fig. 5.25 below.

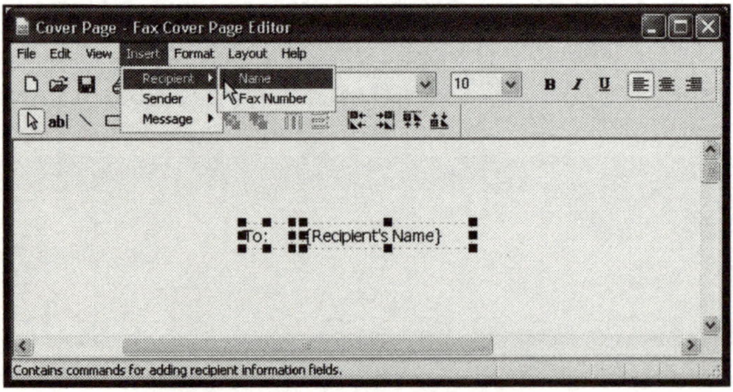

Fig. 5.25 The Fax Cover Page Editor.

As demonstrated above, you must use the **Insert** menu command to insert what you would like to appear on your fax template, such as recipient's name and fax number, sender's name, fax number, company, address and other details - the field **Note** is where you type the body of your fax. Inserted options can be moved to the desired position on the plate (use the <Ctrl> key to group together fields you want to move together) and formatted accordingly. A simple example is given in Fig. 5.26 below.

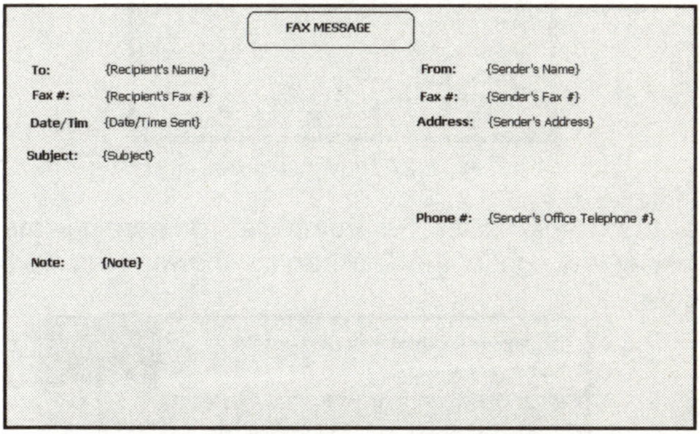

Fig. 5.26 The Designed Cover Page.

The designed template (we hope yours is more imaginative than ours) is saved in the **My Documents\Personal Coverpages** folder with the .cov extension.

Send a Fax Sends a fax that consists only of a cover page. Clicking this menu option starts the Send Fax Wizard. This facility should only be used for short messages. If you want to fax a document you should use your word processor and print the document to the Fax printer.

Receiving a Fax

If your computer is switched on and is attached to a fax device, such as a fax modem, a fax sent to you is intercepted by Windows XP which displays the Fax Monitor box shown in Fig. 5.27 below.

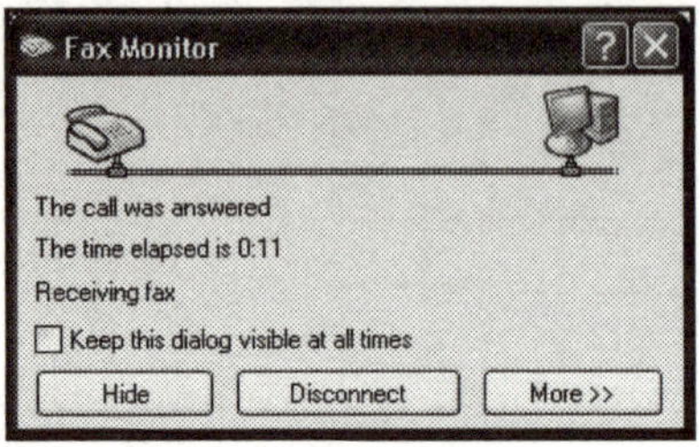

Fig. 5.27 The Fax Monitor.

Once the transmission is complete, a warning message appears on the right of the Taskbar, as shown in Fig. 5.28.

Fig. 5.28 The Fax Warning Message.

Clicking the **Fax received** icon on the Taskbar opens the Fax Console and displays the contents of its **Inbox**.

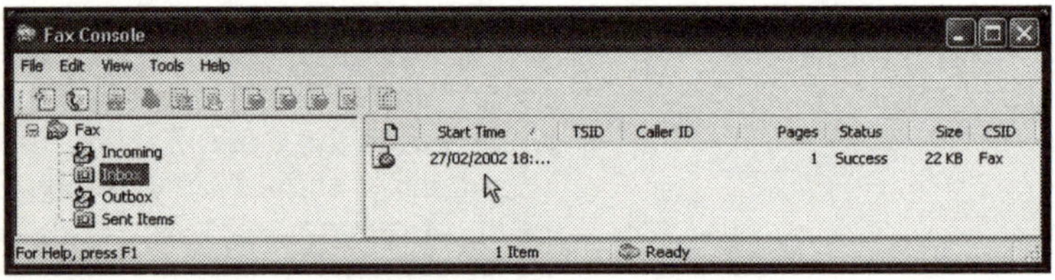

Fig. 5.29 The Fax Console Screen.

Double-clicking an **Inbox** entry, opens the selected Fax in its own window.

Scanners and Cameras

Click the **Scanners and Cameras** link pointed to in Fig. 5.30, to add a scanner or a camera to your computer, or to check their configuration.

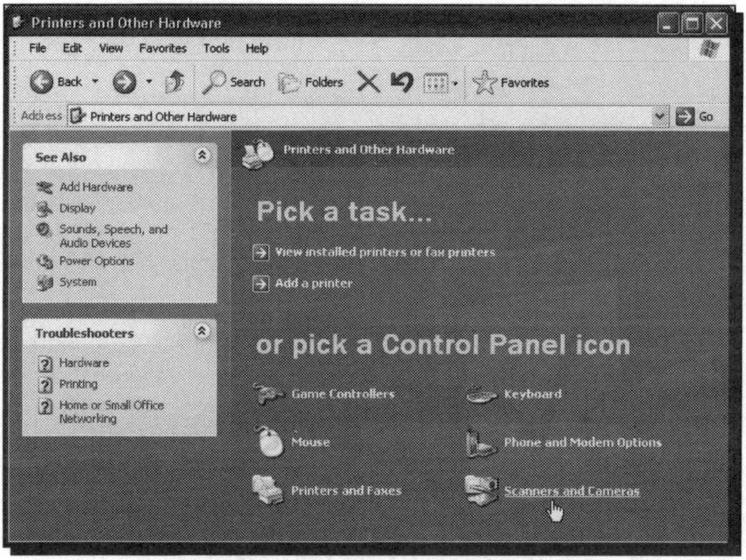

Fig. 5.30 The Printers and Other Hardware Screen.

This opens the Scanners and Cameras folder shown in Fig. 5.31. Plug and Play Scanners and digital Cameras are detected by Windows XP when they are connected to your PC.

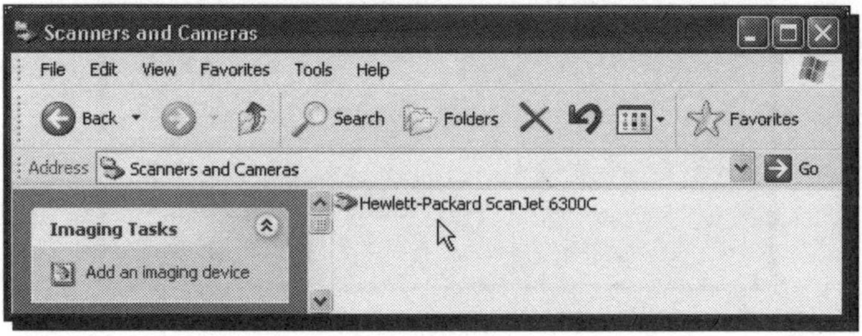

Fig. 5.31 The Scanners and Cameras Folder.

Getting Pictures from a Scanner or Camera

After installation, you can start the Scanner and Camera Wizard by right-clicking the camera or scanner entry in the Scanners and Cameras folder to display a shortcut menu, then click the appropriate option for that device. In Fig. 5.32 we show the shortcut menu for our scanner.

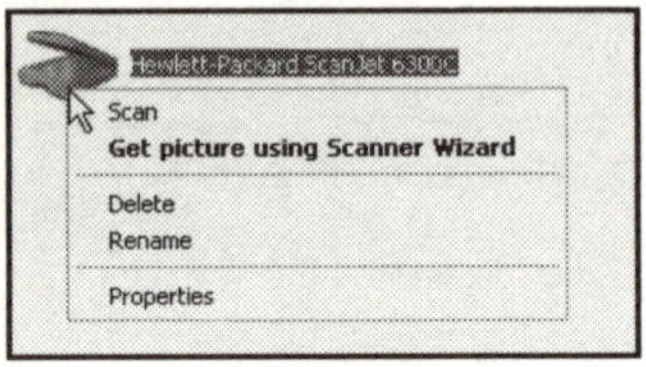

Fig. 5.32 The Scanner Shortcut Menu.

If your scanner or camera are not Plug and Play, follow the instructions that came with that device. It is possible, however, that you might need to get the latest driver for your device which is compatible with Windows XP.

To begin the process, place the picture you want to scan on your scanner's glass plate, then select the **Get picture using Scanner Wizard** option from the shortcut menu in Fig. 5.32. This starts the Wizard and opens the dialogue box in Fig. 5.33 shown below. As you can see, in this instance we have three scanning choices; colour, grey-scale, or black and white.

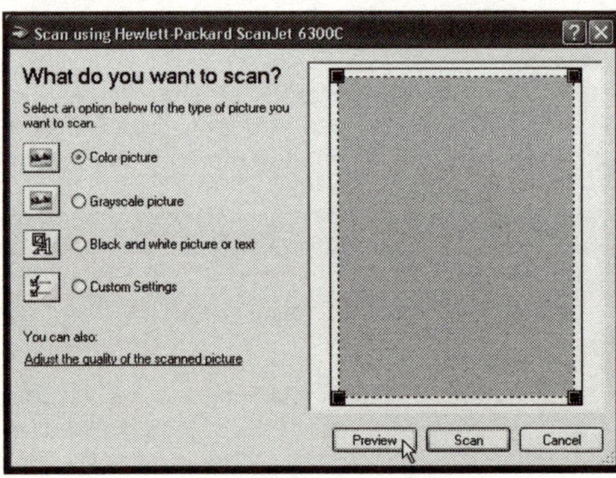

Fig. 5.33 The Scanner Dialogue Box.

Clicking the **Preview** button will activate the scanner and a preview of the object will appear on the right side of the Scanner dialogue box, as shown in Fig. 5.34.

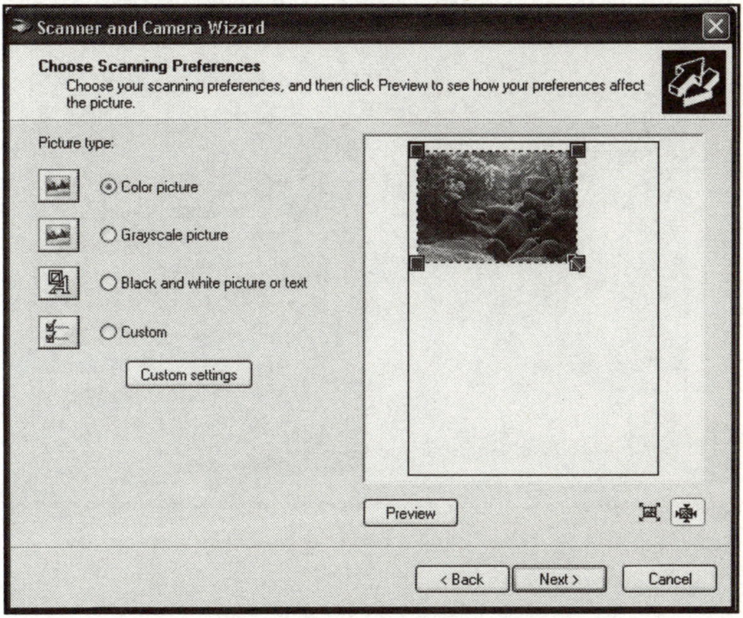

Fig. 5.34 Cropping a Scanned Picture in Preview.

In the picture preview in Fig. 5.34 above, we also show how you can crop the size of the scanned image to the required size of the picture by dragging the square handles to the correct position.

Clicking the **Next** button displays additional Wizard screens asking you to specify the name of the picture and where you would like its file to be saved. As usual, you move through successive Wizard screens by clicking the **Next** button, until the penultimate screen where you are asked whether you would like to 'Publish the picture to a Web site', 'order prints from a photo printing Web site', or do 'Nothing' because you have finished. Selecting the last option, saves your picture in the specified folder, opens the folder and highlights its filename.

Double-clicking the selected filename, displays your picture in the **Windows Picture and Fax Viewer**, as shown in Fig. 5.35 - it looks better in colour!

Fig. 5.35 A Scanned Picture in the Windows Picture and Fax Viewer.

Clicking the button pointed to at the bottom of the picture, closes the Picture and Fax Viewer and opens the displayed picture in the Microsoft Photo Editor (see Chapter 3, page 46) where you can use your editing skills to completely change it to something you would rather have in place of the original. For example, you can apply various effects, such as 'Sharpen', 'Soften', 'Emboss', etc., change the image by 'Cropping', 'Resizing', or 'Rotating' it. You can certainly spend hours changing your original picture beyond recognition! Therefore, it might be a good idea to experiment on a copy of the original picture. Good luck!

6

Network & Internet Connections

In this chapter we will examine how you can connect your PCs to create a home network and how to connect to the Internet. We begin by using the **Start**, **Control Panel** menu command which displays the screen in Fig. 6.1 below.

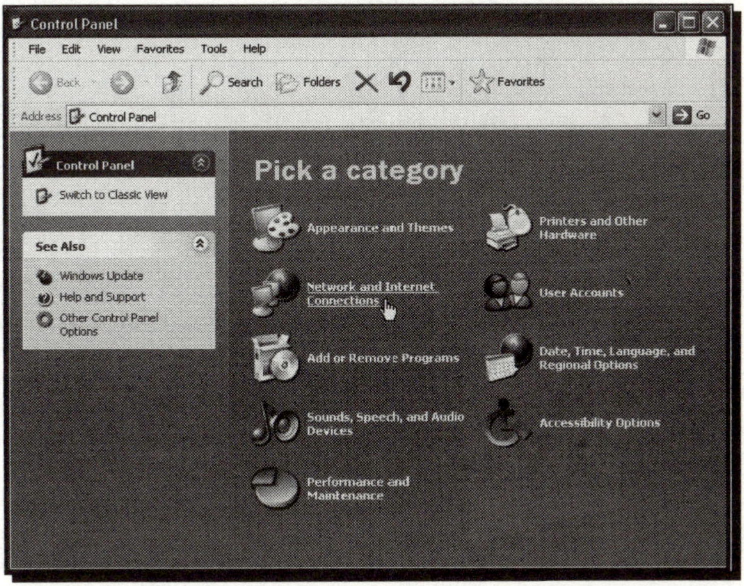

Fig. 6.1 The Control Panel Screen in Category View.

If the **Control Panel** screen displays in Classical View, click the **Switch to Category view** option to be found at the top-left panel of the screen.

Next, click the **Network and Internet Connections** link (pointed to) under the **Pick a category** panel to display the screen shown in Fig. 6.2 on the next page.

The Internet Options

Clicking the **Internet Options** link under the **or pick a Control Panel icon** link pointed to in Fig. 6.2, opens the multi-tab dialogue box shown in Fig. 6.3.

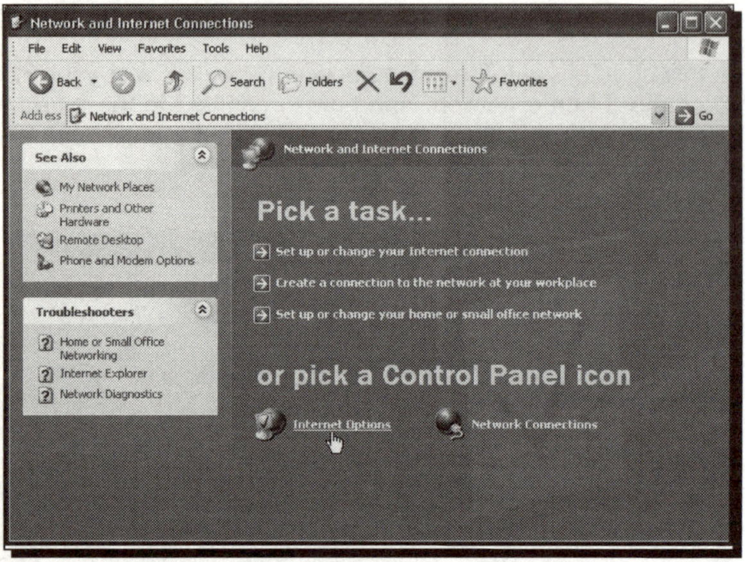

Fig. 6.2 The Network and Internet Connections Screen.

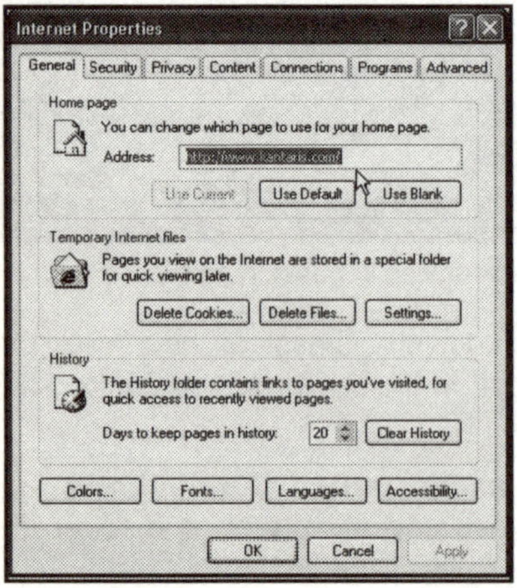

In the General tab sheet, you specify which page to use for your Home page (the one that is displayed when you first open Internet Explorer). You can also **Delete Cookies** (information created and stored on your hard disc by Web sites you visited on your preferences when visiting that site).

Fig. 6.3 The Internet Properties Dialogue Box.

You can also **Delete Files** which are temporary Internet files holding information on pages you visited before on a Web site. These files allow you to browse quickly through such pages because your Internet browser checks and uses these files (if the information in them has not changed) in preference to downloading them from the Internet, which takes much longer.

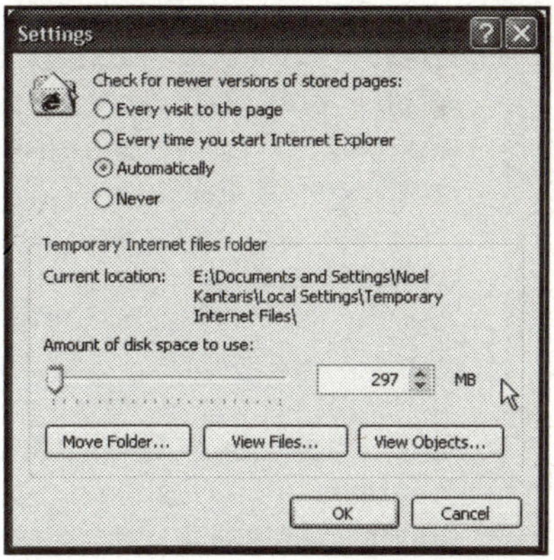

Fig. 6.4 The Settings Dialogue Box.

Obviously such temporary Internet files can take a lot of hard disc space, but you can control it by clicking the **Settings** button to open the dialogue box shown in Fig. 6.4. In here you can select from several options for checking for newer versions of stored Web pages, and you can limit the amount of hard disc space used by them. Click the **View Files** button to see a list of such temporary files held on your computer.

Going back to the General tab sheet of the Internet Properties dialogue box, you will see options at the bottom of the dialogue box dealing with **History**. This is a folder that holds links to pages you have visited, for quick access to recently viewed Web site pages without having to connect to the Internet.

To view history links, click the **History** Toolbar button, shown here to the right, on a Windows XP application such as the **Internet Explorer** or **My Computer** (to do this, use the **View**, **Toolbars**, **Customize** menu command), to open the History panel, shown in Fig. 6.5. You can choose History links from **Today** to several **Weeks Ago**.

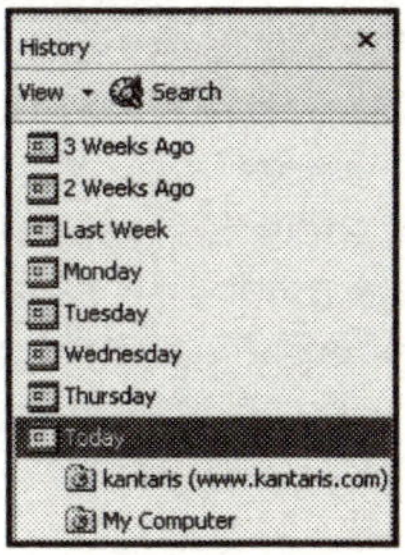

Fig. 6.5 The History Panel.

Internet Security

If you want to stop people getting at your data or tracking what you are doing, then Internet security is important to you. Clicking the Security tab of the Internet Properties dialogue box displays the sheet shown in Fig. 6.6. As each item under **Select a Web content zone to specify its security settings** at the top of the screen is selected, its security settings are shown below the selection area. For example, when **Internet** is selected, you are told that 'This zone contains all Web sites you haven't placed in other zones'. To change the settings, click the **Custom Level** button to display the Security Settings dialogue box shown in Fig. 6.7. In this screen you can select settings for various **ActiveX controls**. These are potentially risky actions, with some of the options not providing a **Prompt** setting.

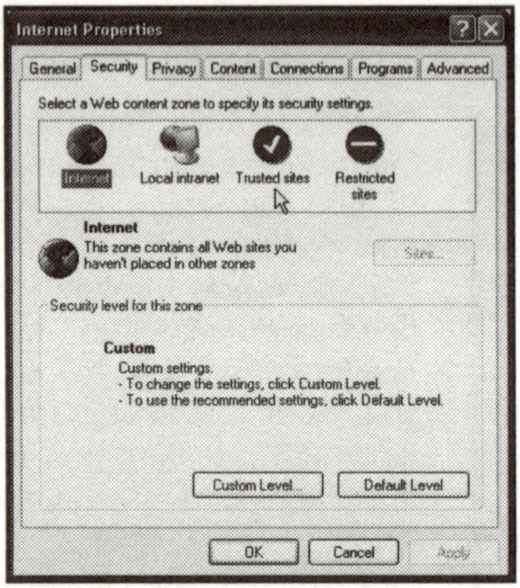

Fig. 6.6 The Internet Security Screen.

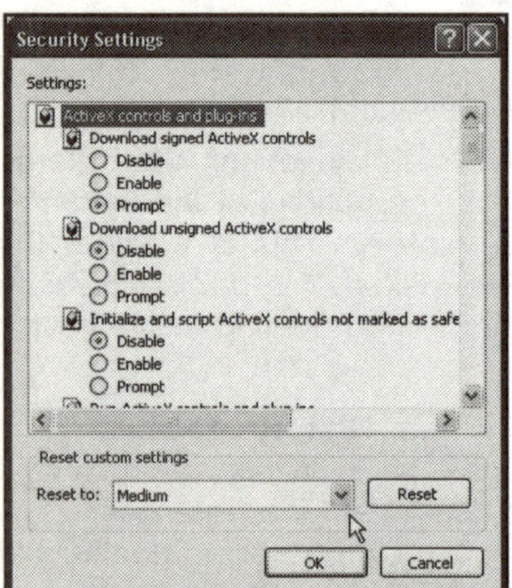

Fig. 6.7 The Security Settings Screen.

None of these options apply to FTP folders, which are folders you upload or download to or from Web sites using the File Transfer Protocol which, however, does not use encryption or other security mechanism to protect your password when you log on to a server. If you want such security, then use Web folders instead.

Internet Privacy

Clicking the Privacy tab of the Internet Properties dialogue box displays the screen in Fig. 6.8. On here you can specify the security level for the Internet zone. As you move the slide up a notch at a time, you impose higher and higher security, while moving the slide downwards diminishes it. An explanation on what is allowed and what is not, is given next to the slide as you move it to a different level. You can also override cookie handling for individual Web sites by clicking **Edit** and filling in the displayed sheet.

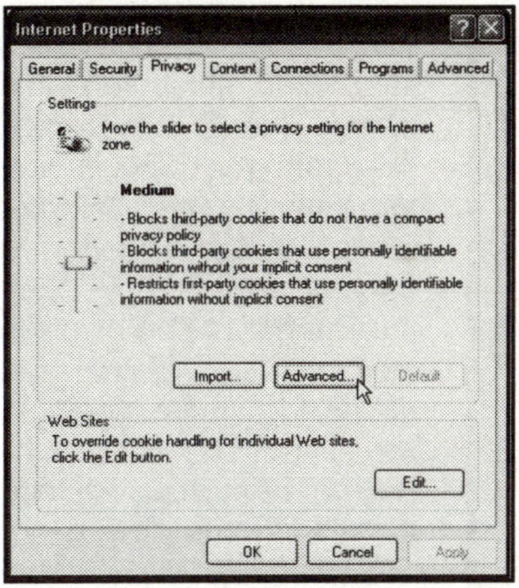

Fig. 6.8 The Internet Privacy Screen.

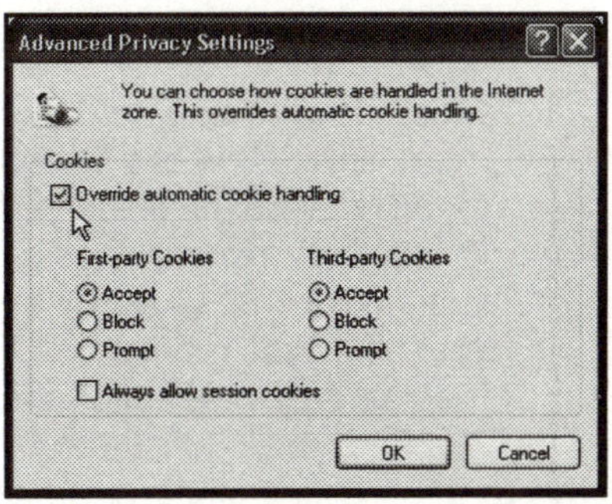

Fig. 6.9 The Advanced Privacy Settings Screen.

Clicking the **Advanced** button, displays the screen shown in Fig. 6.9, in which you can control cookies. If the override box (pointed to) is not checked, the options under it are greyed out. In that case, the Web site's privacy policy, if it exists, is displayed by **Internet Explorer**, which tells you what kind of information the Web site collects, and how it uses it. Also, Web sites might provide a (P3P) (Platform for Privacy Preferences Policy), in which case **Internet Explorer** might be able to compare your privacy settings to that of the P3P privacy policy, and determine whether or not to allow the Web site to save cookies on your computer.

If you check the override box, then you must decide how first-party and third-party cookies should be treated.

Internet Content

Clicking the Content tab of the Internet Properties dialogue box displays the screen in Fig. 6.10. The most important option on this screen is the **Content Advisor** which helps you to control the Internet content that can be viewed on your computer. Clicking the **Enable** button displays the screen shown in Fig. 6.11, where you can set ratings on Language, Nudity, Sex, and Violence permitted to be viewed.

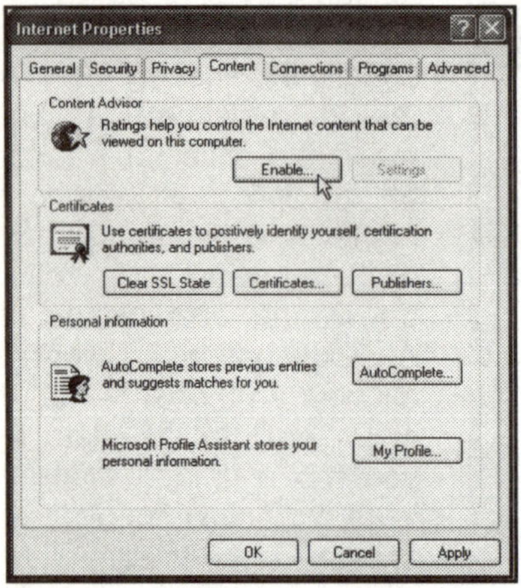

Fig. 6.10 The Internet Content Screen.

You set these ratings by selecting each option and moving the slide to the right a notch at a time, which lowers the level of restriction. What is allowed to be viewed is displayed in the **Description** box as you move the slide. Once you have set ratings to all the listed options, click the **Apply** button followed by **OK**. This displays the Create Supervisor Password dialogue box so that you can protect these ratings.

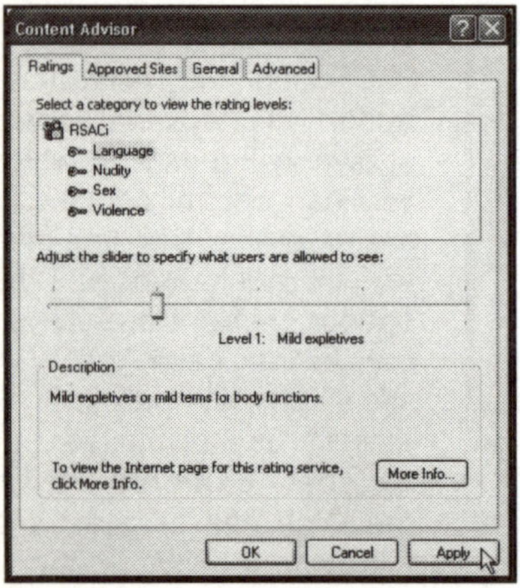

Fig. 6.11 The Content Advisor Screen.

Other options on the Content tab screen of the Internet Properties dialogue box, allow you to use **Certificates** to identify yourself, change the **AutoComplete** settings, or specify **Personal information** you can share when a Web site requests information from its visitors.

Internet Connections

Clicking the Connections tab of the Internet Properties dialogue box displays the screen in Fig. 6.12. Under the **Dial-up and Virtual Private Network settings** you will see a list of our Internet connections which are already available on this computer. However, to show you how to make such a connection, we will take you through the steps required.

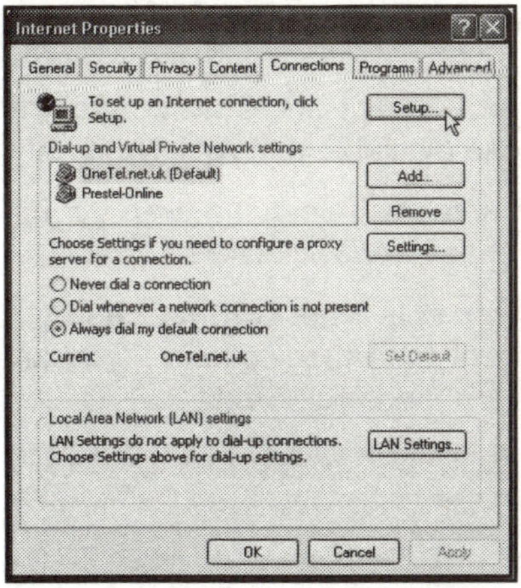

Fig. 6.12 The Internet Content Screen.

To set up a new Internet connection, click the **Setup** button which starts the New Connection Wizard shown in Fig. 6.13 below.

Fig. 6.13 The New Connection Wizard.

As you can see, the New Connection Wizard can be used to connect to the Internet or a private network, or set up a home or small office network. To proceed with the Wizard, click the **Next** button and do the following:

- In the first Wizard screen, select the **Connect to the Internet** option from those available and click **Next**.
- In the second Wizard screen, select the **Set up my connection manually** option and click **Next**.
- In the third Wizard screen, select the **Connect using a dial-up modem**, or one of the other options if you are connecting via one of them, and click **Next**.
- In the fourth Wizard screen, shown in Fig. 6.14, type in your ISP's name and click **Next**.
- In the fifth Wizard screen, type in the phone number of your ISP.
- In the sixth Wizard screen, shown in Fig. 6.15, type in the **User Name** and **Password** given to you by your ISP, tick the boxes relevant to you, then click **Next**.
- The final Wizard screen displays a summary of your entries, and clicking **Finish** creates the connection and closes down the Wizard.

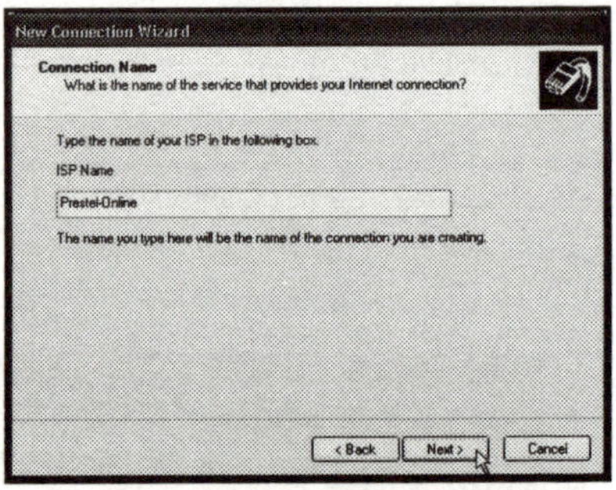

Fig. 6.14 The Fourth New Connection Wizard Screen.

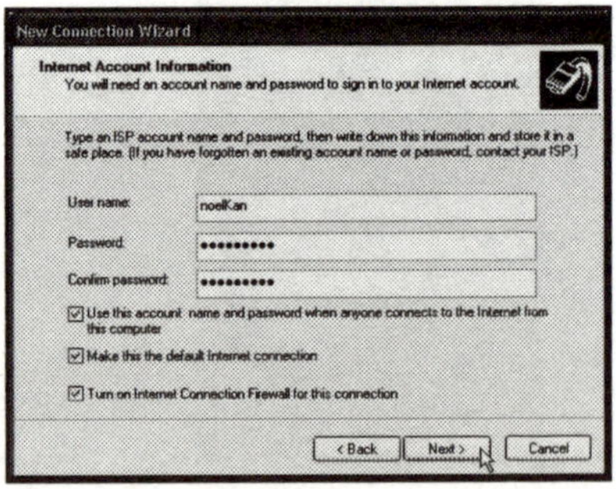

Fig. 6.15 The Sixth New Connection Wizard Screen.

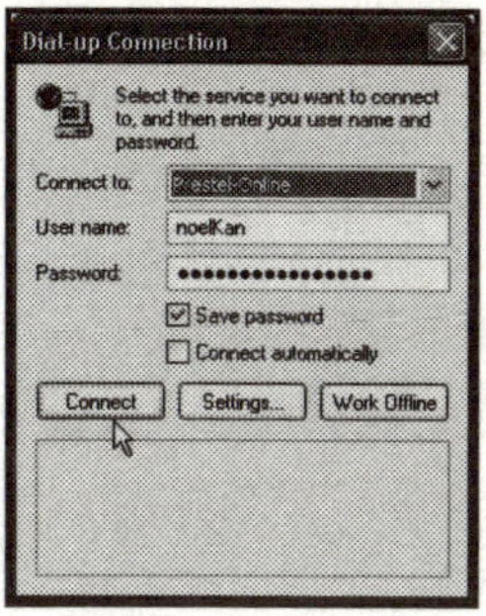

Now, whenever you activate Internet Explorer of your e-mail program, such as Outlook Express, the screen shown in Fig. 6.16 is displayed on your screen, ready for you to make the connection to your ISP.

Fig. 6.16 The Dial-up Connection Screen.

Programs for Internet Services

Clicking the Programs tab of the Internet Properties dialogue box displays the screen in Fig. 6.17. On this tab screen you can choose from drop-down lists which program Windows should use automatically for Internet services such as HTML editor, E-mail, Newsgroups, Internet call, Calendar, and Contact list.

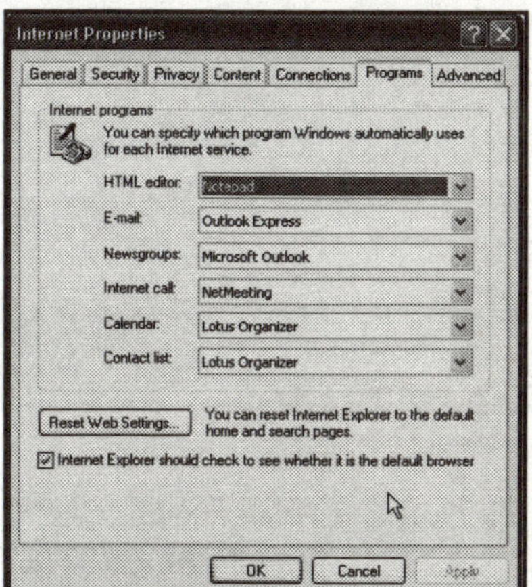

Fig. 6.17 The Internet Programs Screen.

You can also select to have Internet Explorer check to see whether it is the default browser - you might prefer to use another browser such as Netscape.

Advanced Options

You can use the Advanced tab of the Internet Properties dialogue box to select options on such diverse topics as: Accessibility, Browsing, Connection Protocols, Multimedia, Printing, Searching, and Security.

We found that these options are normally set when you customise your printer, browser, media player, etc., therefore we will not spend any more time on this tab sheet.

Network Connections

Clicking the **Network Connections** link (pointed to) under the **or pick a Control Panel icon** option in Fig. 6.18, opens the Network Connections screen shown in Fig. 6.19.

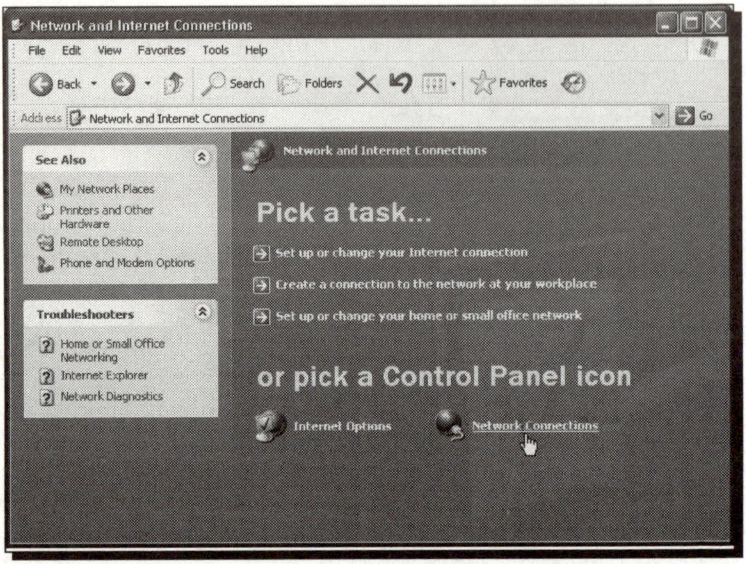

Fig. 6.18 The Network and Internet Connections Screen.

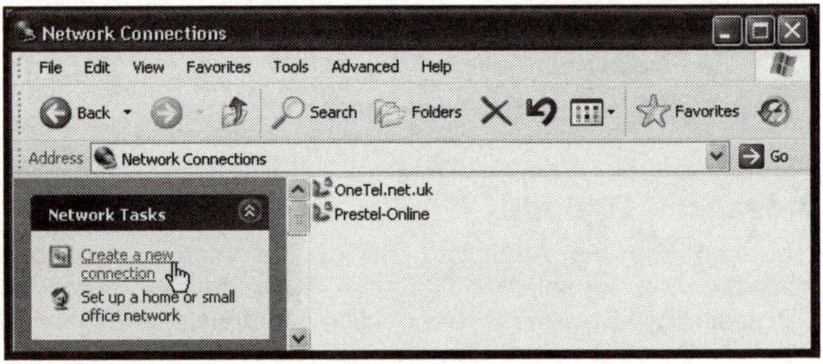

Fig. 6.19 The Network Connections Screen.

Clicking **Create a new connection** link under **Network Tasks** starts the New Connection Wizard as we discussed previously.

However, clicking the **Set up a home or small office network** link starts the Network Setup Wizard, as shown in Fig. 6.20.

Fig. 6.20 The Network Setup Wizard.

To proceed with the Wizard, click the **Next** button and do the following:

- In the first Wizard screen, click the **checklist for creating a network** link, as shown in Fig. 6.21

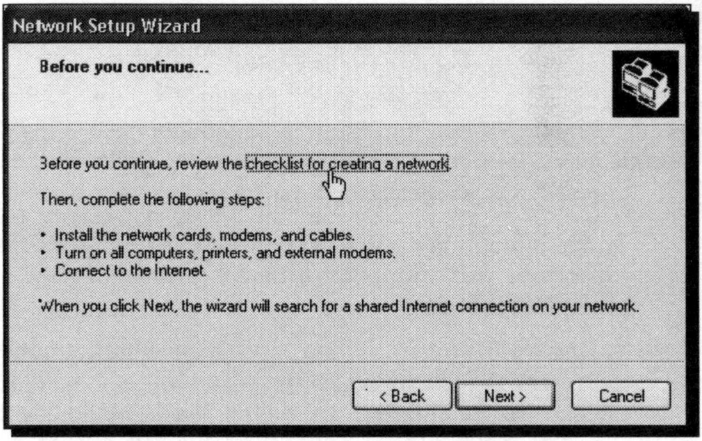

Fig. 6.21 The First Network Setup Wizard Screen.

This activates the **Help and Support Center** and gives you a detailed screen on the steps you need to take to create a home or small office network, as shown in Fig. 6.22 below. We suggest that you spend some time with this help screen getting as much information from it as necessary.

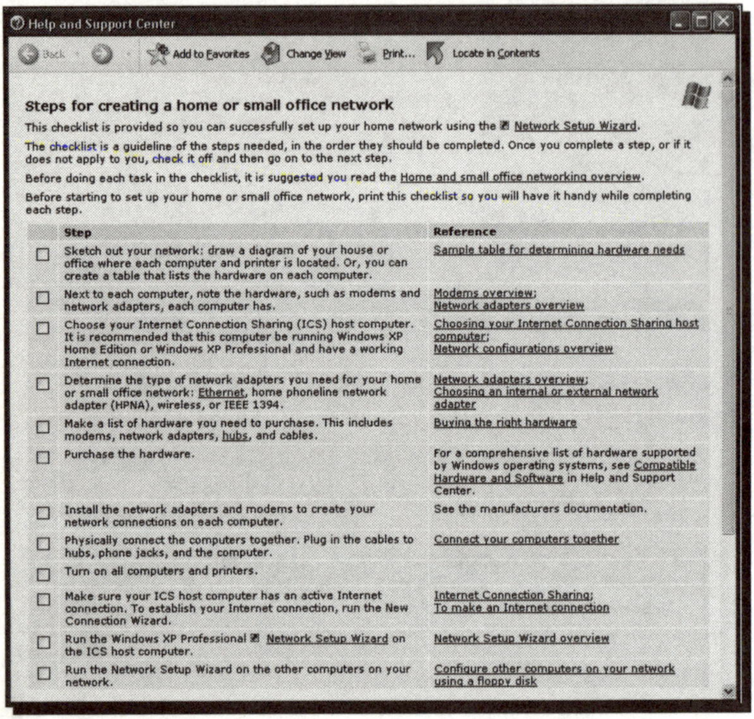

Fig. 6.22 The Help and Support Center's Screen on Networking.

- In the second Wizard screen, select the option that best describes your computer in terms of connectivity, then click the **Next** button.
- In the third Wizard screen, select the Internet connection from the displayed list through which you would like to access the Internet, then click **Next**. Obviously, you need to have set up such a connection before it will appear in the list.

- In the fourth Wizard screen, type in a computer name by which this computer will be known, such as 'Study PC', 'Reception PC', etc., then click **Next**.
- In the fifth Wizard screen, provide a working group name, such as Home or Office, then click **Next**.
- In the sixth Wizard screen, you are given a summary of the settings the Wizard will apply; it might take a few minutes to do so, but once started cannot be interrupted, as shown in Fig. 6.23.

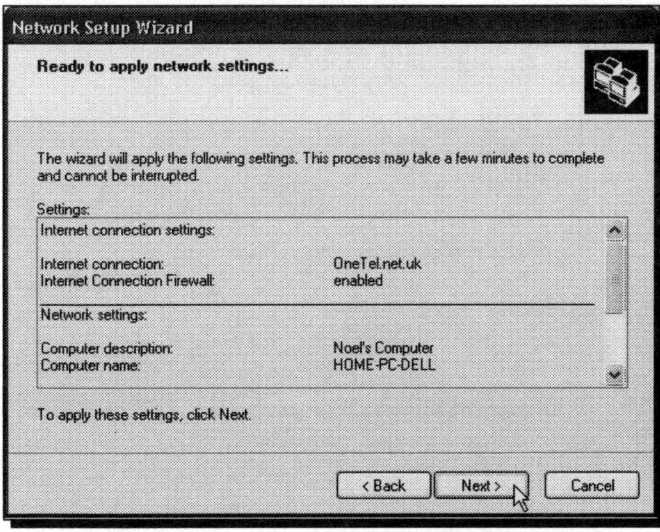

Fig. 6.23 The Sixth Network Setup Wizard Screen.

- In the seventh Wizard screen computers are shown in an animated graphical display in the process of being connected to a group, as shown in the partial screen below.

Fig. 6.24 Part of the Seventh Network Setup Wizard Screen.

- In the eighth Wizard screen, shown in Fig. 6.25, you are given information on what you need to do next. For example, you must run the Network Setup Wizard on all computers on the network which operate under Windows XP, or create a Network Setup disc to be run on computers which do not operate under Windows XP.

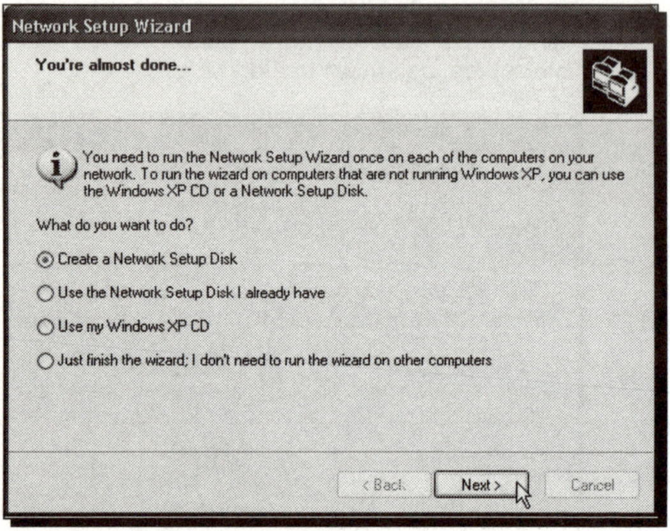

Fig. 6.25 The Eighth Network Setup Wizard Screen.

Obviously, there are one or two other choices available to you on this Wizard screen, so once you have decided what suits your situation, select the appropriate option and click **Next**.

- In the last Wizard screen, shown in Fig. 6.26 on the next page, you are given two links to the Help and Support Center. The first link provides information on how to use the Shared Documents folder, while the second link gives you an overview on shared files and folders. It is worth pursuing both these links.
- Finally, you are asked to restart your computer so that all the settings take effect.

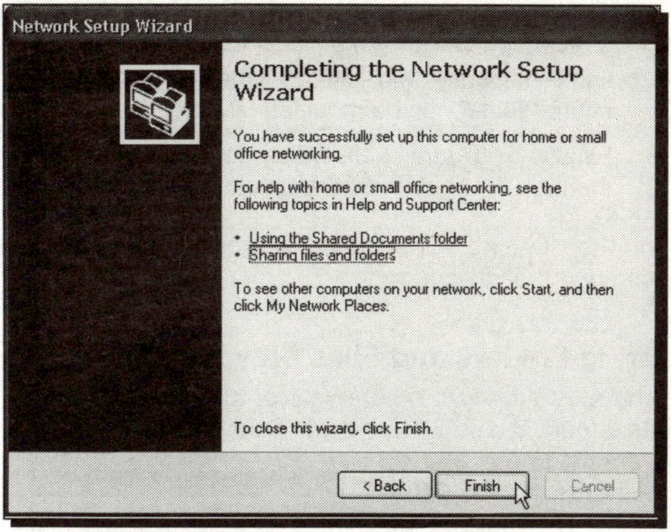

Fig. 6.26 The Final Network Setup Wizard Screen.

As you can see, connecting your computers to a home or small office network is very easy to do. All that remains is to arrange for certain files and folders to be shared.

Sharing Information

You can share files and folders stored on your computer, on a network, and on the Web. The method you choose for sharing information depends on whom you want to share it with and what computer they will use to access it. There are three main categories:

- Everyone who uses your computer can share information by using 'Shared folders' which are counterparts to your personal folders, such as My Documents, with its sub-folders My Pictures, and My Music. Shared Documents, with its sub-folders Shared Pictures, and Shared Music provide a place for you to store files, pictures, and music that can be accessed by all users of your computer.

- You can also share information and resources, such as a disc, folder or printer, between computers on the same network and control whether the files on the shared folder can be modified by other users.
- Finally, you can share your files online by publishing them on the Web in a private folder that you control.

In what follows, we will examine in turn how you can achieve sharing under each category.

Sharing Folders and Files on your PC

To share a folder with other users of the same computer, first locate it (ours is a sub-folder in **My Documents** folder), select it and drag it to the **Shared Documents** link in **Other Places**. The folder will then be moved from its present position to within the **Shared Documents** folder.

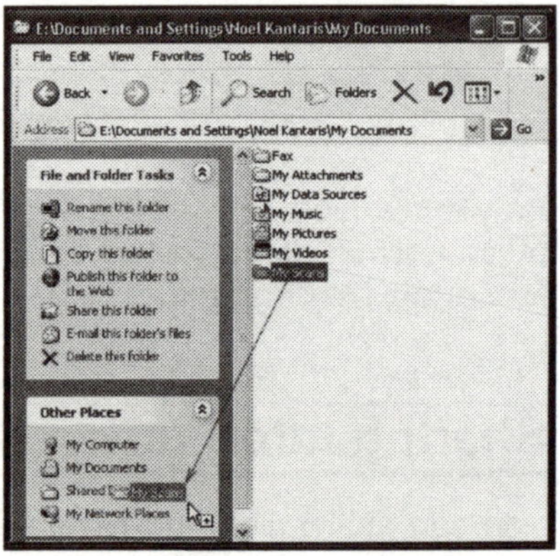

Fig. 6.27 Drag-copying a Folder.

If you want to make a copy of the folder rather than move it, hold down the <Ctrl> key while dragging. You will be able to tell that the intended move will copy the folder by the display of the small plus (+) sign next to the mouse pointer, as shown in Fig. 6.27. When you release the mouse button a small dialogue box appears at the top-left of your screen, as shown here. To start the copying process, you must click the **Copy Here** entry which then displays the copying box shown in Fig. 6.28.

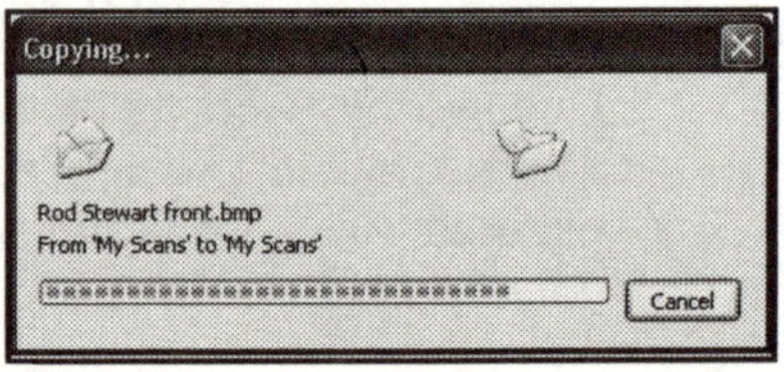

Fig. 6.28 The Copying Information Box.

To move or copy a file into the **Shared Documents** folder, select the file and click either the **Move this file** or the **Copy this file** link. This opens the Move Items (or Copy Items) screen in which you select into which sub-folder in the **Shared Documents** you want to move or copy your selected file.

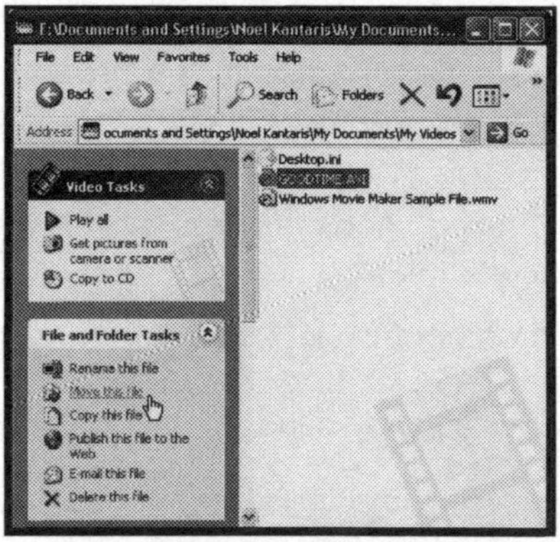

Fig. 6.29 The Internet Programs Screen.

It is a good idea to always move or copy an item into a meaningful sub-folder rather than moving or copying files into the main **Shared Documents** folder. If such a sub-folder does not exist, create it by using the **Make New Folder** button, while the **Shared Documents** folder is selected. The created folder will always be created within the folder you highlight in the Move or Copy dialogue box. To complete the Move or Copy command, select the sub-folder into which you want to place your file and click the **Move** (or **Copy**) button on the dialogue box in Fig. 6.30. As you can also see, the two folders, **Shared Music**, and **Shared Pictures** were created by Windows XP during installation for your convenience.

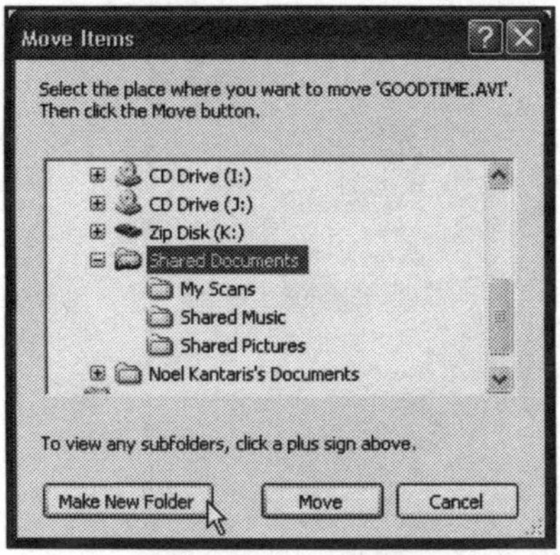

Fig. 6.30 The Move Items Screen.

If you now use **My Computer** and open the **Shared Documents** folder, you will find the file you chose to share inside the newly created sub-folder.

Sharing a Drive or Folder on the Network

If you are connected to a network, you can share a drive or folder on your computer with others connected to the network. To start the process, you must log on as the administrator, then:

- Use the ***start***, **All Programs**, **Accessories**, **Windows Explorer** cascade menu command.
- Select **My Computer**, then right-click the drive you want to share, and click the **Sharing and Security** option from the drop-down menu, as shown in Fig. 6.31 below.

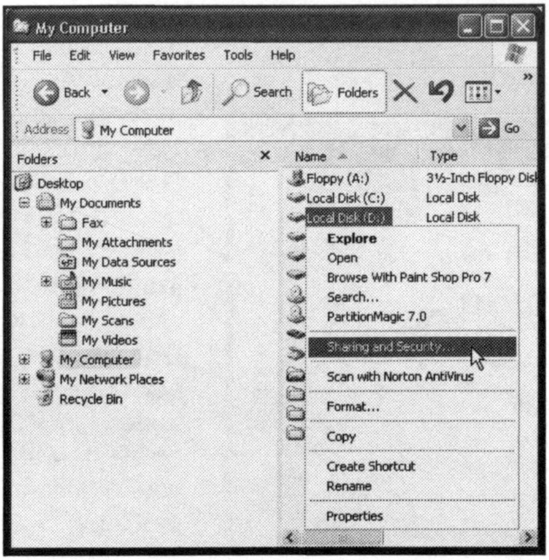

Fig. 6.31 An Item's Shortcut Menu.

- On the Sharing tab of the displayed dialogue box, click the **If you understand the risk but still want to share the root of the drive, click here** link.
- On the displayed screen, shown in Fig. 6.32 on the next page, you now have the option of allowing the sharing of the selected folder (drive D: in our case) with other users on the network, by clicking the **Share this folder on the network** check box. The letter D appears automatically in the **Share name** text box.

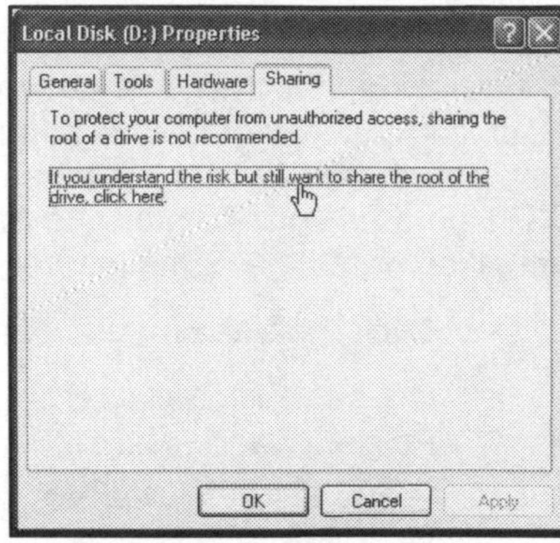

Fig. 6.32 The Sharing Properties Screen.

To change the name of the folder on the network, type a new name in the **Share name** text box. This does not change the name of the original folder on your computer.

If the **Share this folder on the network** check box is not available to you, then either your computer is not connected to the network, or you are not logged in as the administrator of this computer.

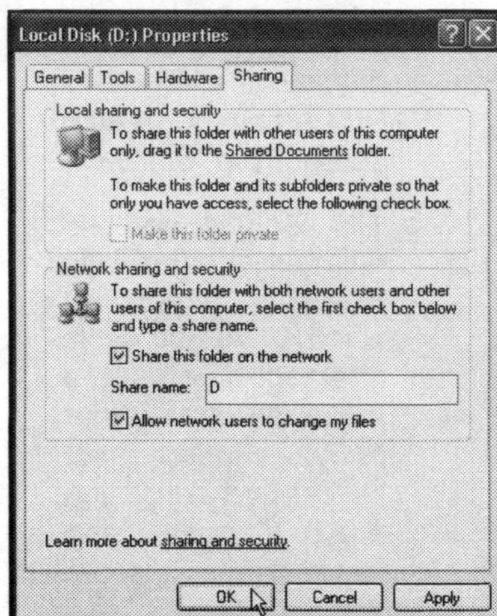

Fig. 6.33 The Sharing Folder Screen.

- To share a single folder with other users on the network, follow the same procedure as explained above, but this time right-click the folder you want to share instead of right-clicking a whole drive. Windows will jump straight to the dialogue box shown in Fig. 6.33, without opening the warning box in Fig. 6.32.
- In the dialogue box in Fig. 6.33 you have the option to allow or disallow network users to change your files by selecting or deselecting the appropriate check box. Think hard before allowing anyone to change your files!

Sharing your Printer

If you are connected to a network, you can share a printer on your computer with others connected to the network. Printers are not shared by default when you install them on Windows XP Home edition. To start the process of sharing a printer, you must log on as the administrator, then:

- Click the ***start*** menu command **Printers and Faxes**.
- On the displayed Printers and Faxes dialogue box, right-click the printer you want to share and select **Sharing** on the drop-down menu shown in Fig. 6.34 to display the Printer's Properties Sharing screen (Fig. 6.35).

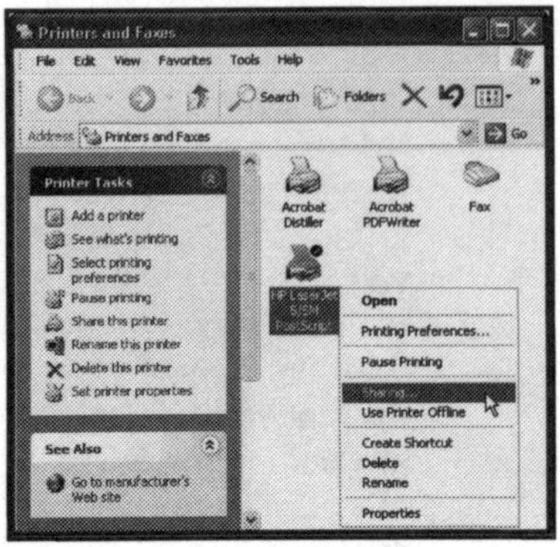

Fig. 6.34 The Printers and Faxes Dialogue Box.

The options you see on the Sharing tab differ depending whether 'sharing' is enabled. If you see a message stating that printer sharing must be turned on, you must run the Network Setup Wizard which can be started by clicking the link on the Sharing tab.

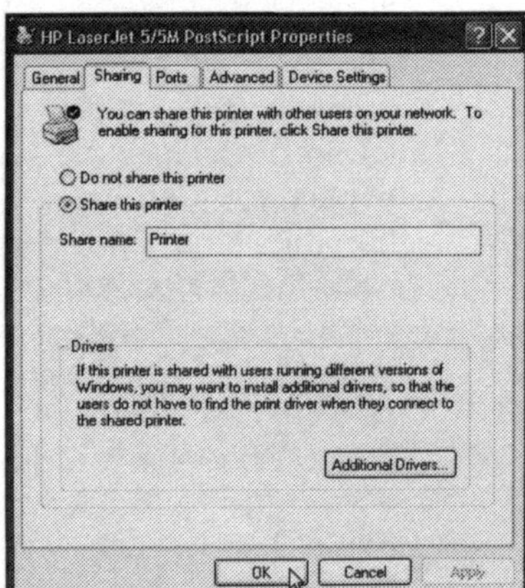

Fig. 6.35 The Printer's Sharing Properties Screen.

If the **Share this printer** option appears on the screen, as in Fig. 6.35, type in a name for the shared printer and click the **OK** button.

Publishing a File or Folder to the Web

To publish a file or folder to the Web, open **My Computer**, then:

- Double-click a drive or folder.
- Click the file or folder you want to publish to the Web to select it, as shown in Fig. 6.36 below.

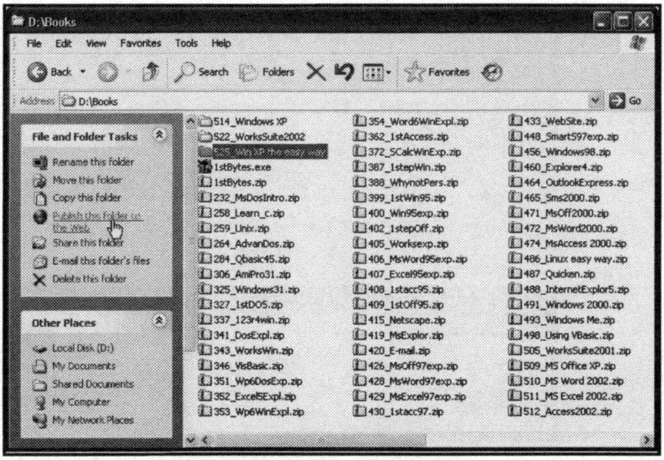

Fig. 6.36 Selecting Files to Publish on the Web.

- Under **File and Folder Tasks**, click the **Publish this folder to the Web** link to start the Web Publishing Wizard. The second Wizard screen displays the contents of the folder, as shown in Fig. 6.37 on the next page, where you can select all the files or some of the files you intend to publish. Having made your selection, click the **OK** button.
- The Web Publishing Wizard now initiates a connection to the internet and once you are connected the screen in Fig. 6.38, also shown on the next page, is displayed.

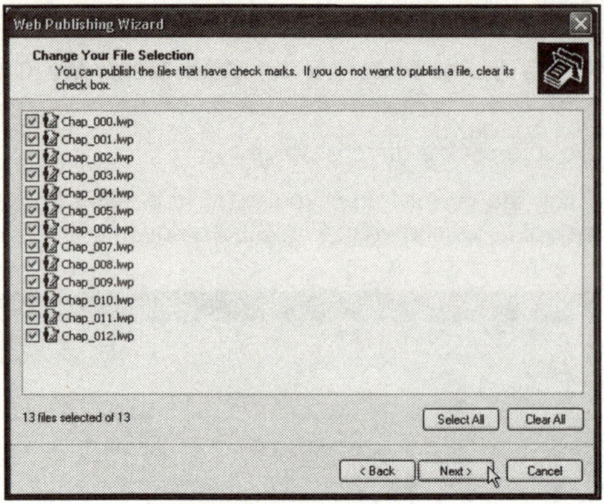

Fig. 6.37 Changing the Selection of Files to Publish on the Web.

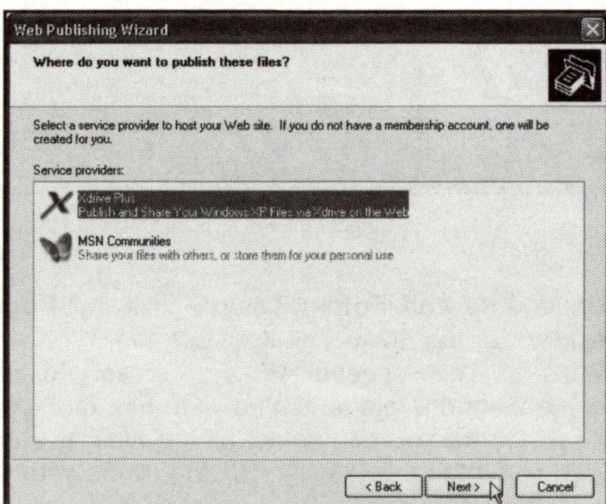

Fig. 6.38 Selecting a Service Provider to Host your Web Site.

Note that there is no option to add to the list of Service Providers who could host your Web site. If you want to publish material to your own Web site, then you must use the File Transfer Protocol (FTP) procedure, to be discussed shortly.

File and Folder Permissions

If you are connected to a network, you can set, view, change, or remove file and folder permissions for a drive or folder on your computer which you share with others connected to the network. However, you can only set file and folder permissions on drives formatted to use NTFS - the advanced file system that includes features not found in any version of FAT. To change permissions you must be the owner of the file or folder, or be the administrator of the system. Then do the following:

- Use the ***start***, **All Programs**, **Accessories**, **Windows Explorer** cascade menu command.
- Locate, select and right-click the shared file or folder, and click the **Properties** option from the drop-down menu, as shown in Fig. 6.39 below.

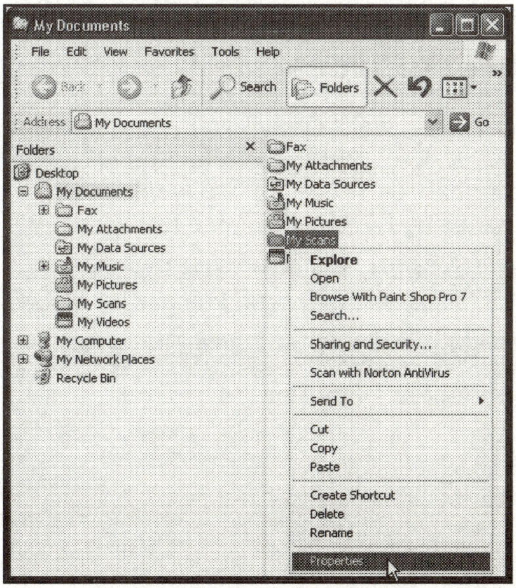

Fig. 6.39 An Item's Shortcut Menu.

- On the displayed dialogue box, click the Security tab. If you are using NTFS and the Security tab does not appear on the Properties dialogue box do the following:

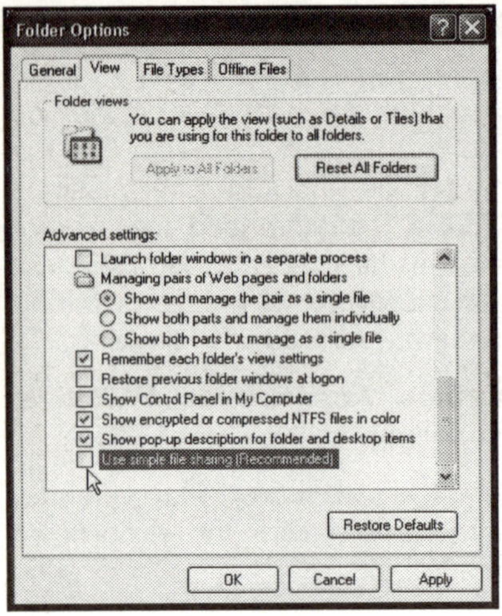

Click ***start***, **Control Panel**, **Appearance and Themes**, and then click **Folder Options**.

On the **View** tab, under **Advanced settings**, clear **Use simple file sharing (Recommended)**, shown in Fig. 6.40.

Fig. 6.40 The View Folder Options Screen.

My Network Places

You can use this option on the ***start*** menu to gain access and information on files and folders on other computers on a network. You can also use this facility to send files and folders to a Web site using FTP by doing the following:

- Use the ***start***, **My Network Places** menu command which displays the screen in Fig. 6.41 below.

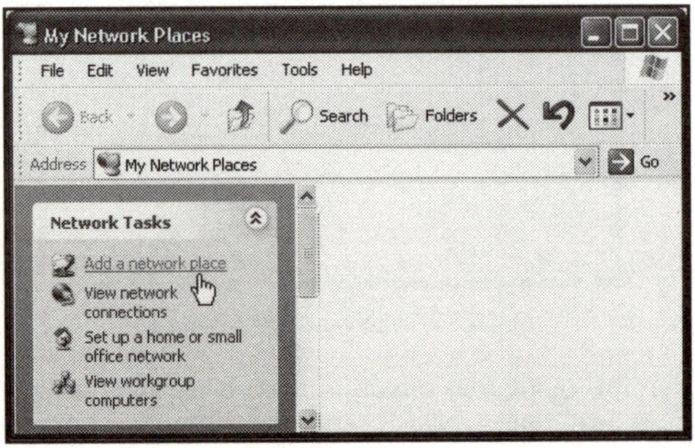

Fig. 6.41 The My Network Places Screen.

- Click the **Add a network place** link under **Network Tasks** to start the Add Network Place Wizard, which helps you sign up for a service that offers online storage space, such as your Web site host.
- On the second Wizard screen, shown in Fig. 6.42 below, type in the Internet or network address. Examples are displayed on the Wizard screen, as shown below, by clicking the appropriate link.

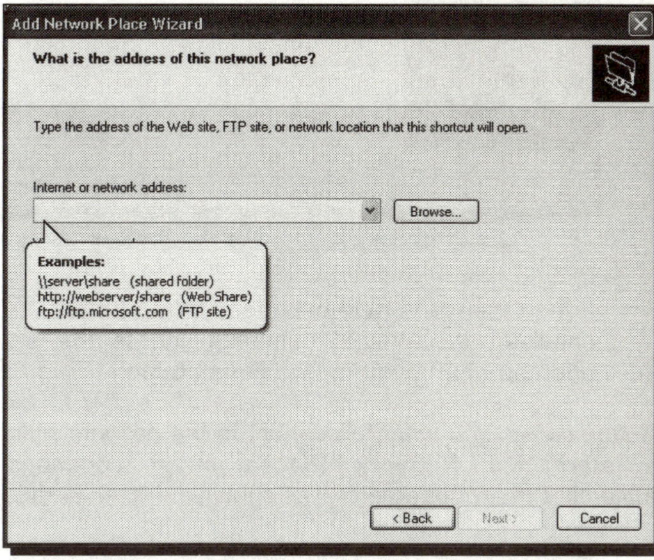

Fig. 6.42 The Second Add Network Place Wizard Screen.

What you type in the **Internet or network address** text box for uploading files using FTP should have been given to you by your Web site host. If it is a network address you are entering, then look at the examples above, or consult you network administrator.

- On the third Wizard screen, you are asked to provide a suitable name for the connection which will appear in **My Network Places**, and can be anything you like. After typing it in, click the **Next** button to take you to the final Wizard screen, shown in Fig. 6.43 on the next page.

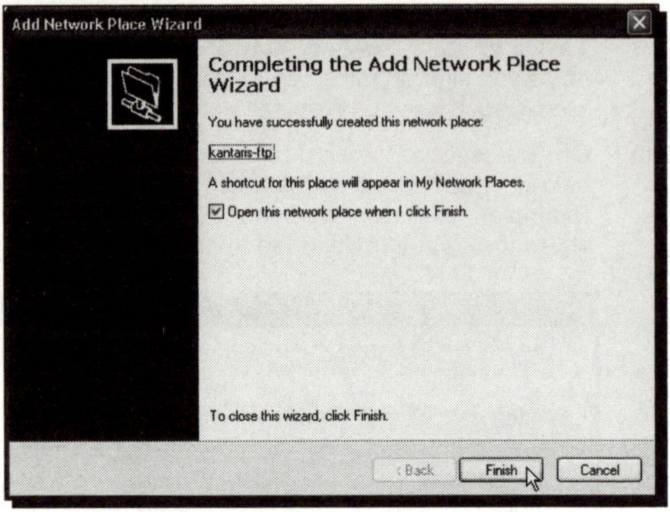

Fig. 6.43 The Final Add Network Place Wizard Screen.

- If the **Open this network place when I click Finish** is checked, the Wizard connects you to the specified address when you click the **Finish** button.

In future, when you want to connect to the network place, use the ***start***, **My Network Places** menu command and double-click the required entry, as shown in Fig. 6.44 below.

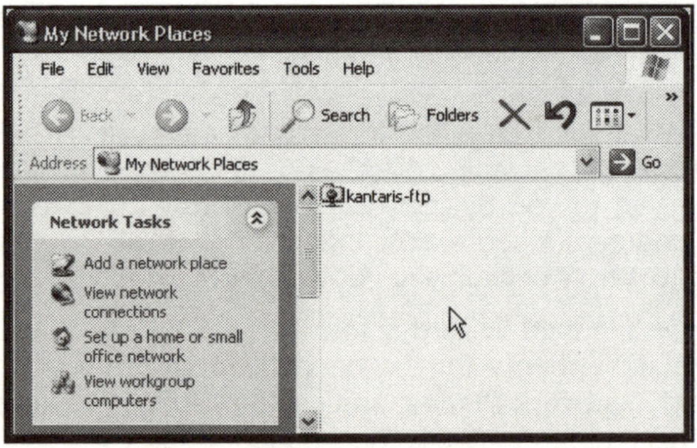

Fig. 6.44 The My Network Places Screen.

7

User Accounts

In this chapter we will examine how you can change user accounts settings, passwords, and pictures on your PC. We begin by using the **Start**, **Control Panel** menu command which displays the screen in Fig. 7.1 below.

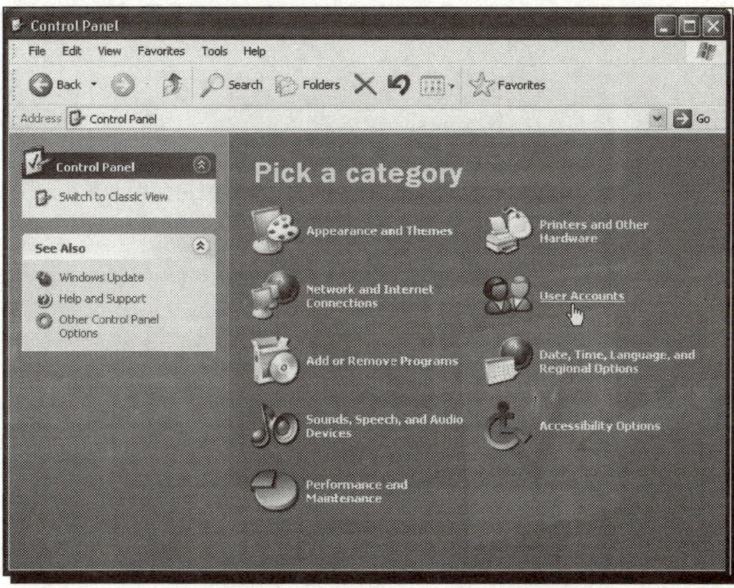

Fig. 7.1 The Control Panel Screen in Category View.

If the **Control Panel** screen displays in Classical View, click the **Switch to Category view** option to be found at the top-left panel of the screen.

Next, click the **User Accounts** entry under the **Pick a category** panel to display the screen shown in Fig. 7.2 on the next page.

The Computer Administrator

In the User Accounts screen, shown below, click the **Computer administrator** link under the **or pick an account to change** entry to display the screen in Fig. 7.3.

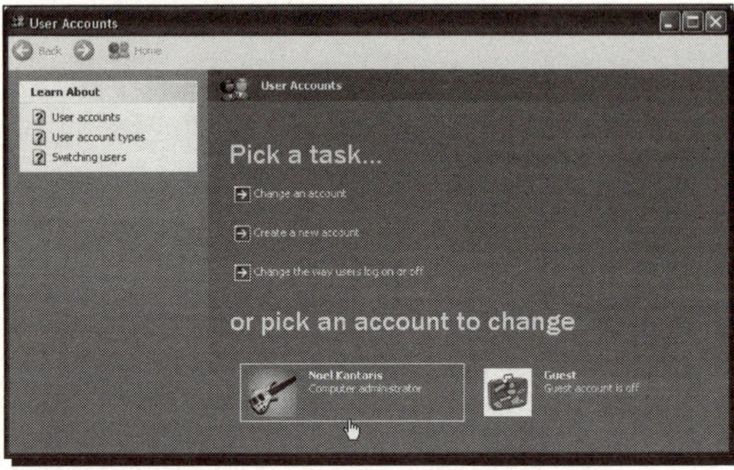

Fig. 7.2 The User Accounts Screen.

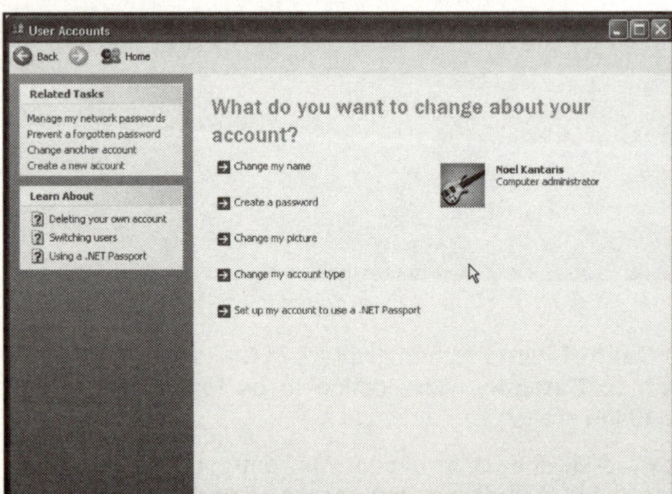

Fig. 7.3 The Computer Administrator's Account Screen.

Obviously you need to log on as the computer's administrator before most of the options on the administrator account screen can be accessed or acted upon. From here, you can change your name, change the picture representing you (see pages 4 and 140), or create a password, as shown in Fig. 7.4 below.

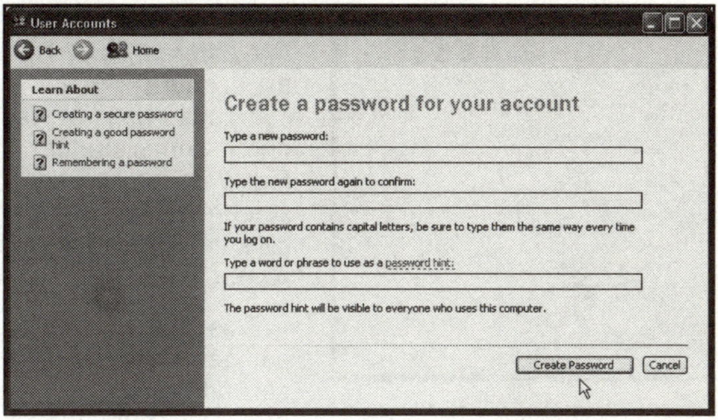

Fig. 7.4 Creating a Password for your Account.

Do have a look at the topics listed under **Learn About** on the left panel of the screen. It is worth finding out how to create a secure password and how to remember it. Another option in Fig. 7.3 allows you to change the account type, as shown in Fig. 7.5 below.

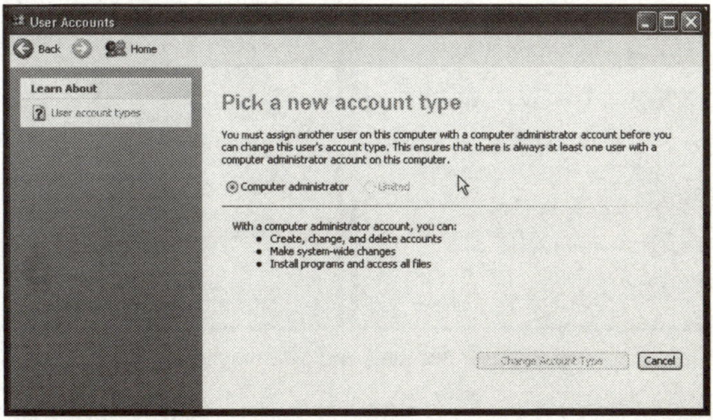

Fig. 7.5 Picking a New Account Type.

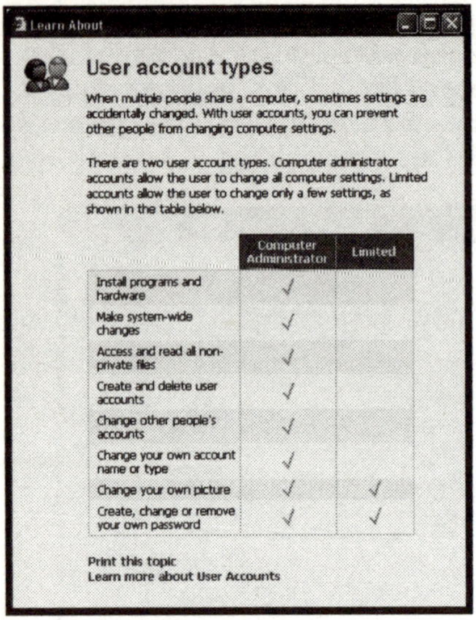

Fig. 7.6 User Account Types.

As you can see, you must assign another user on this computer with an administrator's privileges before you can change the currently logged in user's account to a different type. This is to ensure that this computer has at least one administrator. In Fig. 7.6, we display the screen you will get if you click the link under **Learn About** in Fig. 7.5.

This screen can also be opened by clicking the second link under **Learn About** in Fig. 7.2. The other two links on this screen display information on 'User accounts' and 'Switching users', as shown in Fig. 7.7 below.

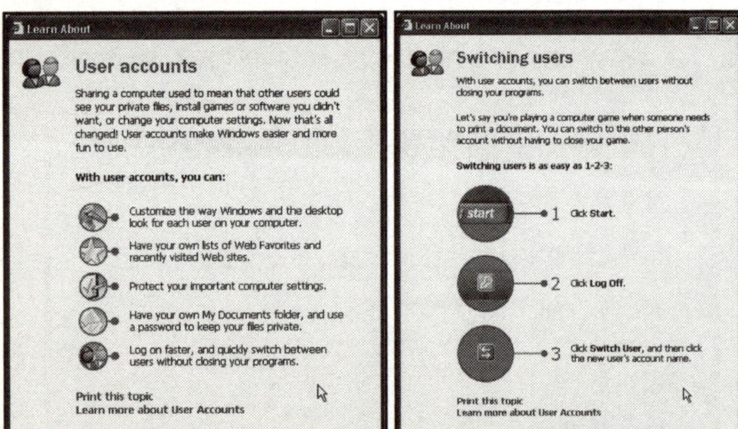

Fig. 7.7 User Accounts and Switching Users.

Obviously, before you can switch between users you must first create their accounts, as we shall see next.

Creating a New Account

If more than one person is to use your computer, then you will need to create an account for each person. Windows XP allows each user on your computer the means of customising their account to their own requirements. For example, they can customise their desktop, and they can customise the way windows display on screen.

Each user also benefits from having their own documents folder so their personal files are kept separate from those of other users, they have separate Internet settings, separate favourites and separate e-mail folders. Individual users can also password protect their accounts so everyone can feel safe in the knowledge that their individualised settings will not be changed by accident or otherwise. Most definitely, the computer administrators should password protect their accounts.

To create a new user account do the following:

- Log on as the administrator, then use the ***start***, **Control Panel** menu command and in the displayed **User Accounts** screen, shown in Fig. 7.8, click the **Create a new account** link under the **Pick a task** entry.

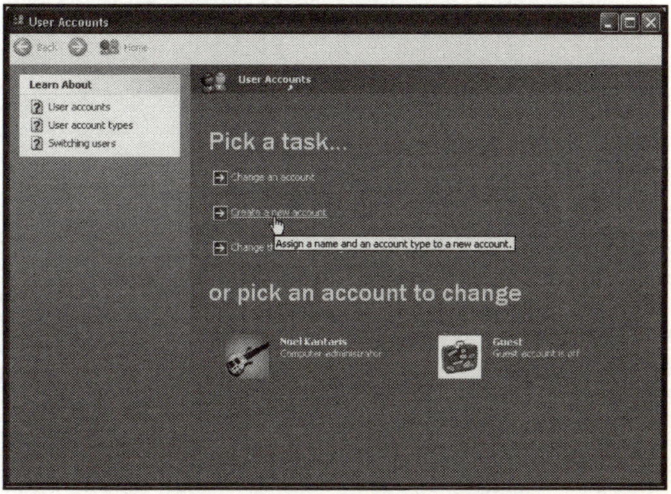

Fig. 7.8 Creating a New Account.

- In the displayed 'Name the new account' window, shown in Fig. 7.9, type in the name of the new account holder and click the **Next** button.

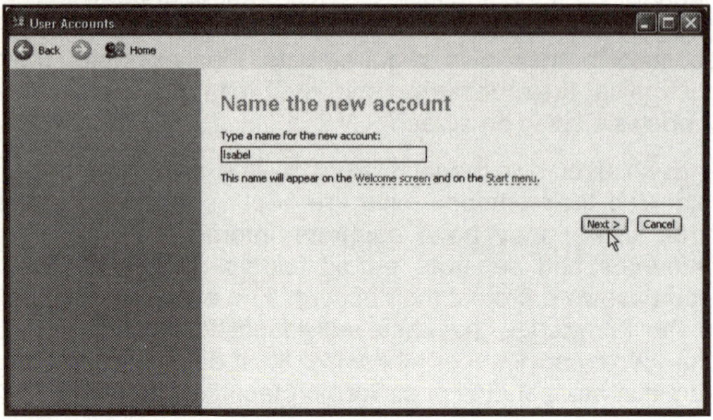

Fig. 7.9 Naming a New Account.

- Since Isabel is rather young at present, select **Limited** as the account type as shown in Fig. 7.10, and click the **Create Account** button.

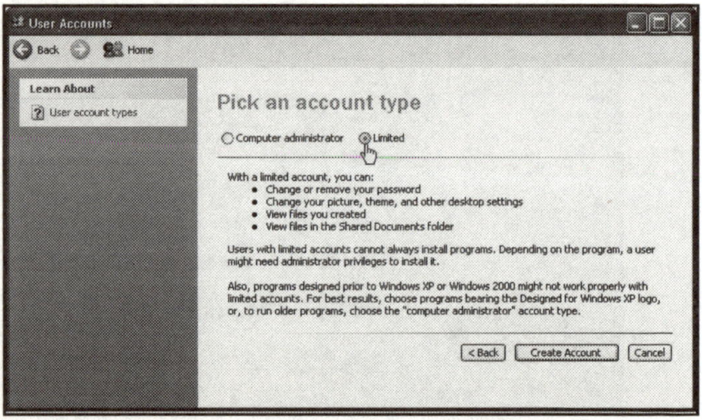

Fig. 7.10 Selecting a New Account Type.

- On the next displayed window, shown in Fig. 7.11 on the next page, click on the newly created account under the **or pick an account to change**.

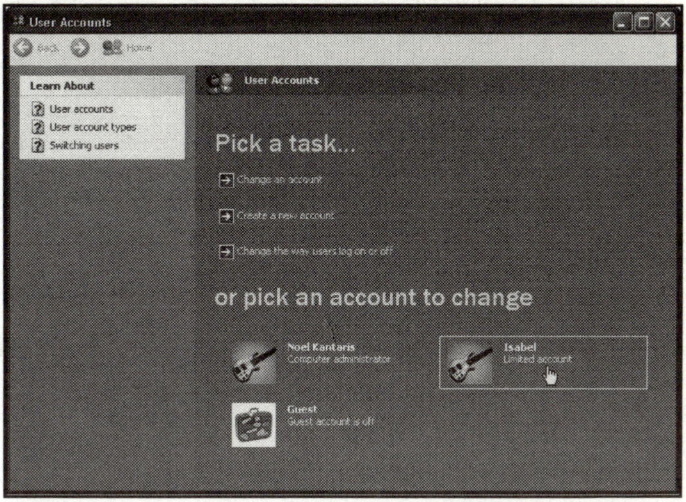

Fig. 7.11 Picking an Account to Change.

- On the displayed 'What do you want to change' window, shown in Fig. 7.12 below, click the **Change the picture** link (pointed to).

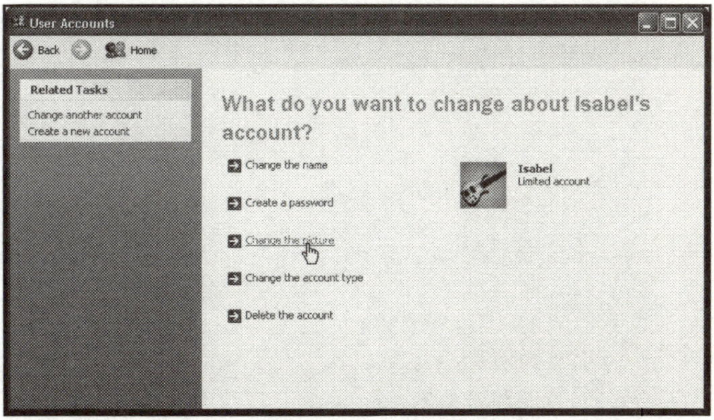

Fig. 7.12 Changing an Account Picture.

- In the displayed 'Pick a picture' window, shown in Fig. 7.13 on the next page, select an appropriate picture and click the **Change Picture** button.

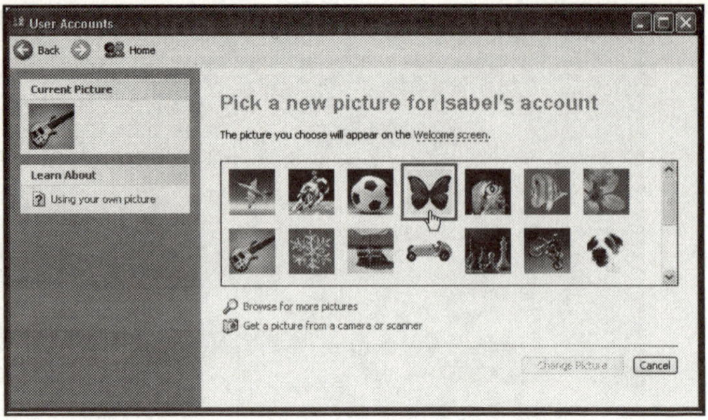

Fig. 7.13 Selecting an Account Picture.

- Next, the window of Fig. 7.12 is displayed once more where you can **Create a password** or click the **Home** Toolbar button to return to the 'Welcome screen' shown in Fig. 7.14 below.

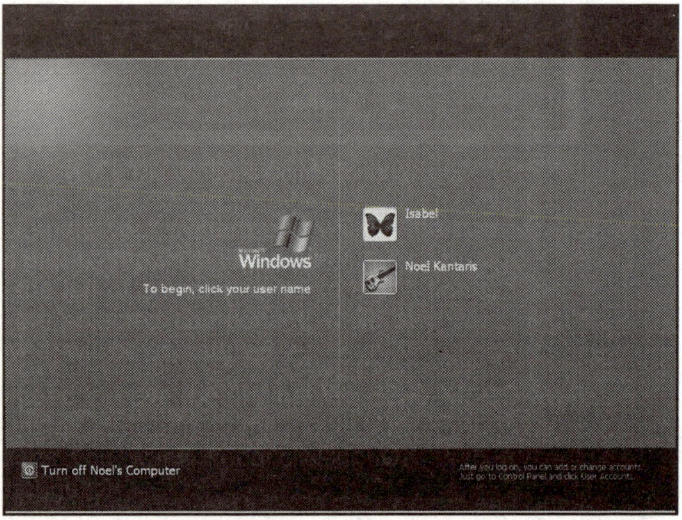

Fig. 7.14 The New Welcome Screen.

Switching Accounts

In Windows XP there are two simple ways of switching users without having to restart the computer. However, if you are using Offline Files, as described on Chapter 4 (page 71) you can only switch users by using the ***start***, **Log Off** command and restarting the computer.

To use Fast Switching, you will have to disable the Offline Files option as follows:

- Log on as the administrator, then use the ***start***, **Control Panel** menu command and in the displayed **User Accounts** screen, shown in Fig. 7.15, click the **Change the way users log on or off** link (pointed to) under the **Pick a task** entry.

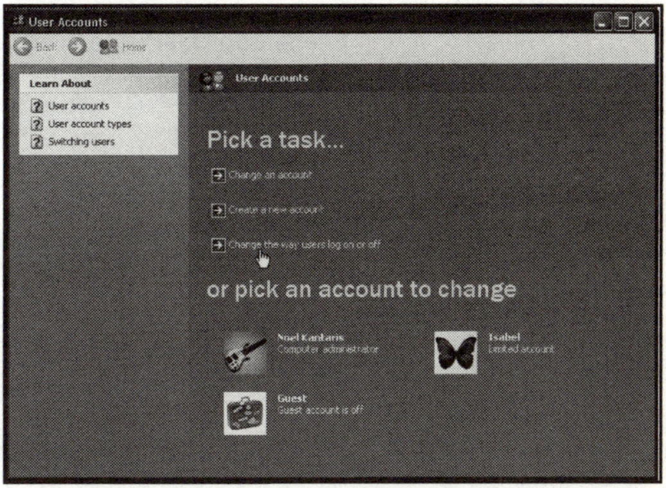

Fig. 7.15 Changing the Way Users Log On or Off.

- On the displayed Offline Files Settings dialogue box (see Fig. 4.22 on page 71), remove the check mark from the **Enable Offline Files** box, then click the **Apply** button followed by the **OK** button.
- On the next window to open, shown in Fig. 7.16, select the **Use fast user switching** option and click the **Apply Options** button.

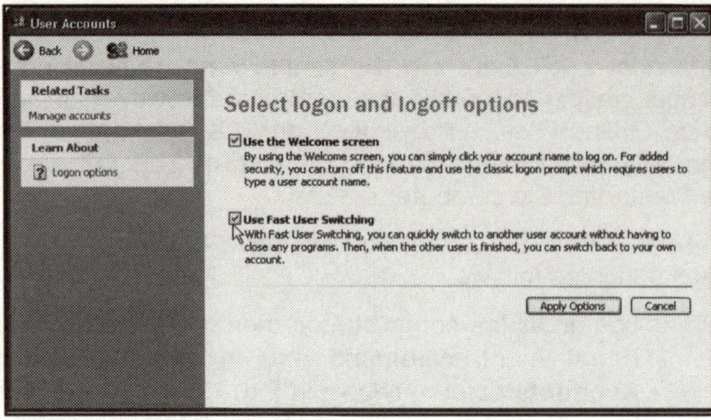

Fig. 7.16 Selecting Log On and Log Off Options.

Now using the ***start***, **Log Off** command displays the box shown in Fig. 7.17 below. Clicking the **Switch User** option displays the Welcome screen shown in Fig. 7.18, showing all the users of the computer so that you can select one.

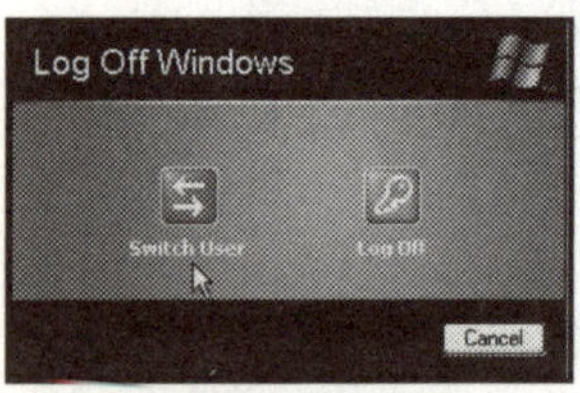

Fig. 7.17 The Log Off Windows box.

A faster method of getting to the Welcome screen is by pressing the <Windows> and <L> keys together.

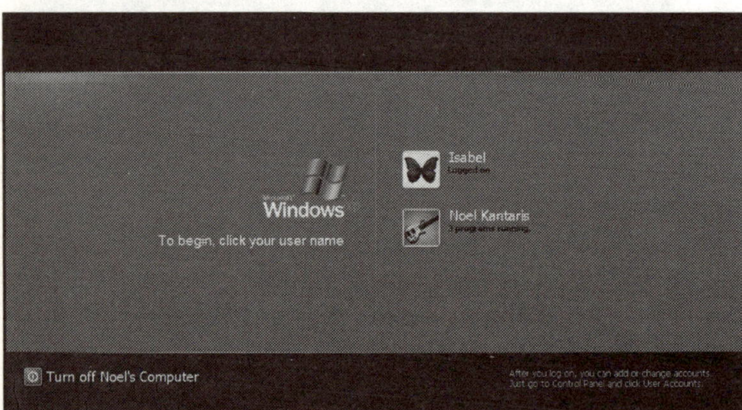

Fig. 7.18 The Windows Welcome Screen.

Using the E-mail Program

When the newly created user first attempts to use the e-mail facilities provided by, say, Outlook Express, the first screen of the Internet Connection Wizard, shown in Fig 7.19 below, is displayed. In this and subsequent screens you need to provide the new user's e-mail connection details.

If the Wizard does not open, or if you want to change your connection details, use the **Tools**, **Accounts** menu command in Outlook Express, select the mail tab and click the **Add** button and select **Mail**.

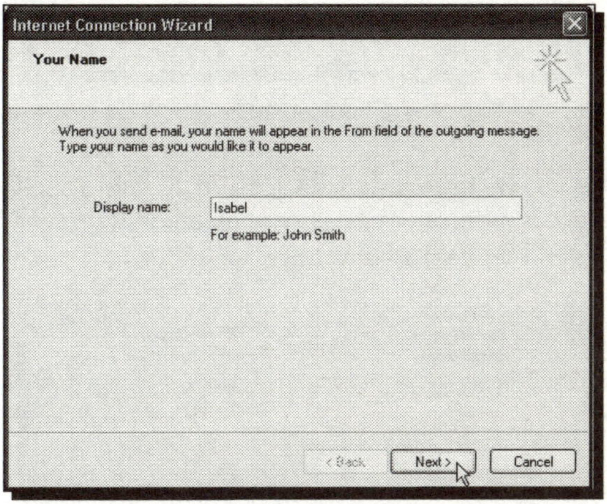

Fig. 7.19 The First Internet Connection Wizard Screen.

In the first screen of the Wizard, type the user's name in the text box, shown above, and click the **Next** button to display the second screen, shown in Fig. 7.20 on the next page. Enter their e-mail address in the text box, if they have not organised one yet you could always sign up for free e-mail with Hotmail (see the extreme right column of the screen dump in Fig. 7.24). Hotmail is a free browser-based e-mail service owned by Microsoft.

In the third Wizard screen enter the e-mail server details, as shown for us in Fig. 7.21. To complete some of the details here you may need to ask your e-mail provider, or your system administrator, for help.

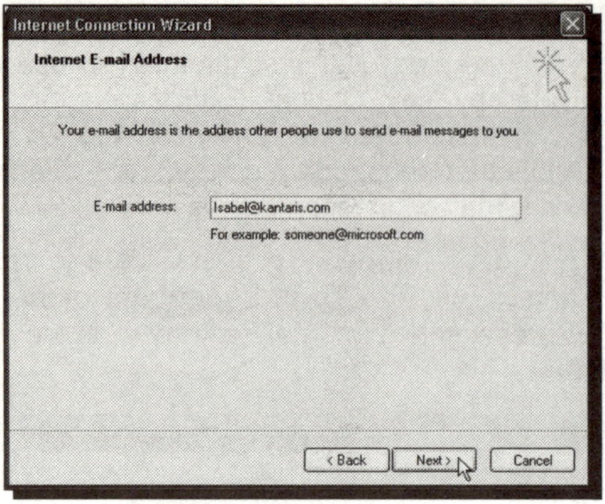

Fig. 7.20 The Second Internet Connection Wizard Screen.

The details given here must be unique to the specified user, and should be different from those of other users of this PC, otherwise you might receive e-mail not intended for your eyes!

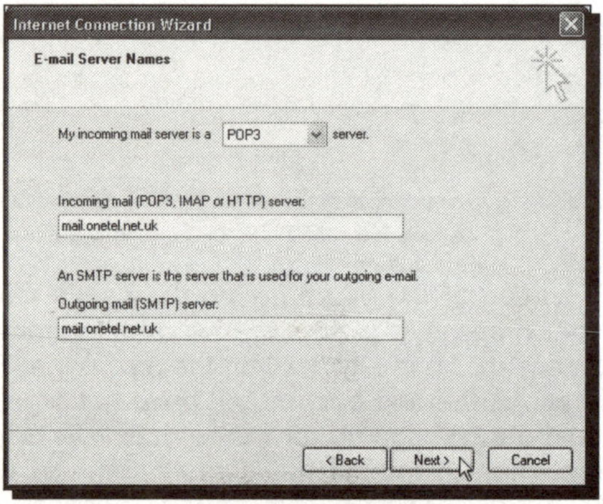

Fig. 7.21 The Third Internet Connection Wizard Screen.

The next Wizard screen asks for a user name and password. Both these would have been given by your e-mail provider. Type these in, as shown here in Fig. 7.22 on the next page, and click the **Next** button.

If you select the **Remember password** option in this box, you will not have to enter these details every time you log on. **BUT** it may not be wise to do this if your PC is in a busy office - for obvious security reasons.

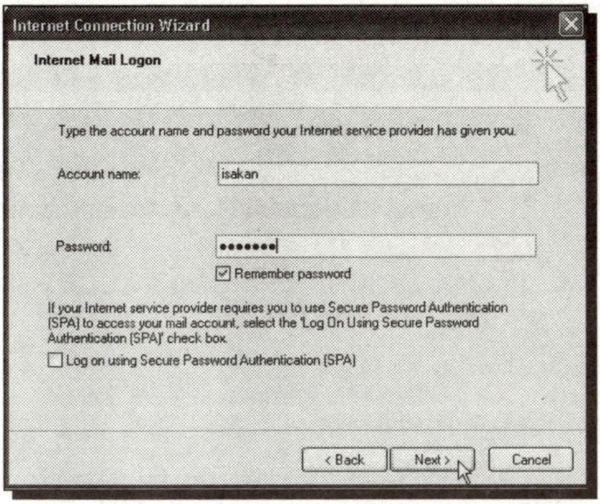

Fig. 7.22 The Fourth Internet Connection Wizard Screen.

This leads to the final Wizard screen informing you of your success, which completes the procedure, so press **Finish** to return you to the Network Connections dialogue box, asking you to select a connection. These connections to the Internet via an Internet Service Provider (ISP), are the same for all users of this PC and were first established by the computer's administrator.

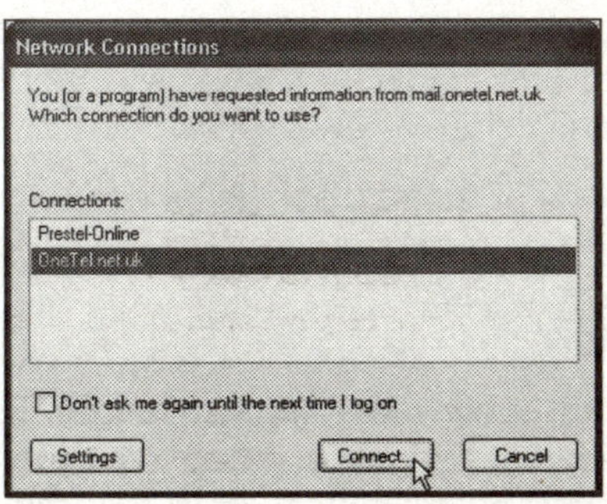

Fig. 7.23 The Internet Accounts Dialogue Box.

Once a connection is established, you can click the Read Mail coloured link, or the **Inbox** entry in the Folder List on the left side of the Outlook Express opening window. Both of these actions open the Inbox, which when opened for the first time, will probably contain a message from Microsoft, like that shown in Fig. 7.24 below.

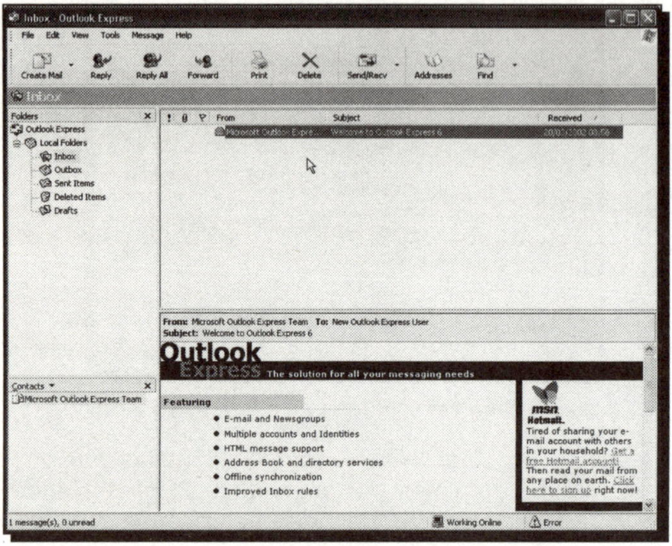

Fig. 7.24 The Inbox Outlook Express Screen.

This shows the default Outlook Express Main window layout, which consists of a Folders List to the left with a Contacts List (from the Address Book) below it, a Message List to the right and a Preview Pane below that. The list under Folders contains all the active mail folders, news servers and newsgroups.

Clicking on one of these displays its contents in the Message List, and clicking on a message opens a Preview of it below for you to see. Double-clicking on a message opens the message in its own window.

If you want to know more about Outlook Express, may we suggest you have a look at our book *Internet Explorer 6 and Outlook Express 6 explained* (BP513), also published by Bernard Babani (publishing) Ltd.

Activating the Guest Account

You can provide limited computer access to guests to your home who might require to look and process their e-mail, by activating the Guest account. To do so, however, you must log on as the computer administrator, and then on the User Accounts window click the Guest icon as shown in Fig. 7.25.

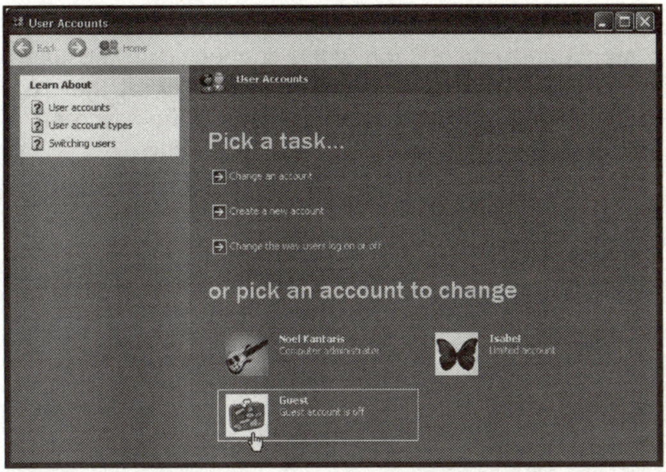

Fig. 7.25 Activating the Guest Account.

This opens the screen shown in Fig. 7.26 below in which you click the **Turn On the Guest Account** button.

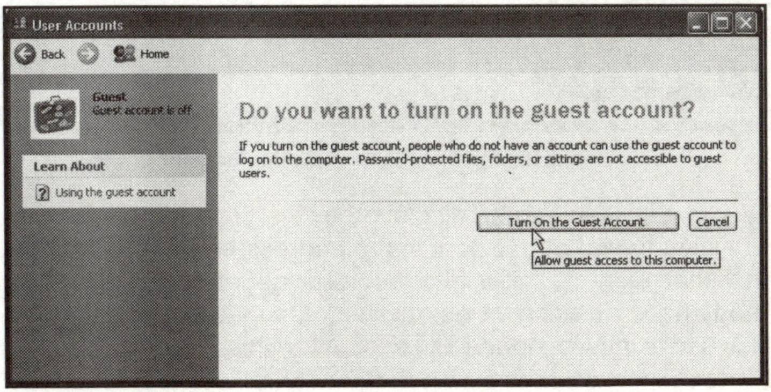

Fig. 7.26 Turning on the Guest Account.

As with other users of this computer, a Guest account needs information about the person's e-mail provider, as discussed previously. An alternative option would be for the guest to use the Microsoft Hotmail facility, but to do so they must be online. Whichever e-mail facility you choose, as a Guest user you cannot connect to the Internet - they must get another user of this computer to first connect to the Internet before they can proceed. The same applies to disconnecting from the Internet after use.

As mentioned earlier (and when connected to the Internet), clicking the **Get a free Hotmail account** link at the extreme right column of the Outlook Express Inbox screen (see Fig. 7.24), displays the screen in Fig. 7.27 below.

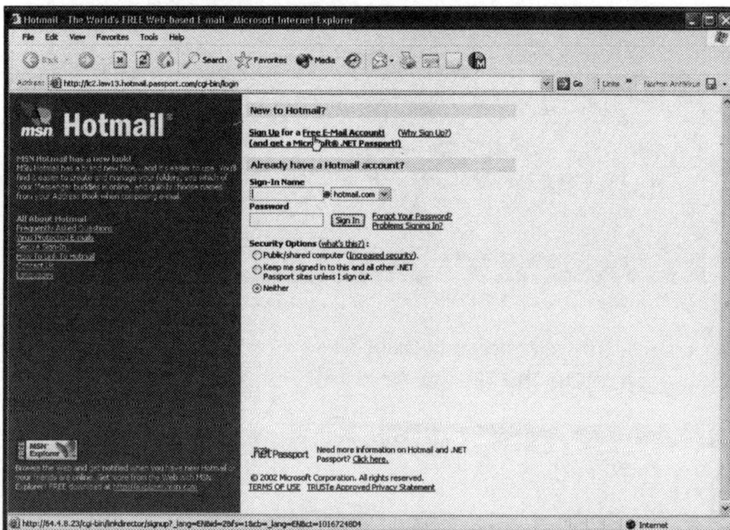

Fig. 7.27 The MSN Hotmail Sign-in Screen.

The same screen can be displayed by starting Internet Explorer and typing www.hotmail.com in the address box. From here you can either sign up for a free e-mail account or sign-in, if you already have an account established. One word of caution; you must use a newly signed up account within 10 days before it becomes activated, and after that you must use it at least once every 30 days if the account is not to be lost.

Increasing Computer Security

You can increase your computer's security by first disabling fast switching between users. To do so, log on as the computer's administrator, log off all other users by switching to their account and using the ***start***, **Log Off** command, then do the following:

- Use the ***start***, **Control Panel** menu command and click the **User Accounts** link.
- In the displayed 'Select logon and logoff options' screen, shown in Fig. 7.28, click the **Logon options** link under the **Learn About** entry on the left panel of the screen.

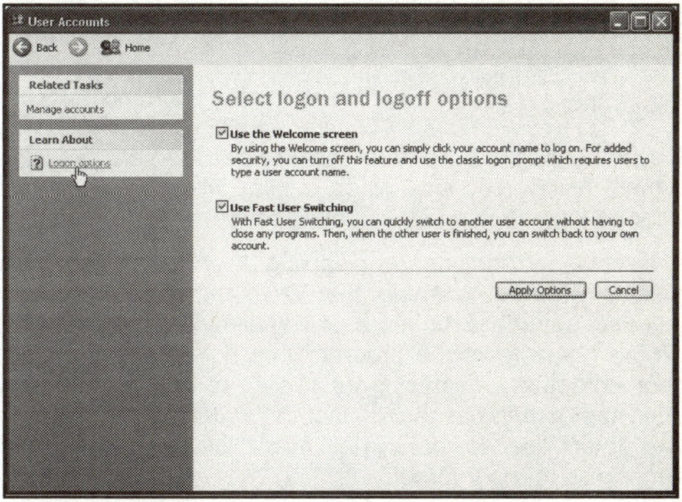

Fig. 7.28 Selecting Log On and Log Off Options.

- The displayed screen, shown in Fig. 7.29 on the next page, contains information on what happens when either or both of the check marks in Fig. 7.28 are removed.

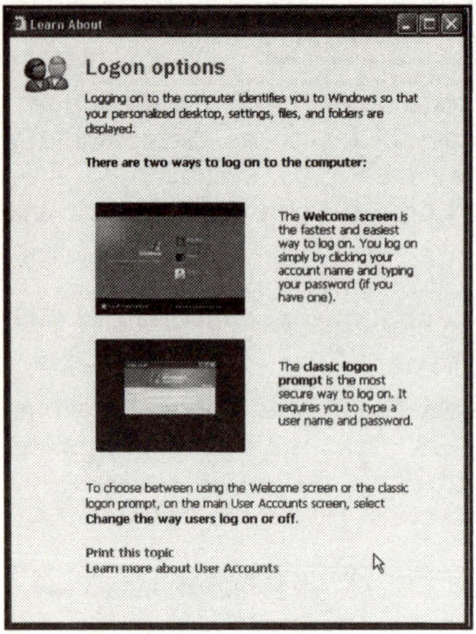

Fig. 7.29 The Learn About Log-on Options Screen.

Obviously, disabling the Fast User Switching option adds a bit more security to the system and allows you to use Offline Files (see Chapter 4, page 71), but it still retains the friendly way of logging in, as it allows you to click your name on the Welcome screen and type a password, if you have one, to log on.

However, if Fast User Switching is disabled, using the <Windows+L> key combination, locks the computer and only the administrator of the PC can unlock it. Also the Guest user is barred from browsing the Web or using any e-mail facility, because when a user who has access to the Internet logs off, the connection is shut down automatically.

If now, in addition to disabling the Fast User Switching option, you also disable the Welcome screen option, you increase security even more as you eliminate the possibility of a Trojan horse (a rogue program that collects information from your computer) disguising as a system log-on and retrieving user names and passwords that the writers of the Trojan horse can later use to break into your system when you are connected to the Internet.

In other words, increasing security decreases convenience of use of your computer, and vice versa. The choice is yours to make!

8

Adding or Removing Programs

In this chapter we will examine how you can install or remove programs and Windows components from your PC. We begin by using the **Start**, **Control Panel** menu command which displays the screen in Fig. 8.1 below.

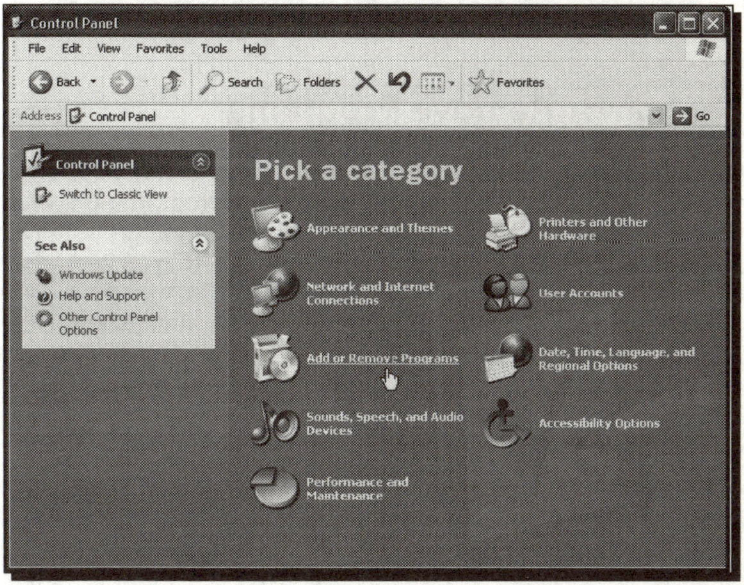

Fig. 8.1 The Control Panel Screen in Category View.

If the **Control Panel** screen displays in Classical View, click the **Switch to Category view** option to be found at the top-left panel of the screen.

Next, click the **Add or Remove Programs** entry under the **Pick a category** panel to display the screen shown in Fig. 8.2 on the next page.

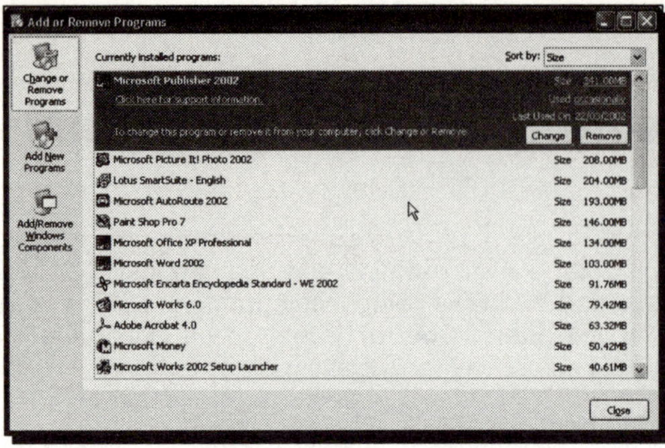

Fig. 8.2 The Add or Remove Programs Screen.

Change or Remove Programs

The **Change or Remove Programs** option icon on the left panel of the above screen, only works for programs on your system that were specially written for Windows and are listed in the Add or Remove Programs screen above (Fig. 8.2). Using this option removes all trace of the selected program from your hard disc. However, with earlier Windows programs, you will be left with the usual application set-up files on your system which will have to be removed manually.

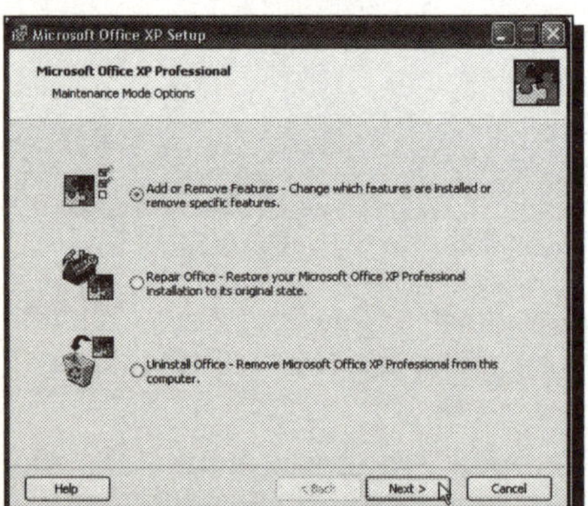

Fig. 8.3 The Office XP Setup Screen.

To change or remove a listed application, highlight it, then click either the **Change** or **Remove** buttons to the right of the highlighted area. For example, selecting the Microsoft Office XP Professional entry from the above list and clicking the **Change** button, displays the screen in Fig. 8.3.

Adding New Programs

To add new Windows programs to your computer's hard disc, click the **Add New Programs** button on the left panel of the Add or Remove Programs screen shown in Fig. 8.2. This displays the screen shown in Fig. 8.4 below.

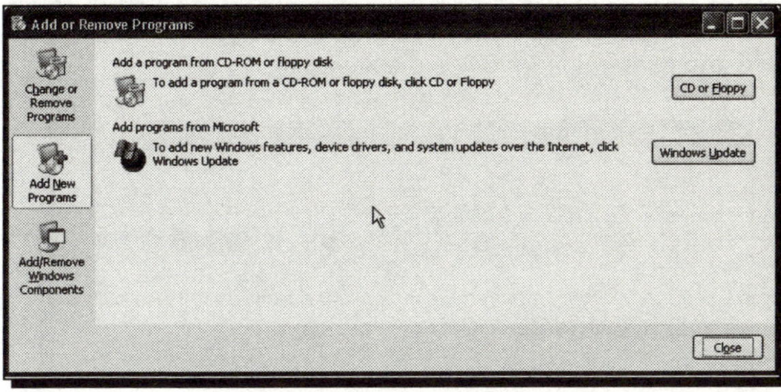

Fig. 8.4 The Add New Programs Screen.

The facility to add a program seems superfluous because installing new Windows programs on your computer's hard disc is made very easy these days. Almost all Windows applications are distributed on one or more CDs the first one of which uses an auto-start program which in turn runs the SETUP program.

Furthermore, most applications vendors give you instructions that if the auto-start program does not start the installation process, to click the Windows ***start*** button, and select the **Run** command which opens the Run dialogue box shown in Fig. 8.5 and type in the **Open** text box the command

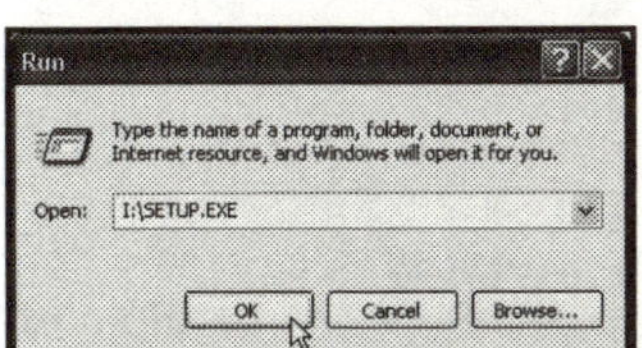

Fig. 8.5 The Run Dialogue Box.

```
i:\setup
```

where i: is our CD-ROM drive; yours will probably be different. Clicking the **OK** button, starts the installation process.

In the end, which method you use, if the auto-start facility fails, is up to you.

The Manual Windows Update Utility

An essential part of keeping your Windows system healthy and up-to-date is the Update program. Microsoft provides fixes and updates to Windows XP and its many other components on their Web site to which you are automatically connected by clicking the **Windows Update** button in Fig. 8.4. The first time you invoke the Update program you are asked to connect to the Internet - in our case via our Dial-up Connection. Once this is done, the screen in Fig. 8.6 is displayed.

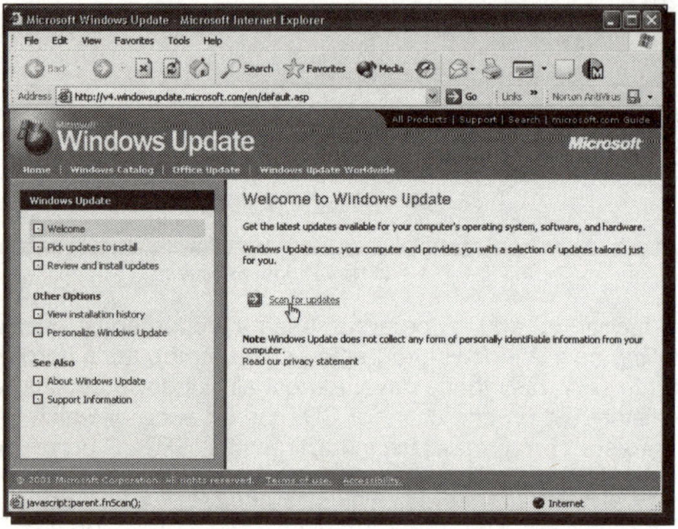

Fig. 8.6 The Windows Update Screen.

As you can see, you are given a promise that the Update program does not collect any form of personal information from your computer. Clicking the **Scan for updates** link, starts the process by first looking into your computer's configuration to see what your system might need, before displaying the updates relevant to your system. In our case the screen in Fig. 8.7 on the next page was displayed. In your case the contents of this screen will most certainly be different from ours. It all depends on when you updated your system last time, and what you selected to download from the site at the time.

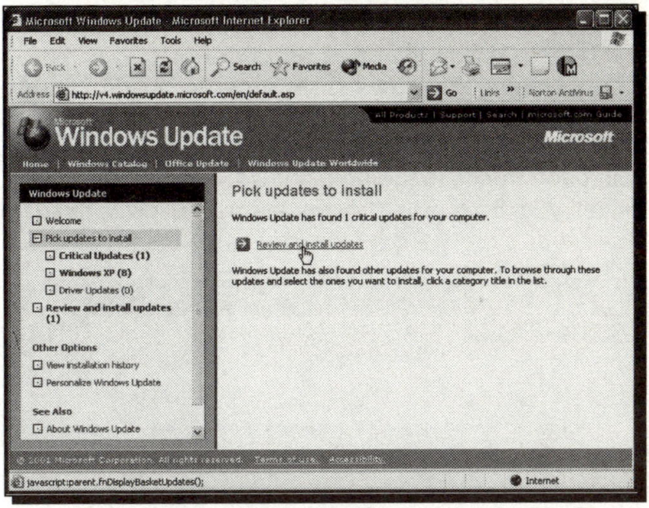

Fig. 8.7 The Windows Updates List.

Using the above screen you can **Review and install updates** you select from the displayed list, as shown in Fig. 8.8 below.

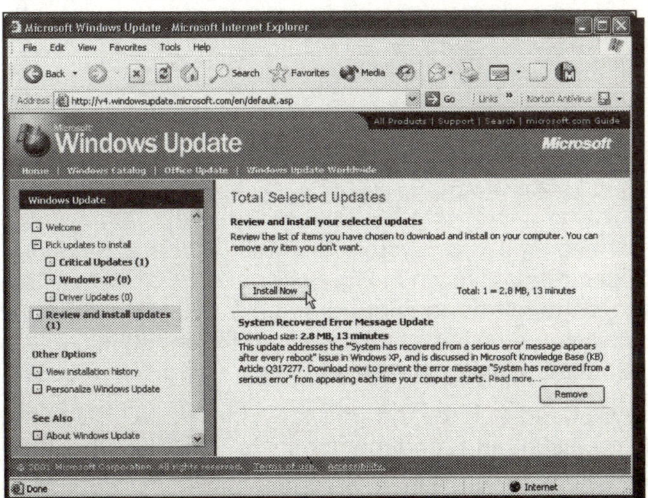

Fig. 8.8 The Windows Updates List.

In Chapter 12, under System Performance and Maintenance, we will discuss how to turn on Automatic Updates.

Adding/Removing Windows Features

The **Add/Remove Windows Components** option icon on the left panel in Fig. 8.2, allows you to install or remove specific Windows components at any time. To install or remove such features, open the dialogue box, shown in Fig. 8.9, highlight the group that you think will contain them and click the **Details** button.

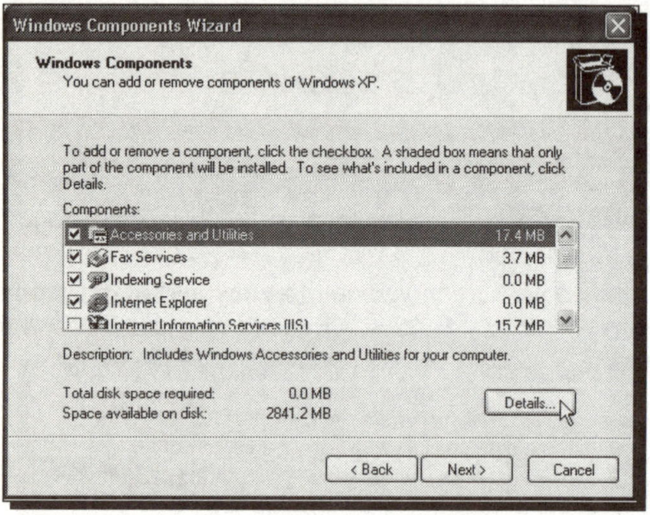

Fig. 8.9 The Windows Components Wizard.

This will examine your system and will list the components of the chosen group, shown in Fig. 8.10 on the next page. Clicking the box to the left of an item name so that a tick appears in it, will install the selected component, while any items with their ticks removed, will be uninstalled.

You will need to have the original Windows XP CD available when you install additional components. Once you have made the selections you want, keep clicking **OK** to carry out the required changes.

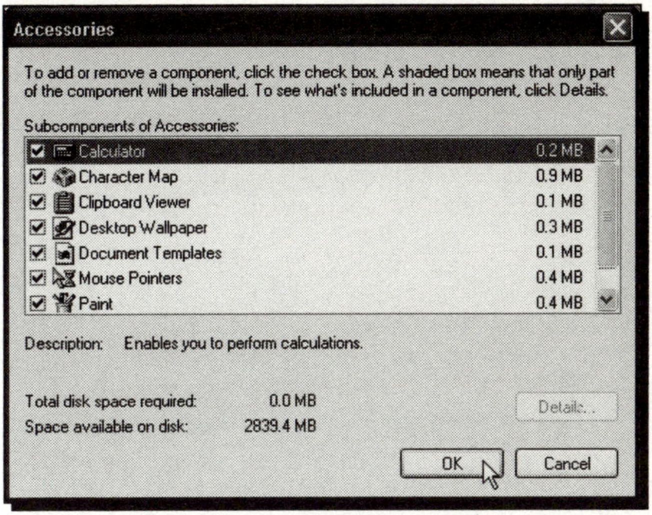

Fig. 8.10 The Accessories Dialogue Box.

It is easy to use up too much hard disc space with Windows features, so keep your eye on the **Total disk space required** entry.

9

Date, Time & Regional Options

In this chapter we will examine how you can change the date, time, language, and regional options of your PC. We begin by using the **Start**, **Control Panel** menu command which displays the screen in Fig. 9.1 below.

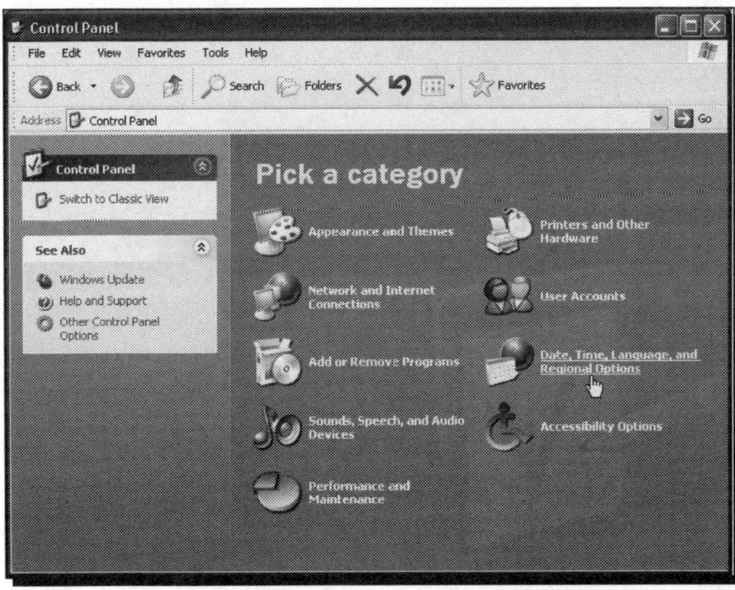

Fig. 9.1 The Control Panel Screen in Category View.

If the **Control Panel** screen displays in Classical View, click the **Switch to Category view** option to be found at the top-left panel of the screen.

Next, click the **Date, Time, Language, and Regional Options** entry under the **Pick a category** panel to display the screen shown in Fig. 9.2 on the next page.

Date and Time

To change the date and time settings of your computer's clock, click the **Date and Time** link (pointed to) in Fig. 9.2 below.

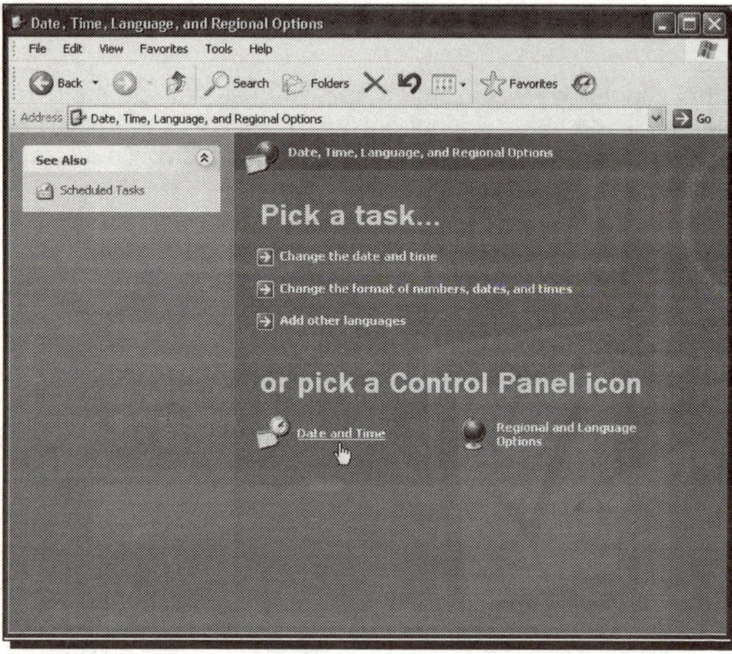

Fig. 9.2 The Date, Time, Language, and Regional Options Screen.

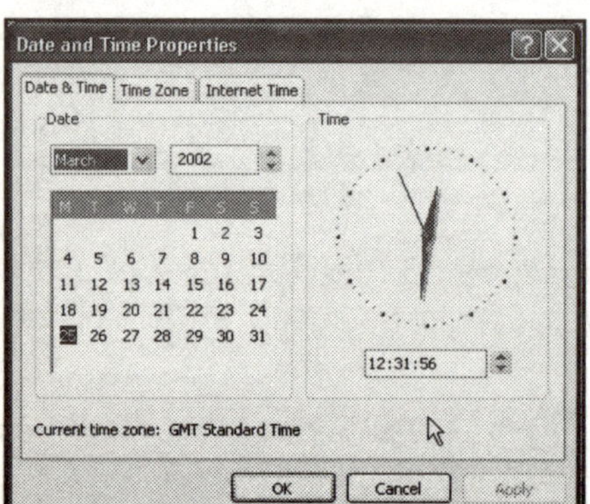

You can use the three tabs on the displayed dialogue box, shown in Fig. 9.3, to make changes to your computer's date and time settings.

Fig. 9.3 The Date and Time Properties Dialogue Box.

Changing the Date and Time

To change the date of your system, simply select the month from the drop-down menu which is displayed when the down arrow to the right of the month box is clicked, as shown here. The actual date within the selected month is selected by clicking the appropriate entry on the calendar. To change the year click the up or down buttons to the right of the year box.

To change the time, click on either the hour, minutes or seconds block you want to change, then click the up or down buttons to the right of the time box, to change the selected block by one unit per click. For example, if you clicked on minutes, then each time you click the up or down time buttons, the time changes by one minute for each click. Alternatively, edit the appropriate blocks directly within the time entry.

After making any changes to the date or time, click the **Apply** button followed by the **OK** button.

Changing the Time Zone

To change the time zone of your computer, click the Time Zone tab in the Date and Time Properties dialogue box (Fig. 9.3) to display the screen shown in Fig. 9.4. To change the time zone from the one shown here, click the down-arrow (pointed to) to display a drop-down list from which you can choose your time zone.

After making any changes to the time zone, click the **Apply** button followed by the **OK** button.

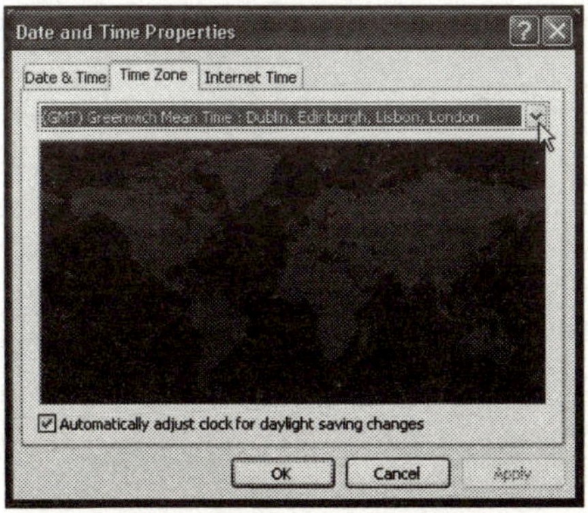

Fig. 9.4 The Time Zone Screen of the Date and Time Properties Dialogue Box.

Internet Time Synchronising

You can synchronise your computer's clock with a time server on the Internet by clicking the Internet Time tab of the Date and Time Properties dialogue box (Fig. 9.3) to display the screen in Fig. 9.5. This tab is only available if you are not a member of a domain (a group of computers that are part of a network).

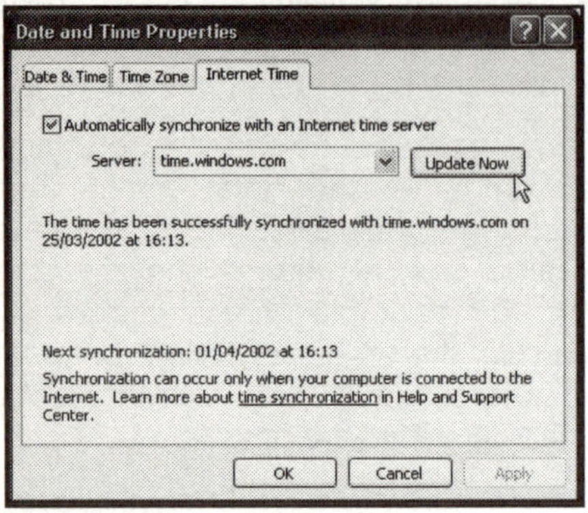

Fig. 9.5 The Internet Time Screen of the Date and Time Properties Dialogue Box.

To synchronise your computer's clock with an Internet time server, you must first connect to the Internet before you select a server from the drop-down list, displayed when you click the down-arrow to the right of the **Server** entry box, and click the **Update Now** button.

If you have a continuous Internet connection, through a cable modem or a high speed digital subscriber line (DSL) modem, and the **Automatically synchronize with an Internet time server** box is ticked, then your computer clock will be synchronised automatically once a week.

If your computer is a member of a domain your computer clock will most likely be synchronised automatically by the network time server so that all computers on the network show the same time.

If time synchronisation fails it could be that either you are not connected to the Internet, your personal Firewall prevents changes to your computer clock, or the time server is busy. Time synchronisation will also fail if you have the wrong date set in the Date and Time screen.

Regional and Language Options

Most Windows application programs use Windows settings to determine how they display and handle language, numbers, and currency. It is important that you ensure your system was correctly set up during the installation process, although these settings can be changed later, as discussed below.

To change the regional and language settings of your computer, click the **Regional and Language Options** link pointed to in Fig. 9.6 below.

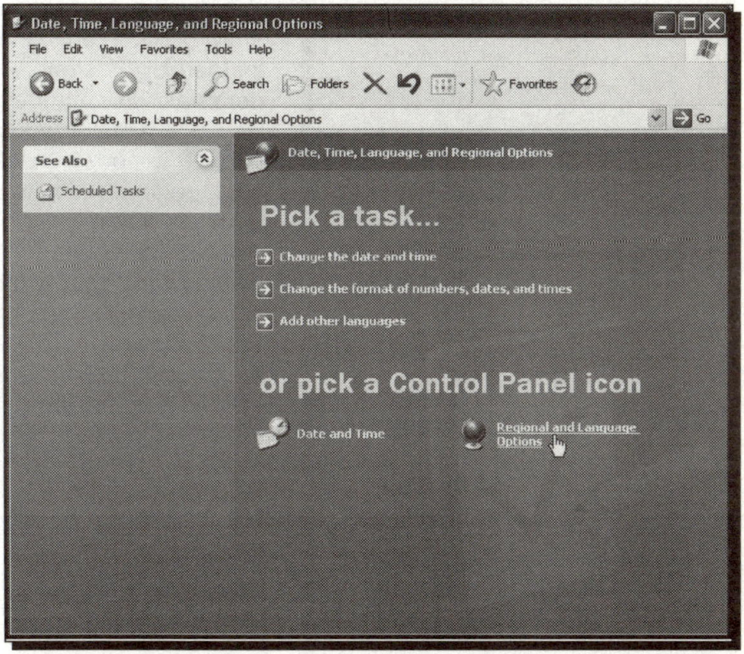

Fig. 9.6 The Date, Time, Language, and Regional Options Screen.

This opens the tabbed Regional and Language dialogue box shown in Fig. 9.7 on the next page.

Changing Regional Options

Make sure the various entries are correct. If not, change them by clicking the down arrow to the right of an entry to display a drop-down list and select the most appropriate country in the Regional Options tab screen of the dialogue box.

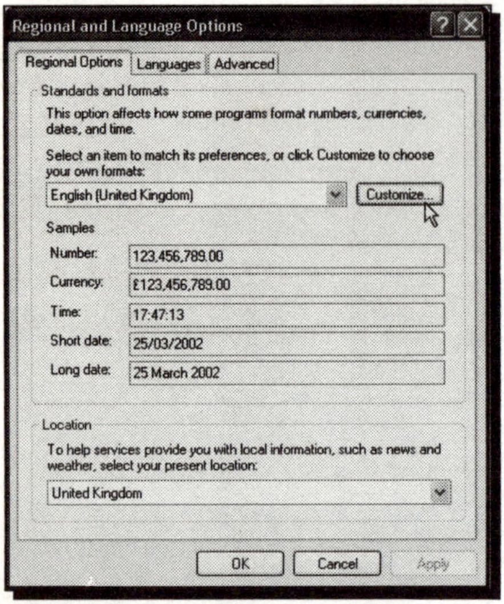

Fig. 9.7 The Regional Options Screen.

If, in the future, you start getting '$' signs, instead of '£' signs, or commas in numbers where you would expect periods, check your regional settings and click the **Customize** button to display the multi-tab screen shown here in Fig. 9.8. You can use the various tab screens of this dialogue box to change the way numbers, currency, time, and date display. You will have to click the **Apply** button before any changes become effective.

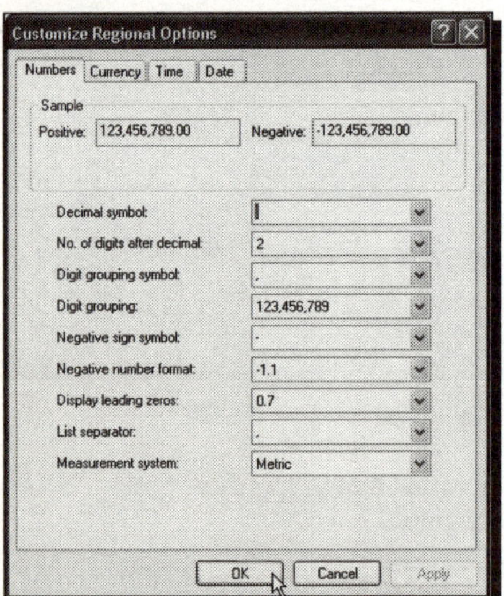

Fig. 9.8 The Regional Options Screen.

To change the actual time and date of your computer's clock, double-click the clock displayed at the bottom right corner of the Windows screen.

Changing Language

Clicking the Languages tab of the Regional and Language Options dialogue box, displays the screen in Fig. 9.9. From here, you can add or remove an 'input language', which is defined as the language in which you enter and display text.

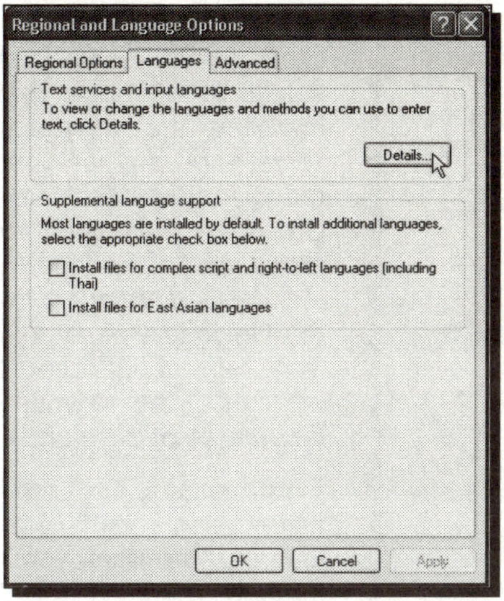

Fig. 9.9 The Regional Options Screen.

To change an input language, click the **Details** button to display the screen in Fig. 9.10. From here you can select one of the installed input languages as the default language from a drop-down list under the **Default input language** area. You can also add or remove an input language or text services by clicking the **Add** or **Remove** button in the **Installed services** entry area.

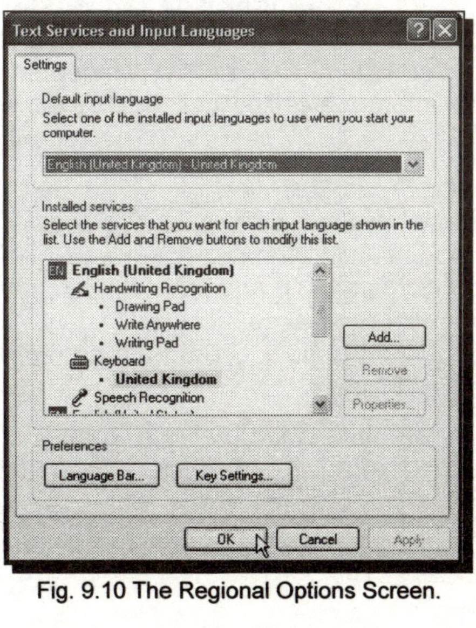

Fig. 9.10 The Regional Options Screen.

Text services include keyboard layouts, Input Method Editors (IMEs) for entering East Asian language characters, and handwriting and speech recognition options.

Advanced Language Options

Clicking the Advanced tab of the Regional and Language Options dialogue box, displays the screen in Fig. 9.11 below.

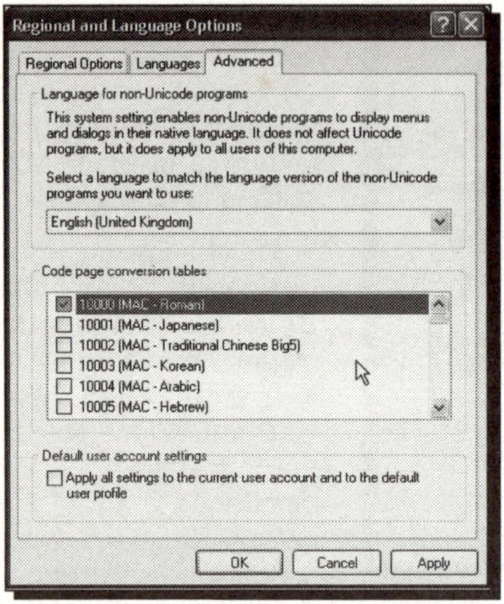

Fig. 9.11 The Advanced Options Screen.

From here you can select a language that matches the language version of any of your programs that don't use Unicode encoding (a character encoding standard developed by the Unicode Consortium that represents almost all of the written languages of the world).

For example, if you are using an older Hebrew program, click to check the box against the Hebrew entry under **Code page conversion tables**, then click the **Apply** button. Windows will ask you to insert the Windows XP distribution CD in the computer's CD-ROM drive so that the appropriate files can be copied to your PC's hard disc.

The selected check boxes in the list of **Code page conversion tables** indicates which code page conversion tables are installed and loaded into memory when you start your computer. Adding a conversion table and selecting it under the **Language for non-Unicode programs**, allows Windows to interpret the letters and characters used in a program correctly and convert them to and from Unicode.

Only the Administrator of the Computer or group of computers is allowed to add or remove code page conversion tables.

10

Sound, Speech & Audio Devices

In this chapter we will examine how you can change the sounds made by your PC, or configure the settings for your recording devices. We begin by using the **Start**, **Control Panel** menu command which displays the screen in Fig. 10.1 below.

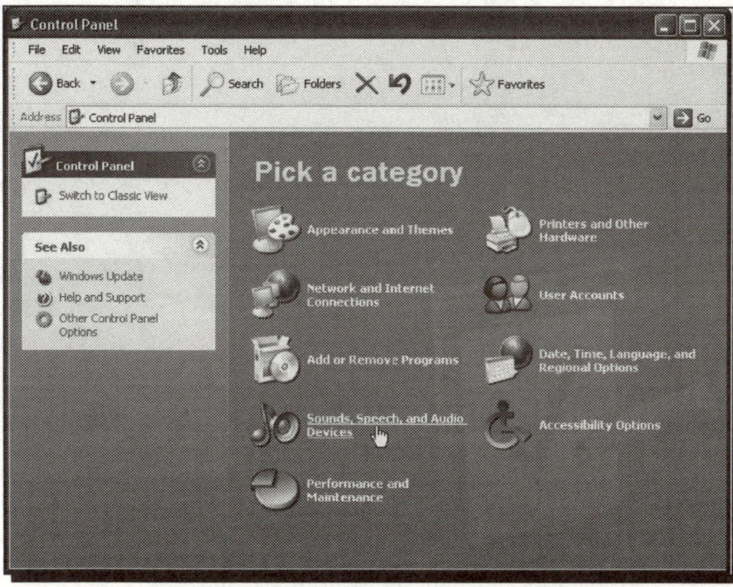

Fig. 10.1 The Control Panel Screen in Category View.

If the **Control Panel** screen displays in Classical View, click the **Switch to Category view** option to be found at the top-left panel of the screen.

Next, click the **Sounds, Speech, and Audio Devices** entry under the **Pick a category** panel to display the screen shown in Fig. 10.2 on the next page.

Sounds and Audio Devices

To change the sounds and audio devices settings on your computer, click the **Sounds and Audio Devices** link pointed to in Fig. 10.2 below.

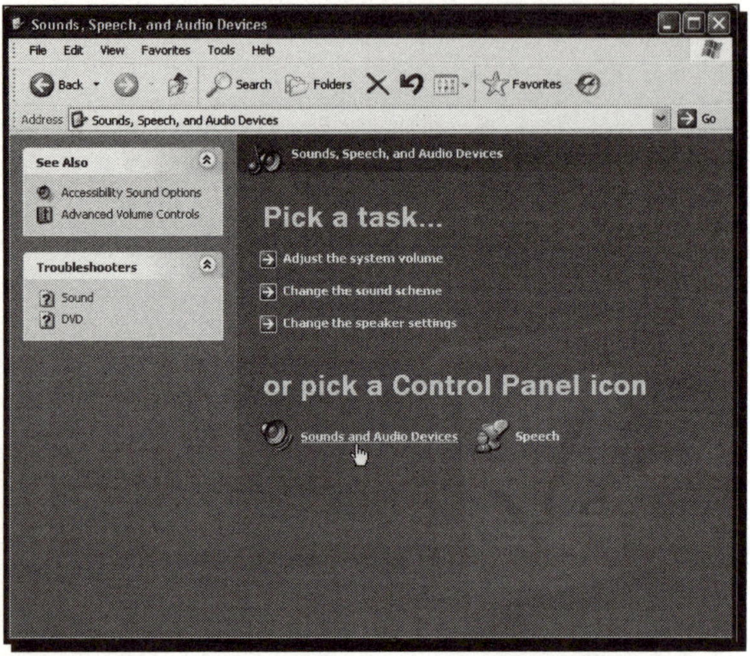

Fig. 10.2 The Sounds, Speech, and Audio Devices Screen.

This displays a multi-tab dialogue box, shown in Fig. 10.3 on the next page, from which you can:

- adjust your computer's system volume
- select from a list of schemes that can be used to allocate sounds to various program events
- select the sound playback and record device
- select the voice playback and record device
- select from a list of devices available on your PC to look at their properties and use the troubleshoot facility.

Changing the Computer's System Volume

You can change the computer's system volume using the Volume tab screen of the **Sounds and Audio Devices Properties** dialogue box, shown below.

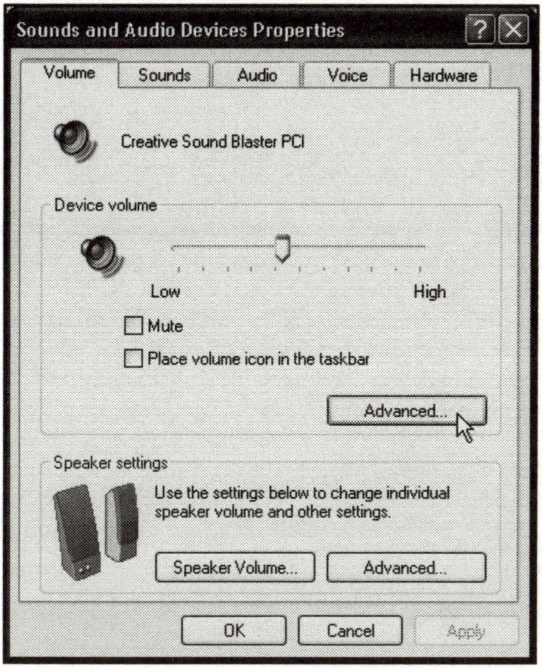

Fig. 10.3 The Volume Tab Sheet of the Sounds and Audio Devices Properties Screen.

For convenience, you can click the **Place volume icon in the task bar** box, so that future changes to the volume can be made easier.

Clicking the **Advanced** button (pointed to in Fig. 10.3 above) displays the Volume Control screen shown in Fig. 10.4 on the next page. You can use this screen to adjust your system's sound source settings, such as CD, MIDI, and other installed devices.

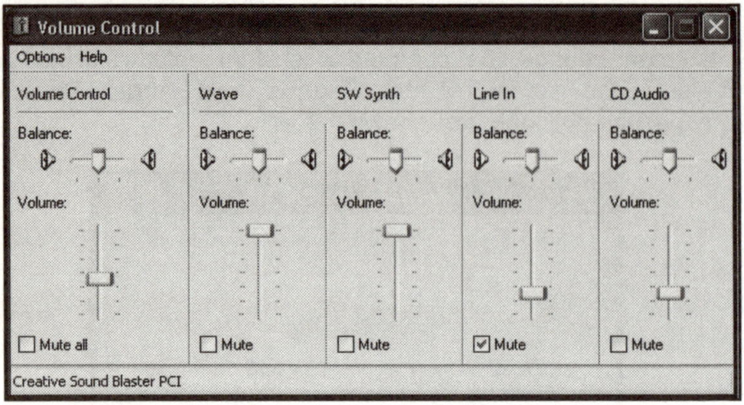

Fig. 10.4 The Sounds and Audio Devices Properties Dialogue Box.

You can also use the buttons under **Speaker settings** in Fig. 10.3 to select the speakers attached to your audio card, adjust audio playback features, and select sound effects you want to apply for audio playback.

Assigning Sounds to Program Events

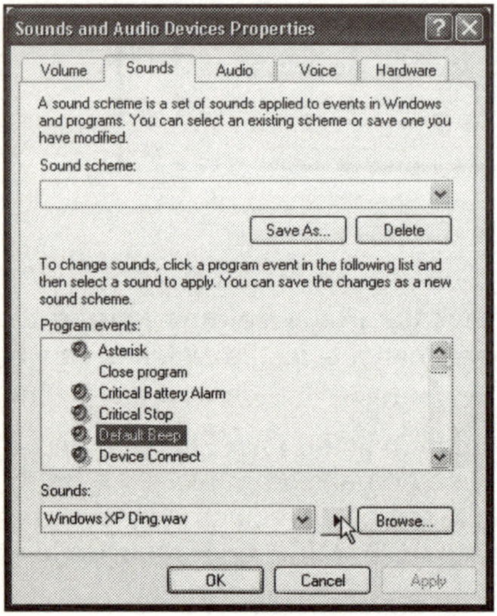

Fig. 10.5 The Sounds Tab Sheet.

The Sounds tab sheet of the Sounds and Audio Devices Properties screen, is shown in Fig. 10.5. You can use this screen to select a **Sound scheme** (from a drop-down list), or change the sound of a selected program event by highlighting it and using the **Browse** button to select a different sound to apply to the event from a displayed list shown in Fig. 10.6 on the next page.

Currently applied sounds to a selected event can be heard by clicking the right-arrow button to the right of the **Sounds** box, pointed to at the bottom of the screen in Fig. 10.5. To hear a proposed sound replacement, click the right-arrow button to the right of **Preview** at the bottom of the screen (pointed to) in 10.6. Finally, you can save the changes you have made to sounds representing different events as a new sound scheme so that you can recall it at will.

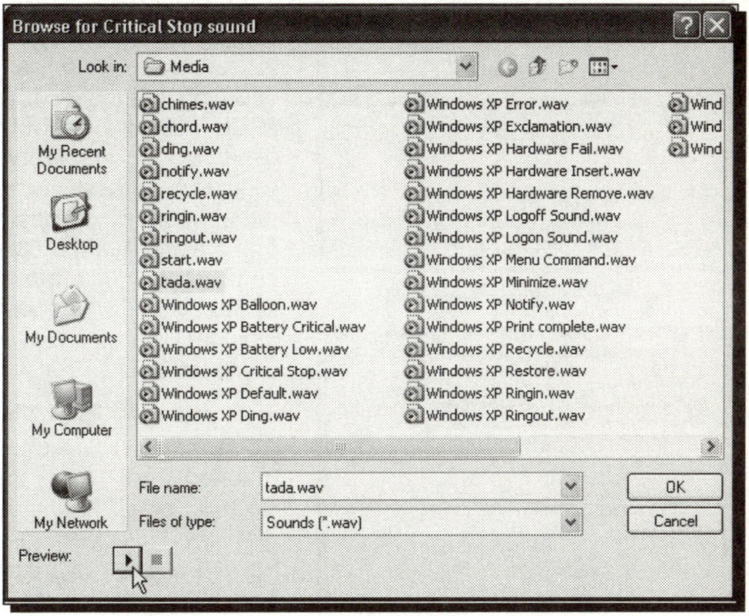

Fig. 10.6 The Browse for a Selected Sound Event.

As you can see from the screen above, you can also **Look in** other places on your hard disc for other sounds to represent the sound event selected in Fig. 10.5.

Audio Devices

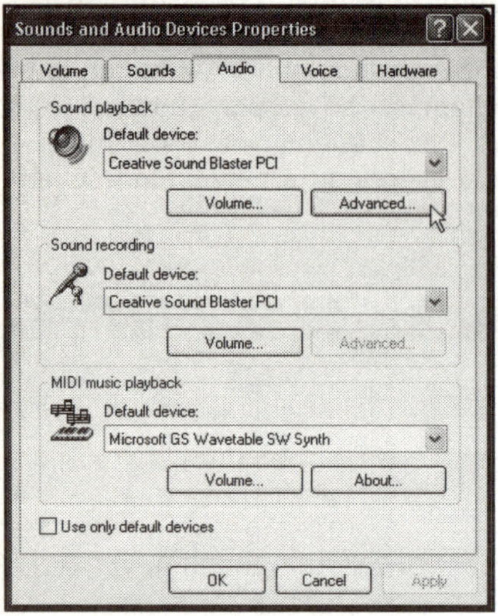

Fig. 10.7 The Audio Tab Sheet.

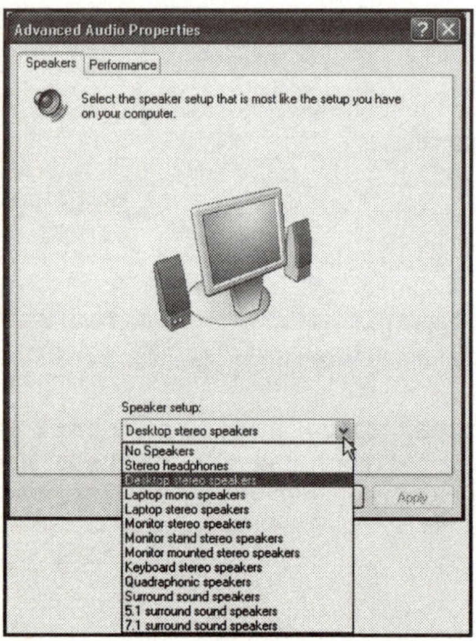

Fig. 10.8 The Advanced Audio Properties Screen.

The Audio tab sheet of the Sounds and Audio Devices Properties screen, is shown in Fig. 10.7. You can use this screen to select the audio playback and recording hardware available on your computer, or specify the instrument normally used by games to play MIDI output. MIDI (Musical Instrument Digital Interface) is a serial interface standard that also allows the connection of music synthesizers and musical instruments to computers.

If you now click the **Advanced** button (pointed to) in the **Sound playback** area of the screen in Fig. 10.7, the Advanced Audio Properties screen is displayed as shown in Fig. 10.8. From here you can configure the available output devices on your system, such as internal or external stereo speakers, stereo headphones, or even route output directly to a mixing console by selecting 'No speakers'.

The Voice Playback or Recording Device

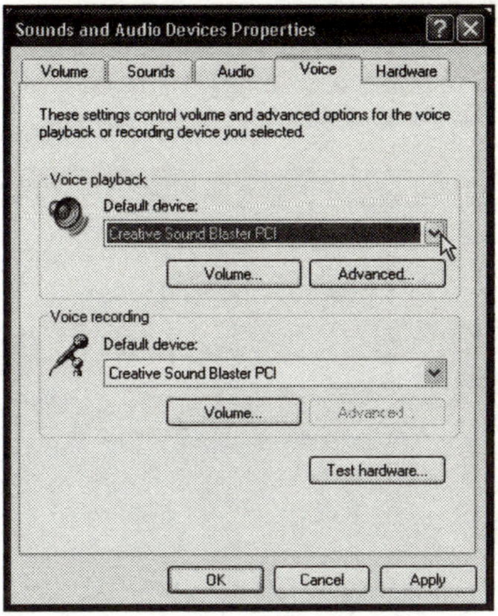

Fig. 10.9 The Voice Tab Sheet.

The Voice tab sheet of the Sounds and Audio Devices Properties screen, is shown in Fig. 10.9. From here you can control the volume and advanced options for the voice playback and recording device you select.

If more than one voice playback or recording device is installed on your system, click the down-arrow to the right of the **Default device** to select one from the drop-down list.

The Hardware Devices

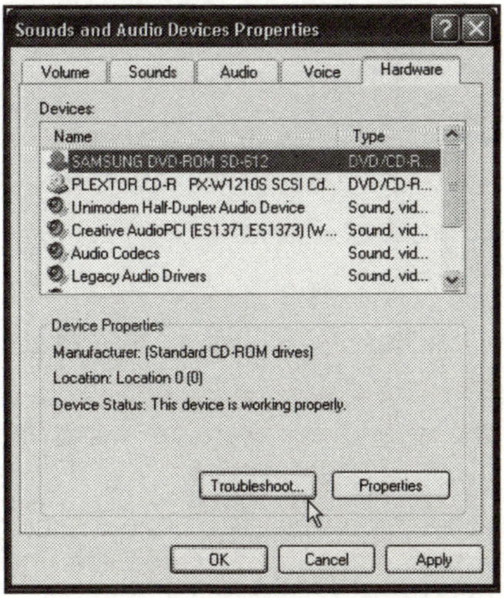

Fig. 10.10 The Hardware Tab Sheet.

The Hardware tab sheet of the Sounds and Audio Devices Properties screen, is shown in Fig. 10.10. To test a device, first select it, then click the **Troubleshoot** button.

If you are playing DVDs you might need to select the playback region. To do this, select the DVD-ROM and click the **Properties** button, then click the DVD Region tab on the displayed screen.

Speech Recognition Settings

To change the sounds and audio devices settings on your computer, click the **Speech** link pointed to in Fig. 10.11 below.

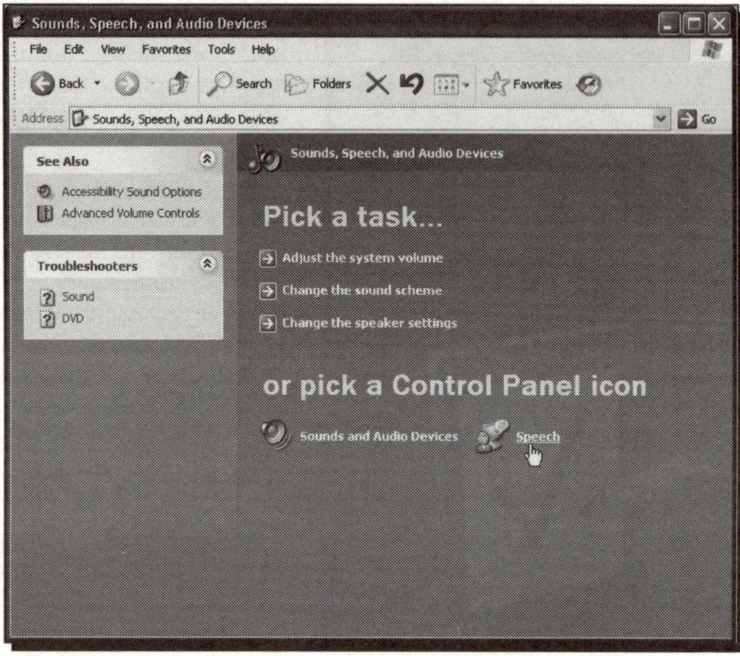

Fig. 10.11 The Sounds, Speech, and Audio Devices Screen.

This displays a multi-tab dialogue box, shown in Fig. 10.12 on the next page, from which you can:

- Create a new user profile by activating the Profile Wizard.
- Calibrate the microphone and speakers by using the Microphone Wizard.
- Create a training profile by using the User Training Wizard and teaching your computer to recognise your speaking style and the sounds of your environment.

Speech Properties

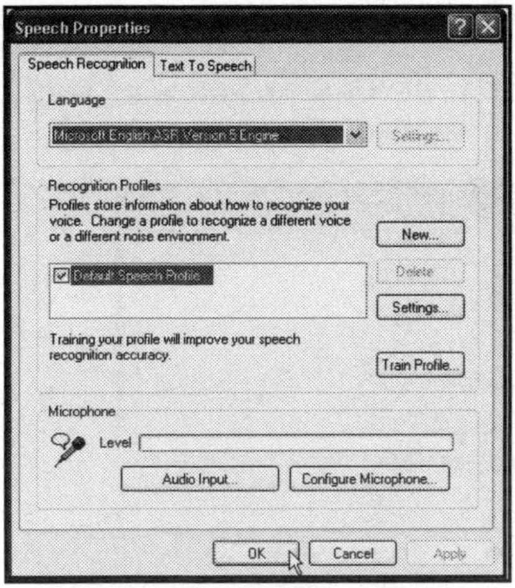

Fig. 10.12 The Speech Recognition Tab Sheet.

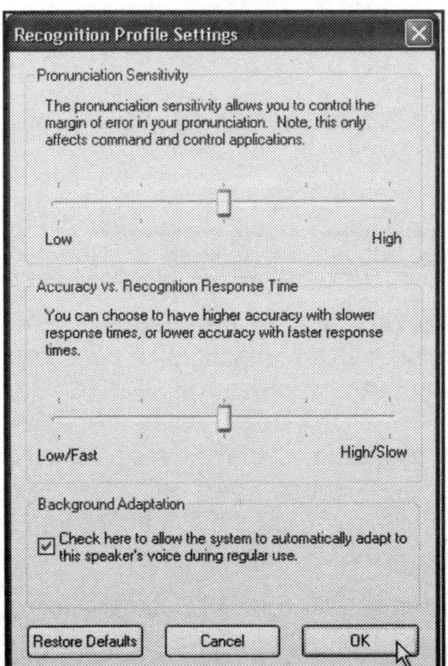

Fig. 10.13 Recognition Profile Settings.

You can change the computer's speech properties by using the Speech Recognition tab screen of the **Speech Properties** dialogue box, shown in Fig. 10.12.

The **Settings** button on the **Recognition Profiles** area of the Speech Properties screen, may provide additional settings or information about the active engine, as shown in Fig. 10.13. However, this screen is specific to the selected language engine type and it is possible that your chosen language engine might not have any additional properties. If that is the case, then the **Settings** button will not be active.

As you can see, you can use the Recognition Profile Settings screen to adjust the pronunciation sensitivity, change the ratio between accuracy and recognition responce time, and allow the system to automatically adapt to the speaker's voice during regular usage.

Text to Speech Translation

In the **Voice selection** box you can choose one of three available Text To Speech (TTS) voices. Once selected, the TTS engine will speak the text in the **Use the following text to preview the voice** box.

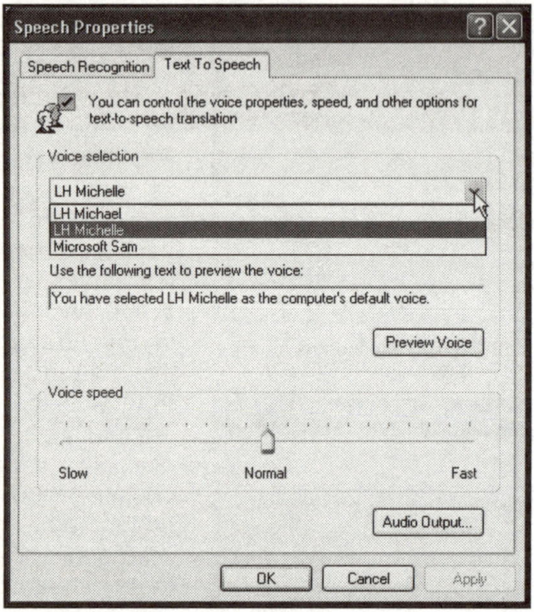

Fig. 10.14 The Speech Recognition Tab Sheet.

The text in the **Use the following text to preview the voice** box can be changed. To illustrate this, highlight a paragraph from a word processed document and press the <Ctrl+C> key combination to copy it onto the Windows clipboard. Next, highlight the entire text in the **Use the following text to preview the voice** box and press the <Ctrl+V> key combination to copy the selected text from the Clipboard into it. To hear the new text, click the **Preview Voice** button.

Do experiment by selecting a different TTS engine or by changing the speed of its speech production with the slider in the **Voice speed** area of the Speech Properties screen, until you are satisfied with the result.

11

Accessibility Options

In this chapter we will examine how you can adjust your PC's settings for vision, hearing and mobility. We begin by using the **Start**, **Control Panel** menu command which displays the screen in Fig. 11.1 below.

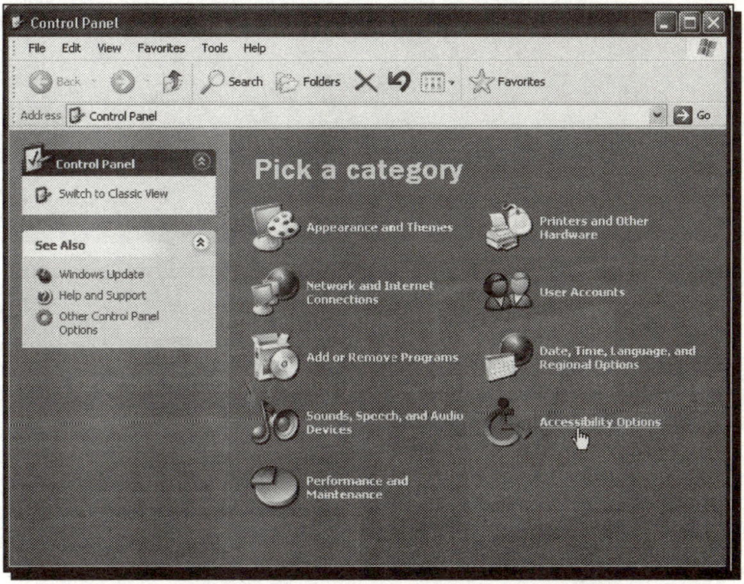

Fig. 11.1 The Control Panel Screen in Category View.

If the **Control Panel** screen displays in Classical View, click the **Switch to Category view** option to be found at the top-left panel of the screen.

Next, click the **Accessibility Options** entry under the **Pick a category** panel to display the screen shown in Fig. 11.2 on the next page.

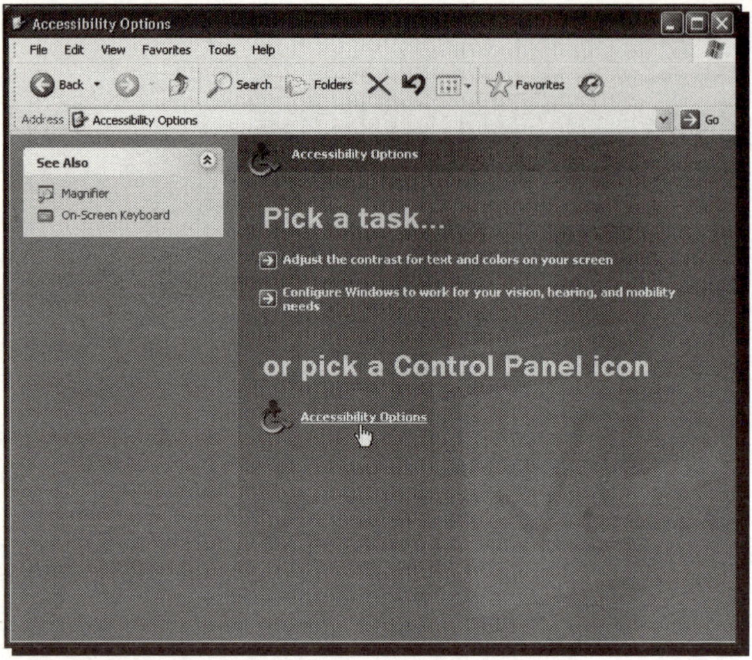

Fig. 11.2 The Accessibility Options Screen.

Windows XP gives you the opportunity to use two ways to make your PC more accessible to individuals who have difficulty typing or using a mouse, have slight impaired vision, or are hard-of-hearing. These are:

- Use of the Control Panel Accessibility Options which include adjusting the behaviour of the keyboard, sound volume, colours and sizes, and the behaviour of the mouse.
- Use the Accessibility Wizard which configures Windows for your vision, hearing, and mobility needs.

Both these approaches to customising Windows XP to your requirements will be examined in the following sections of this chapter.

The Control Panel Accessibility Options

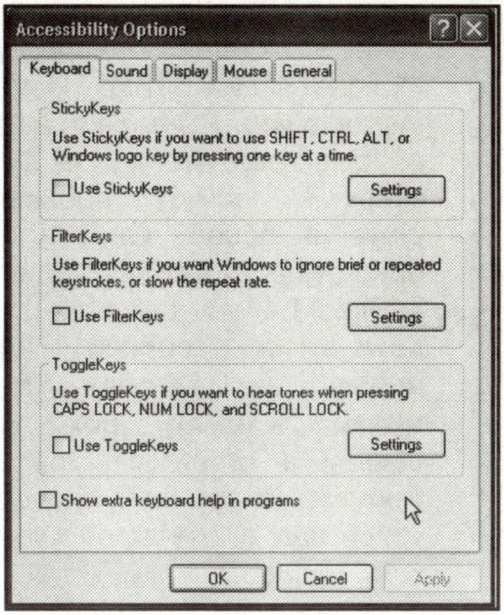

Fig. 11.3 The Accessibility Options Screen.

Clicking the **Adjust the contrast for text and colors on your screen** option under the **Pick a task** entry, or the **Accessibility** option under the **or pick a Control Panel icon** entry, opens the same multi-tab dialogue box, as shown in Fig. 11.3.

Clicking each tab in turn on this Accessibility Options dialogue box displays screens on which you can change the behaviour of the keyboard, sound, display, mouse and other general categories.

The Keyboard Options

Activating the **StickyKeys** option (Fig. 11.3), allows the user to press a modifier key such as <Ctrl>, <Alt>, <Shift>, or the <Windows Logo> and keep it active until another key, but different to the above keys, is pressed. This is useful to people who have difficulty pressing two keys simultaneously.

Activating the **FilterKeys** option, instructs the keyboard to ignore brief or repeated keystrokes. The keyboard repeat rate can also be adjusted.

Activating the **ToggleKeys** option, instructs your PC to play a high-pitched sound when the <Caps Lock> <Scroll Lock>, or <Num Lock> keys are on and low-pitched sound when they are off.

The **Settings** buttons against each of the above options allow for fine tuning of these preferences.

The Sounds Options

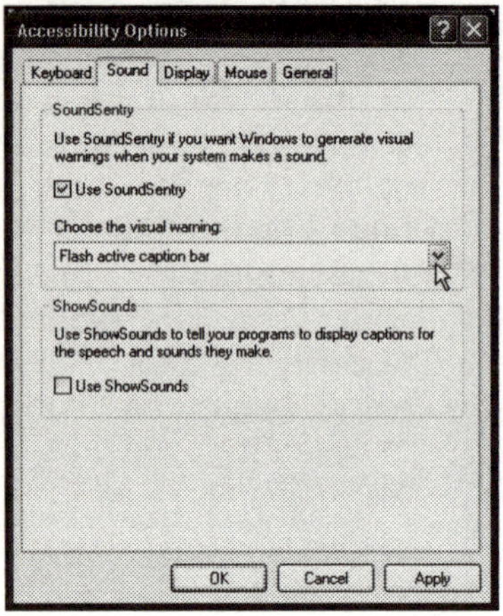

Fig. 11.4 The Sound Accessibility Options Tab Sheet.

Activating the **SoundSentry** option on the Sound tabbed sheet of the Accessibility Options screen, (Fig. 11.4), instructs your PC to flash part of its screen every time the system's built-in speaker plays a sound. Once this option is activated, as shown in Fig. 11.4, you can click the down-arrow (pointed to) against the **Choose the visual warning** box to display a drop-down menu from which you can choose which part of the screen you want to flash.

Activating the **ShowSounds** option, instructs programs that use sound only to provide information on what they are doing at the time, to also provide visual information.

The Display Options

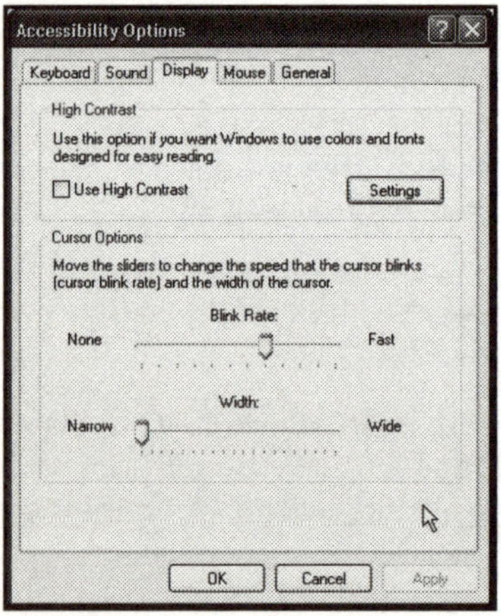

Fig. 11.5 The Display Accessibility Options Tab Sheet.

Activating the **High Contrast** option on the Display tabbed sheet of the Accessibility Options screen, shown in Fig. 11.5, instructs programs to change their colour-specific schemes to the one specified in the **Settings** sheet. Fonts are also changed whenever possible to improve legibility.

You can also change the rate at which the insertion point blinks and its width by dragging the two sliders appropriately.

The Mouse Options

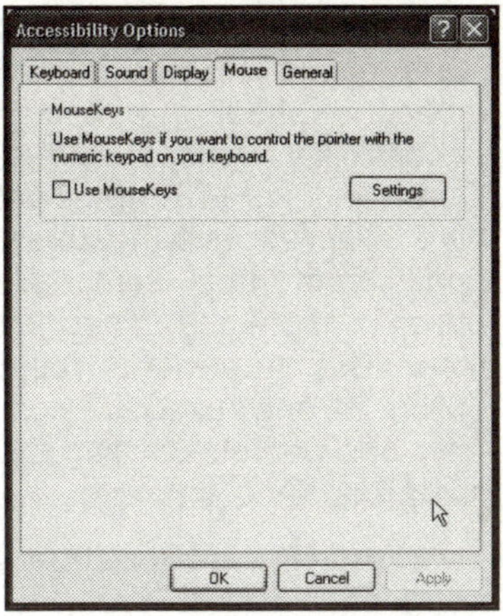

Fig. 11.6 The Mouse Accessibility Options Tab Sheet.

Activating the **MouseKeys** option on the Mouse tabbed sheet of the Accessibility Options screen, shown in Fig. 11.6, allows the keys on the numeric keypad to be used to move the mouse pointer. The shortcut key combination you need to use to activate and deactivate the numeric keypad MouseKeys is displayed in the **Settings** sheet, where you can also change the pointer speed, and specify whether to use the MouseKeys when the Num Lock key is on or off.

Once the MouseKeys option is activated, you can also use the numeric keypad to simulate mouse operations such as click, double-click, or drag. To carry out these operations, do the following:

- To click, press 5 on the numeric keypad.
- To double-click, press the plus sign (+) on the numeric keypad.
- To right-click, press the minus sign (-) on the numeric keypad, and then press 5 to click, or press the plus sign (+) to double-click.
- To click as if you were using both mouse buttons at once, press the asterisk (*) on the numeric keypad, and then press 5 to click or the plus sign (+) to double-click.
- To switch back to standard clicking, press slash (/) on the numeric keypad.

The General Options

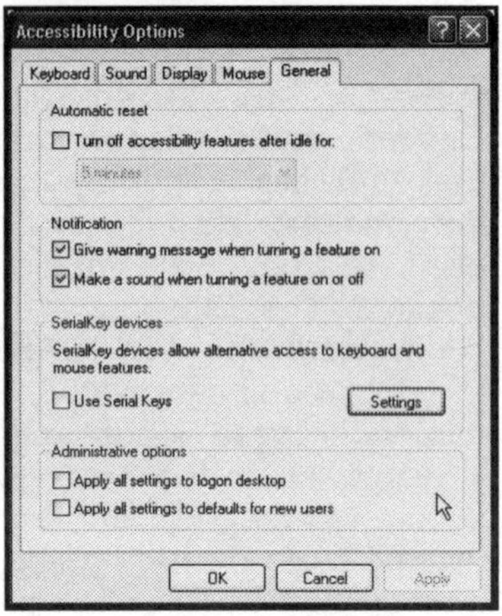

Fig. 11.7 The General Accessibility Options Tab Sheet.

Activating the **Automatic reset** option on the General tabbed sheet of the Accessibility Options screen, shown in Fig. 11.7, turns off all the accessibility features, apart from the SerialKeys option, after the specified time. The **Automatic reset** option is only used if more than one person is using the same User Account.

Activating the **SerialKeys services** allows you to connect an alternative input device to the computer's serial port. Use the **Settings** button to display Settings for SerialKeys screen, shown in Fig. 11.8, to specify which serial port to use. This feature is useful for people who are unable to use the computer's standard keyboard or mouse.

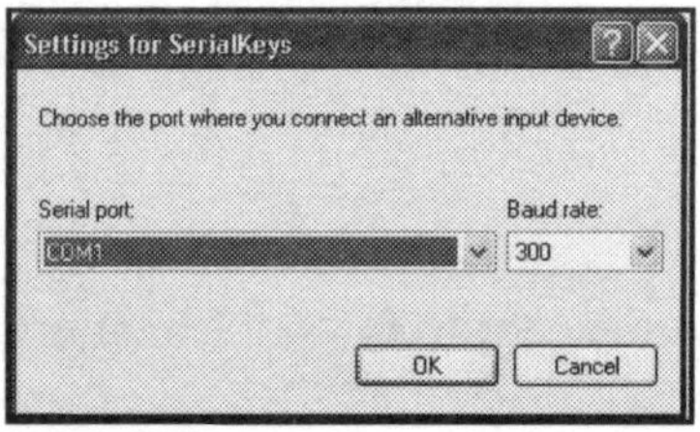

Fig. 11.8 The Settings for SerialKeys Sheet.

To activate the **Administrative options** you must be the computer's or the group's administrator. The first option applies the Accessibility Options currently selected to the Log on desktop. This allows all users (particularly those with disabilities) to use these features to help them log onto the computer. The second option under **Administrative options** applies the Accessibility Options currently selected to all new User Accounts.

The Accessibility Wizard

To start the Accessibility Wizard, use the **start**, **Control Panel** command, then click the **Accessibility Options**. On the displayed screen, shown in Fig. 11.9 below, click the **Configure Windows to work for your vision, hearing, and mobility needs** link (pointed to) under the **Pick a task** entry.

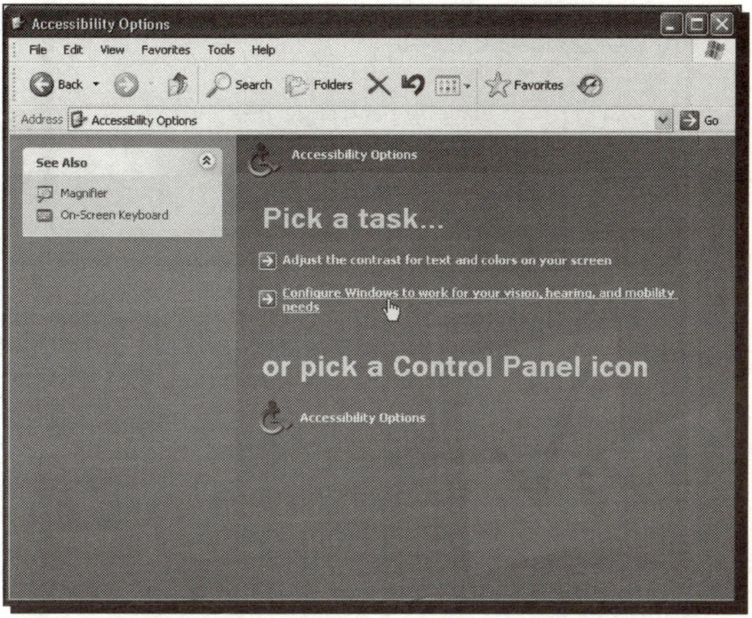

Fig. 11.9 Picking a Task on the Accessibility Options Screen.

This starts the Accessibility Wizard displaying its first 'Welcome' screen. As usual, clicking the **Next** button at the bottom of each Wizard screen moves you to the next Wizard screen. What follows is largely self-explanatory.

On the second Wizard screen, shown in Fig. 11.10 on the next page, you are asked to select the smallest size of text you can read easily. You have three options to choose from; usual Windows text size, large window titles and menus, or Microsoft Magnifier with large window titles and menus.

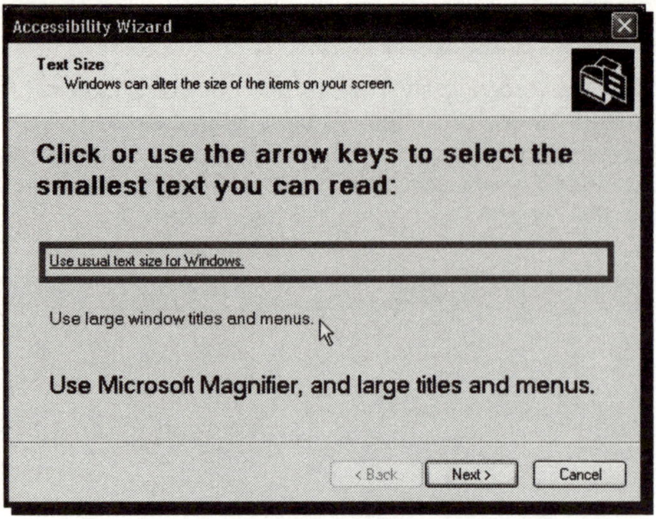

Fig. 11.10 The Second Accessibility Wizard Screen.

We will come back to the Microsoft Magnifier later on in this chapter. In the meantime, select one of the first two options and click **Next** to display the third Wizard screen (Fig. 11.11).

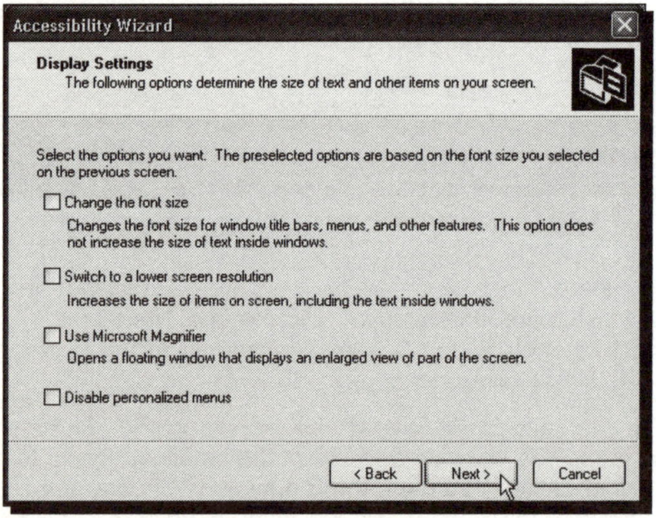

Fig. 11.11 The Third Accessibility Wizard Screen.

What option (if any) is preselected on the third Wizard screen depends on the choices you have made on the second Wizard screen. Clicking **Next** displays the fourth Wizard screen, shown in Fig. 11.12 below.

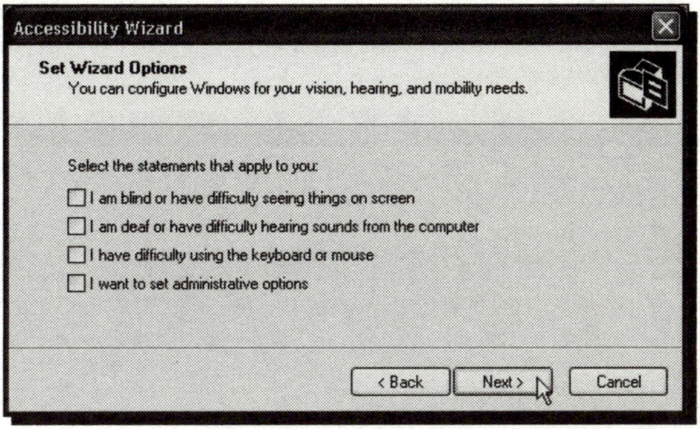

Fig. 11.12 The Fourth Accessibility Wizard Screen.

Obviously, the fifth and subsequent Wizard screens will depend on the choices you have made on the fourth screen above. For example, selecting **I want to set administrative options** and clicking **Next**, displays the screen in Fig. 11.13, followed by another screen before displaying the final Wizard screen.

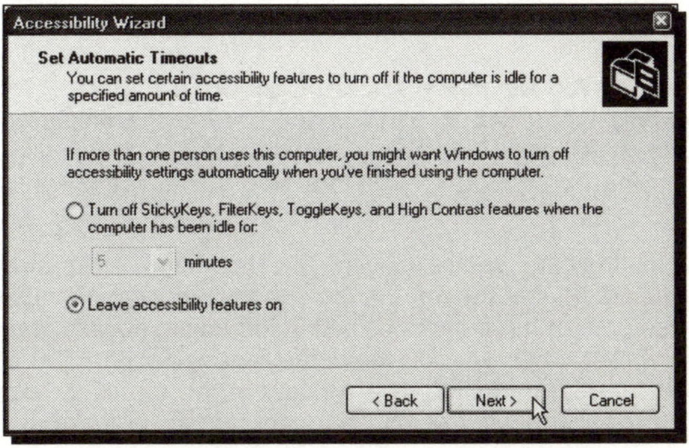

Fig. 11.13 The Fourth Accessibility Wizard Screen.

The Microsoft Magnifier

As we have seen in the previous section, the Microsoft Magnifier could have been started from within the Accessibility Wizard. Another way of starting it is by clicking the **Magnifier** link (pointed to) under the **See Also** entry in Fig. 11.14 below.

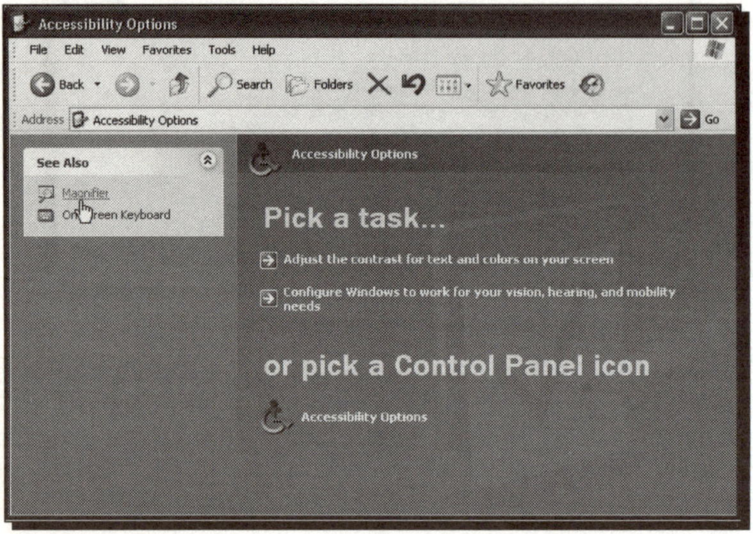

Fig. 11.14 The Magnifier link on the Accessibility Options Screen.

The displayed Magnifier screen is shown in Fig. 11.15 on the next page. The first thing to notice here is the display of the Microsoft Magnifier message, which can be prevented from displaying by clicking the **Do not show this message again** box.

Nevertheless, before closing this message, note that it is magnified at the top of the screen as shown, because the mouse pointer happens to be within the actual (lower) message box. In fact, wherever you move the mouse pointer, that part of the screen is magnified in a window at the top of the screen. This magnifying window can be made bigger in the usual way of manipulating all other application windows.

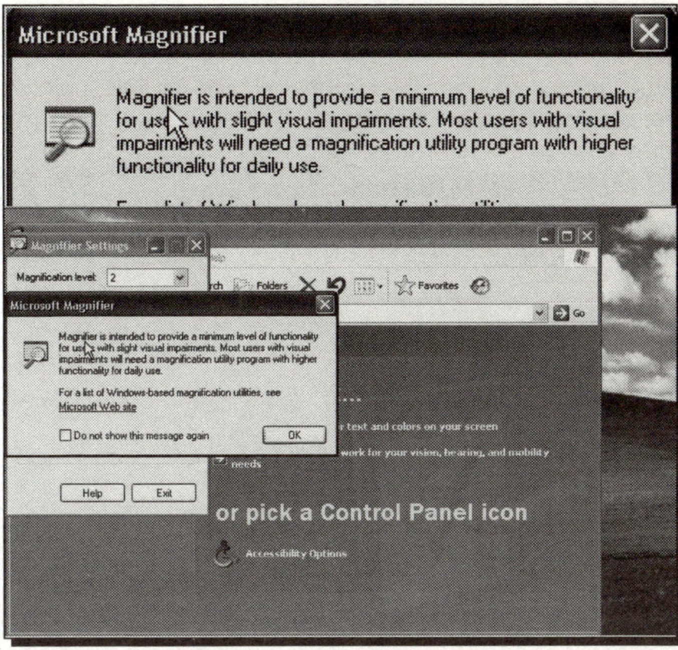

Fig. 11.15 The Magnifier Screen.

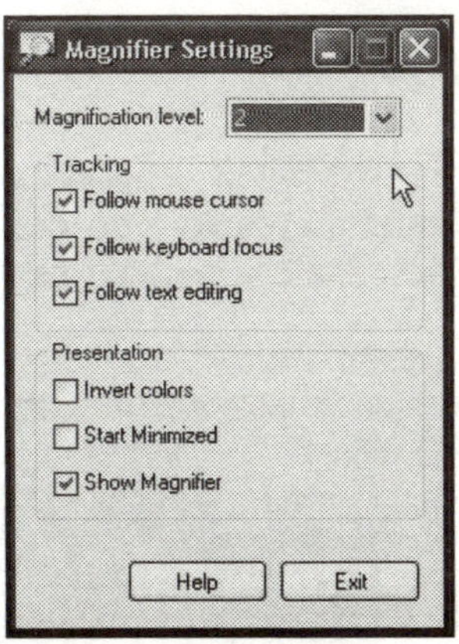

Fig. 11.16 The General Magnifier Settings Box.

After closing the Microsoft Magnifier message box, the Magnifier Settings dialogue box becomes fully visible, as shown in Fig. 11.16. From here you can set the **Magnification level** from 1 (low) to 9 (high), and select **Tracking** and **Presentation** options. Clicking the **Exit** button removes the Magnifier facility from your screen.

Selecting **Start Minimized** under **Presentation**, minimises the Magnifier Settings box on the Task bar next time you start the Magnifier. To now exit the Magnifier, click the Magnifier Settings entry on the Task bar and remove the minimise option.

The On-Screen Keyboard

To activate the On-Screen Keyboard, click its link (pointed to) under the **See Also** entry in Fig. 11.17 below.

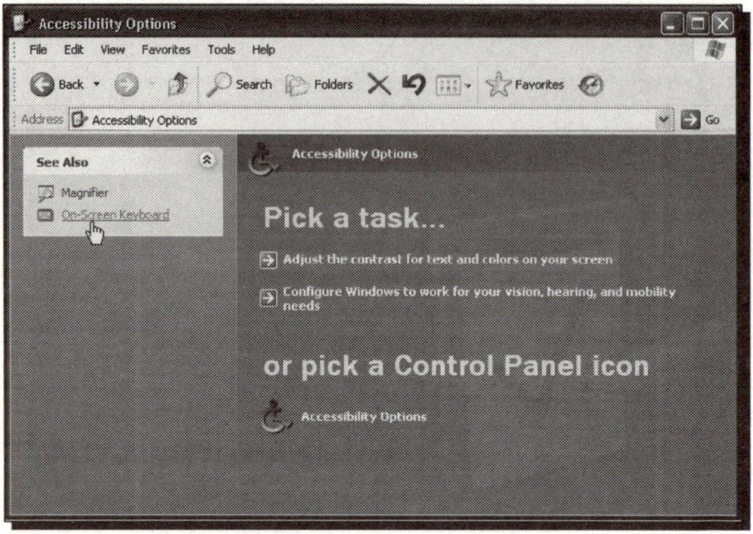

Fig. 11.17 The On-Screen Keyboard link on the Accessibility Options Screen.

This displays the screen shown in Fig. 11.18 below. The virtual keyboard allows users with mobility impairments to type data using a pointing device or joystick. The result is exactly as if you were using the actual keyboard.

Fig. 11.18 The On-Screen Virtual Keyboard.

The On-Screen Keyboard has three typing modes you can use to type data. These are:

- Clicking mode - you click the on-screen keys to type text.
- Hovering mode - you use a mouse or joystick to point to a key for a predefined period of time, and the selected character is typed automatically.
- Scanning mode - the On-Screen Keyboard continually scans the keyboard and highlights areas where you can type keyboard characters by pressing a hot key or using a switch-input device.

The three typing modes are selected by choosing the **Settings Typing Mode** menu command, as shown in Fig. 11.19 below.

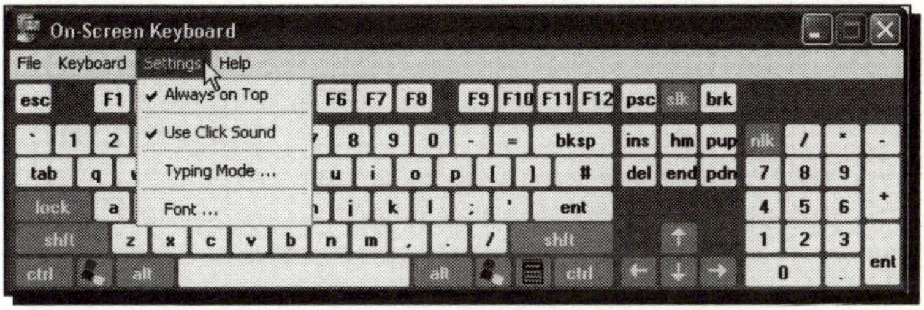

Fig. 11.19 The Settings Menu of the On-Screen Keyboard.

This opens the Typing Mode dialogue box shown in Fig. 11.20 in which you click the option you prefer and, if appropriate, the time interval before the command is actioned.

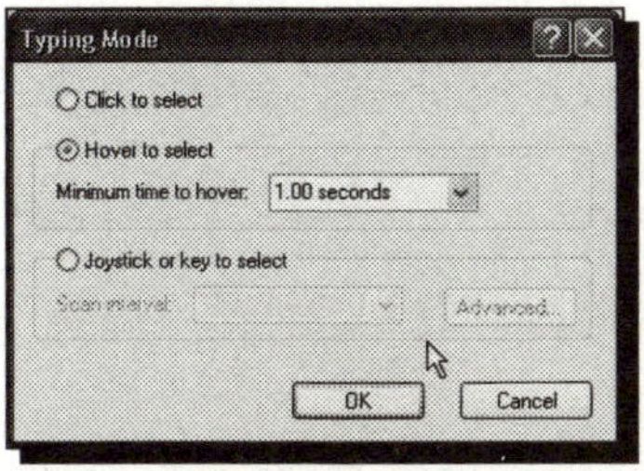

Fig. 11.20 The Typing Mode of the On-Screen Keyboard.

Also, note that you can select from the **Settings** menu to have the virtual keyboard appear **Always on Top** of all other windows displayed on your screen, and select to **Use Click Sound** which is particularly useful if you are using the **Hover to select** option of Typing Mode.

There are several types of On-Screen Keyboards which are chosen from the **Keyboard** menu shown in Fig. 11.21 below.

Fig. 11.21 The Settings Menu of the On-Screen Keyboard.

These are:

- The **Enhanced Keyboard** that includes the numeric keypad.
- The **Standard Keyboard** that does not include the numeric keypad.

You can also display the keyboard with the keys in the **Regular Layout**, or in a **Block Layout** in which the keys are arranged in rectangular blocks. Block layout is especially useful in scanning mode.

You can also select to display the US standard keyboard (**101 keys**), the universal keyboard (**102 keys**), or a keyboard (**106 keys**) with additional Japanese language characters.

As you can see, the Accessibility Options are many and varied, and some of these can also be used by people who have no disability whatsoever. The choice is yours!

12

Performance and Maintenance

In this chapter we will examine how you can enhance the performance of your PC and apply regular maintenance checks. We begin by using the **Start**, **Control Panel** menu command which displays the screen in Fig. 12.1 below.

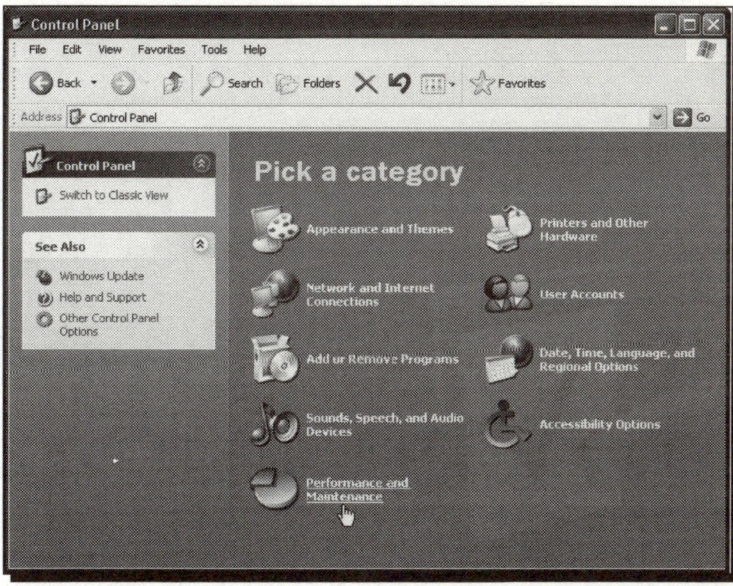

Fig. 12.1 The Control Panel Screen in Category View.

If the **Control Panel** screen displays in Classical View, click the **Switch to Category view** option to be found at the top-left panel of the screen.

Next, click the **Performance and Maintenance** entry under the **Pick a category** panel to display the screen shown in Fig. 12.2 on the next page.

The Administrative Tools

Clicking the **Administrative Tools** link pointed to in Fig. 12.2, opens the Administrative Tools System folder, shown in Fig. 12.3, which provides shortcuts to certain Management tools and services.

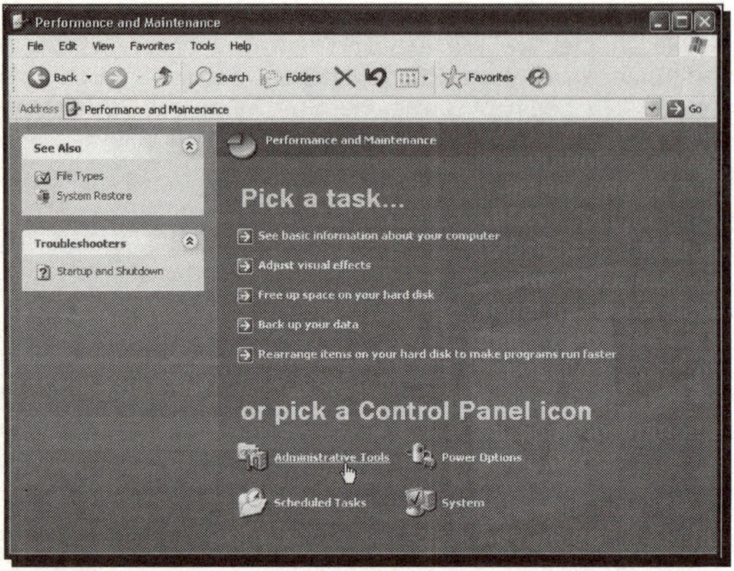

Fig. 12.2 The Performance and Maintenance Screen.

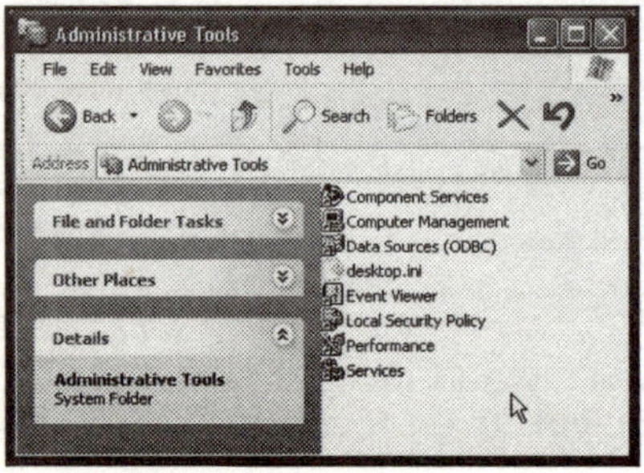

Fig. 12.3 The Administrative Tools Folder.

For example, the Component Services shortcut provides access to the Microsoft Management Services which hosts administrative tools that you can use to administer networks, computers, services, and other system components; while the Computer Management short-cut provides access to a collection of administrative tools that you can use to manage a single local or remote computer.

Clicking the System Monitor shortcut displays a colourful screen which shows the detailed monitoring of the operating system resources, as shown in Fig. 12.4.

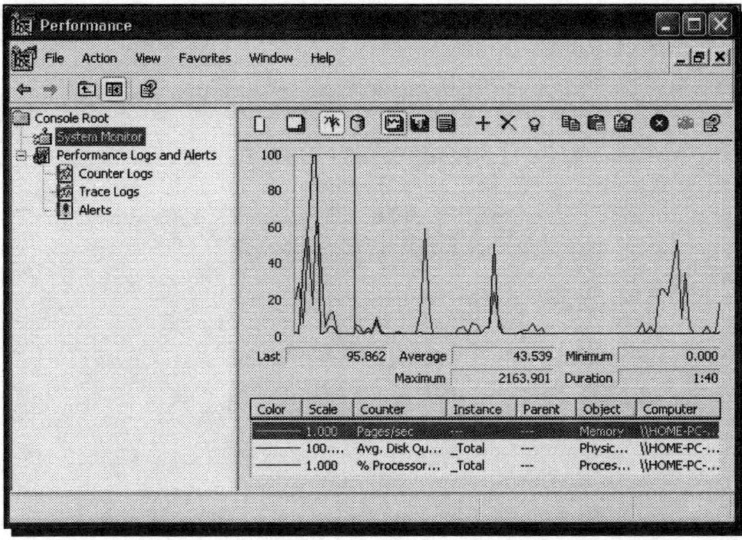

Fig. 12.4 The System Performance Monitoring Screen.

You can get detailed help with each service provided by the Microsoft Management Console by double-clicking each

shortcut in Fig. 12.3, then clicking the **Help** button, shown here, on its displayed Toolbar. The Help screen displays a series of books which can be opened to reveal more books and topics on which you can get help and explanation. We suggest you spend some time with the Help System if you are interested in these topics. We leave it to you.

The Power Options

Clicking the **Power Options** link pointed to in Fig. 12.5, displays the Power Options dialogue box shown in Fig. 12.6 on the next page.

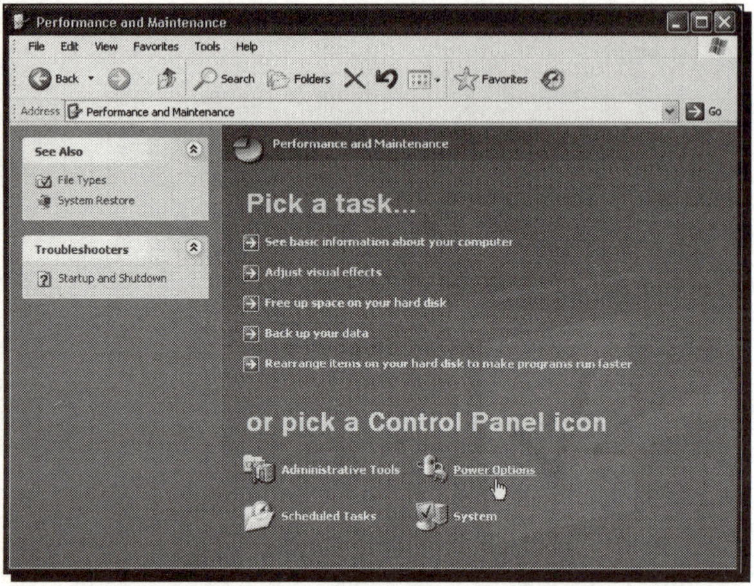

Fig. 12.5 The Performance and Maintenance Screen.

You can use the Power Options dialogue box to automatically put your computer into standby mode (reduces power consumption of your computer) or hibernation mode (turns off your computer after saving everything in memory to your PC's hard disc), provided you log on as an administrator, and your computer is set up by the manufacturer to support these options. If your computer is connected to a network, network policy settings may prevent you from completing these tasks.

Standby Mode

When your computer is put into standby mode, information in computer memory is not saved to your hard disc. You must save all your work before putting your computer into standby mode, because if there is an interruption in power, all information in the computer's memory will be lost.

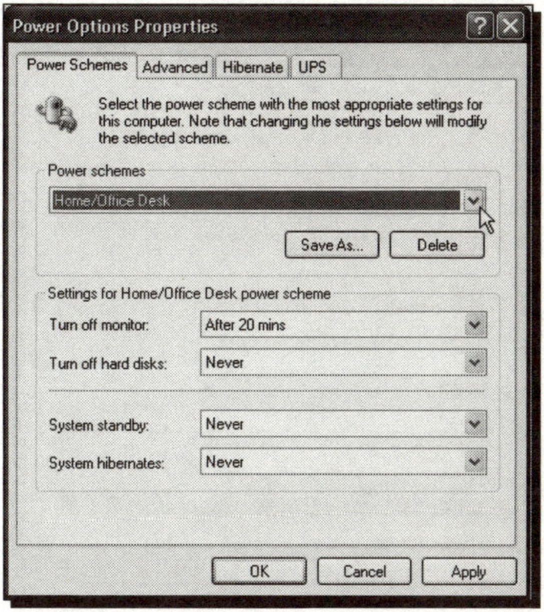

Fig. 12.6 The Power Scheme Tab Sheet of the Power Options Properties Screen.

To put your computer in Standby mode, click the down-arrow to the right of the **System standby** box and select the time lapse before Standby mode takes effect. You can also choose a time interval after which your monitor and/or your hard discs are turned off.

If you are using a portable computer, you can specify one setting for battery power and a different setting for AC power. In fact, you can adjust any power management option that your computer's hardware configuration supports.

Advanced Options

Clicking the Advanced tab in Fig. 12.6, displays the screen shown in Fig. 12.7 below. On this screen you can select what you want under **Options**, then click the down-arrow button against the **When I press the power button on my computer** box and choose what you want to happen from the drop-down options list also shown in Fig. 12.7.

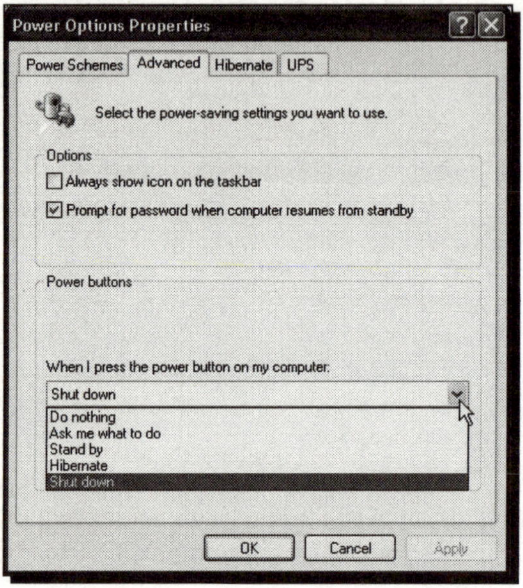

Fig. 12.7 The Advanced Tab Sheet of the Power Options Properties Screen.

As you can see, you can select any one of five options, but if you select the last option, you must also specify what to do by going back to the Power Schemes tab sheet and choosing a short time interval for the required action, be it Standby or Hibernation.

Hibernation Mode

When your computer is put into hibernation mode, everything in the computer memory is saved to your hard disc, and your computer is switched off. When you turn the computer back on, all the programs and documents that were open when you turned the computer off are restored on the desktop.

To initiate hibernation, click the Hibernate tab of the Power Options Properties dialogue box. If the Hibernate tab is unavailable, then this is because your computer does not support this feature. If it does, make sure the **Enable hibernation** box is checked, as shown in Fig. 12.8.

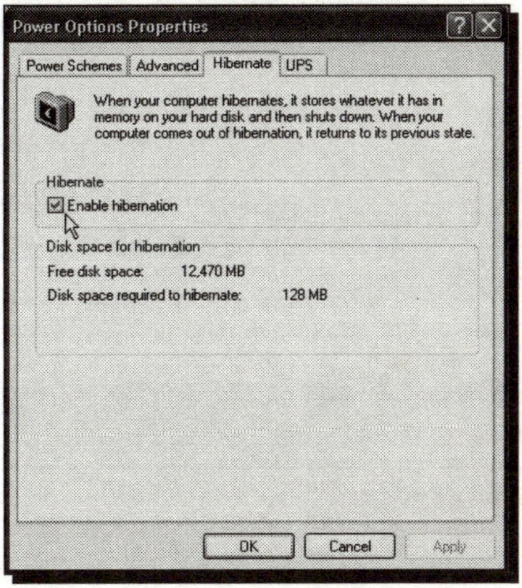

Fig. 12.8 The Hibernate Sheet of the Power Options Properties Screen.

You could test the system by selecting a short time in **System hibernates** (Fig. 12.6), say 'after 1 min', then sit back and see what happens.

If you decide that you do not want your system to hibernate, uncheck the **Enable hibernation** box in the Hibernate sheet of the Power Options Properties screen (Fig. 12.8), then click the Power Schemes tab, and select 'never' for the time the **System hibernates** in Fig. 12.6.

Scheduled Tasks

Clicking the **Scheduled Tasks** link pointed to in Fig. 12.9, displays the Scheduled Tasks dialogue box shown in Fig. 12.10 below.

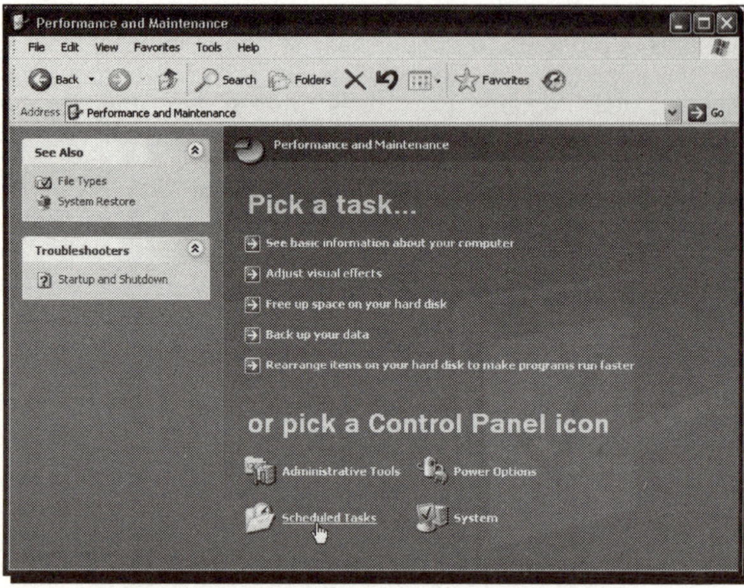

Fig. 12.9 The Performance and Maintenance Screen.

The Scheduled Tasks window allows you to carry out several Windows XP house-keeping tasks, such as disc cleanup, or defrag-menting your data, at times convenient to you.

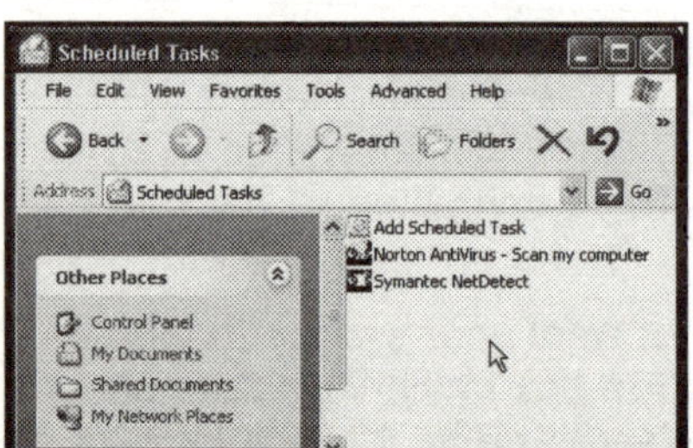

Fig. 12.10 The Scheduled Tasks Window.

If you are running other programs, such as Norton AntiVirus in our case, an entry for that program also appears in the Scheduled window (Fig. 12.10)

To add a scheduled Windows XP task, double-click the **Add Scheduled Task** icon to start the Wizard. Clicking **Next** on the first Wizard screen displays the second Wizard screen, shown in Fig. 12.11 below:

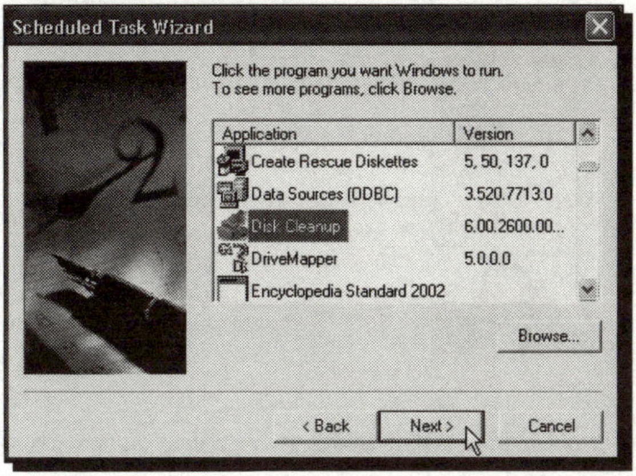

Fig. 12.11 The Second Scheduled Task Wizard Screen.

On this screen (Fig. 12.11), select the task to be scheduled then click the **Next** button to display:

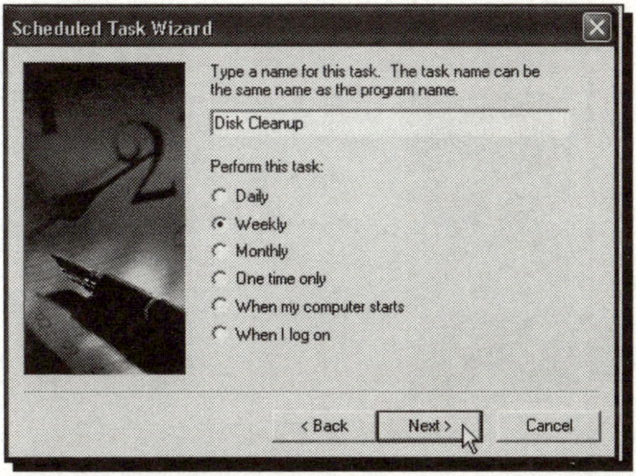

Fig. 12.12 The Third Scheduled Task Wizard Screen.

On this screen (Fig. 12.12) you are asked to specify the frequency at which you would like the selected task to be performed (we selected weekly in our example). Having done so, press the **Next** button to display the fourth Wizard screen.

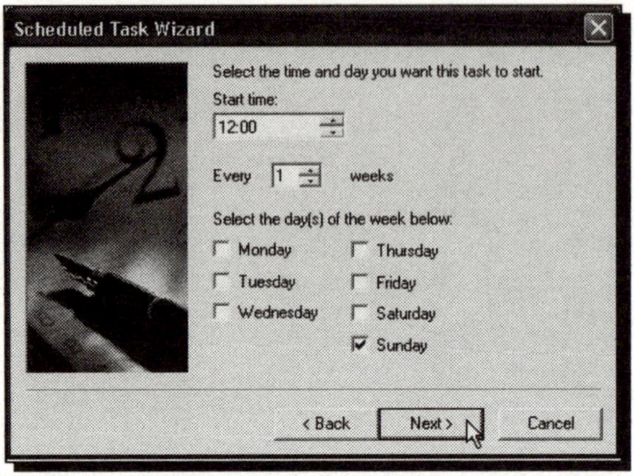

Fig. 12.13 The Fourth Scheduled Task Wizard Screen.

On this screen you are asked to specify when you want the selected task to be carried out. Obviously, your computer must be switched on in order to perform such scheduled tasks, so it's up to you to choose a convenient time. Having done so, press the **Next** button to display the fifth Wizard screen.

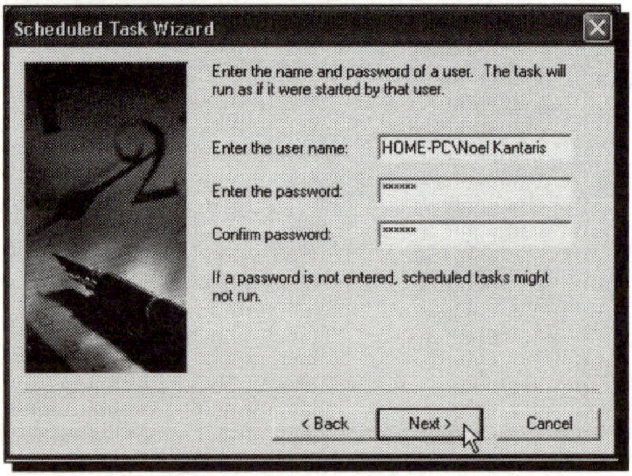

Fig. 12.14 The Fifth Scheduled Task Wizard Screen.

As you can see from this Wizard screen (Fig. 12.14), you can enter the name of a user and a password. The task is then run as if it were started by the specified user. Clicking **Next**, displays the final Wizard screen and clicking the **Finish** button, performs the selected task at its chosen time.

It is a good idea to perform such tasks regularly, but make sure that

- your computer is switched on at the selected times, and
- you are not inconvenienced by your time selection.

It is, of course assumed that your PC's clock is showing the same time as your watch, otherwise you might get some unexpected surprises!

The newly created scheduled task now appears in the Scheduled Tasks window, as shown in Fig. 12.15 below.

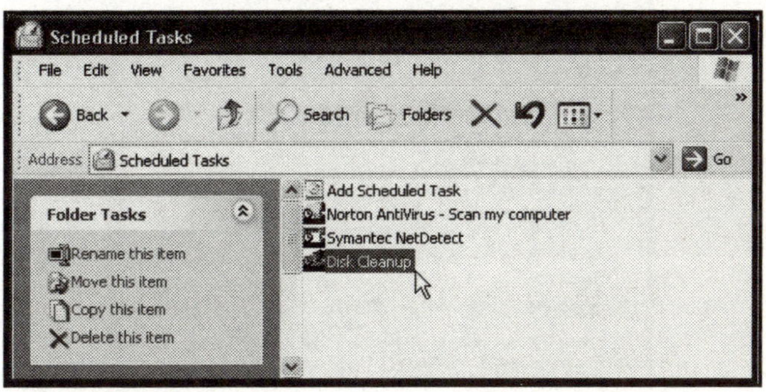

Fig. 12.15 The Additional Entry in the Schedule Tasks Window.

To edit a scheduled task, double-click its entry in the above window, which opens a three-tab dialogue box in which you can make changes to the selected 'Task', its 'Schedule', and its 'Settings'.

Disc Cleanup

The first thing that the **Disk Cleanup** utility does after activation, whether from the **Scheduled Tasks** or by clicking the **Free up space on your hard disk** link under the **Pick a task** entry in Fig. 12.9 (page 198), is to ask you to select the drive you want to clean up, as shown in Fig. 12.16. It then scans the specified drive, and then lists temporary files, Internet cache files, and unnecessary program files that you can safely delete, as shown in Fig. 12.17 below.

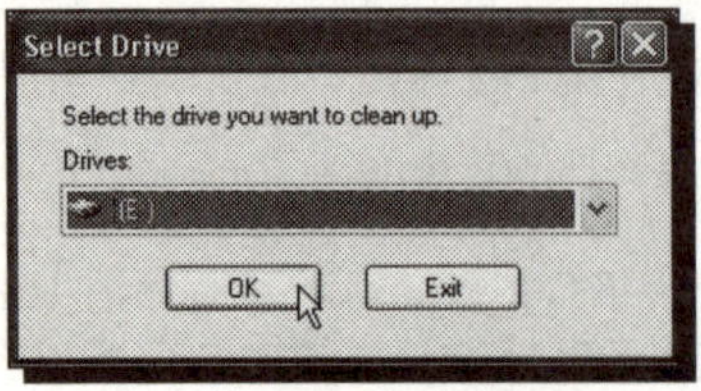

Fig. 12.16 Selecting a Drive.

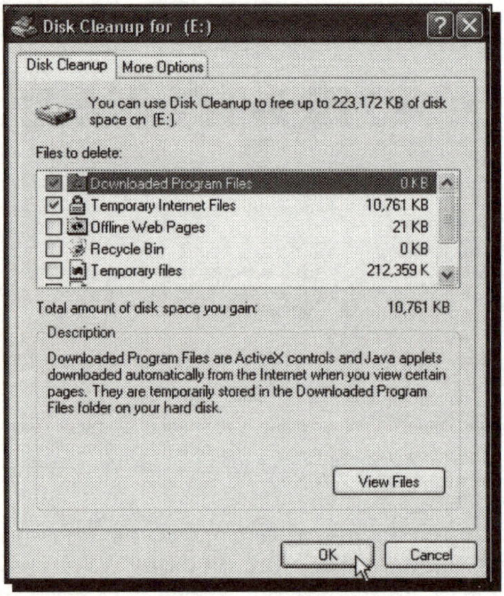

Fig. 12.17 Files Found by Cleanup.

As you can see, in our case, we could free 10,761 KB of disc space by simply deleting the Temporary Internet Files (Web pages stored on your hard disc for quick viewing). The More Options tab allows you to remove Windows components and installed programs that you do not use any more.

Defragmenting your Hard Discs

The **Disk Defragmenter** can also be scheduled to optimise a hard disc by rearranging the data on it to eliminate unused spaces, which speeds up access to the disc by Windows operations. You can also activate this utility by clicking the **Rearrange items on your hard disk to make programs run faster** link under the **Pick a task** entry in Fig. 12.9 (page 198).

You don't need to exit a running application before starting the **Disk Defragmenter**. Once activated, choose which drive to defragment and you can do so in the background while working by minimising the utility onto the Task bar. On the other hand, you can watch the process of the operation.

For example, having selected a drive and clicking the **Analyze** button, you will be told whether defragmentation is needed or not. On the other hand, clicking the **Defragment** button, starts the process which is shown in Fig. 12.18 below.

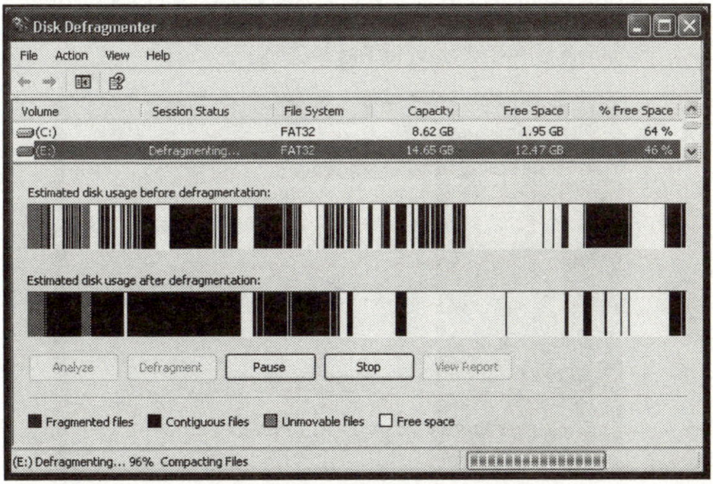

Fig. 12.18 Defragmentation in Progress.

On your screen you can see which files are fragmented (shown in red) and which files are not fragmented (shown in blue), while free space is shown in white. For large drives this process can take a long time, so make time for it!

The Backup Utility

The **Backup Program** (not available with Windows Home Edition) is another utility that can also be scheduled to back up both system set-up and data files from the hard disc to another, removable storage medium, on a regular basis. You can also activate the backup utility by clicking the **Back up your data** link under the **Pick a task** entry in Fig. 12.9 (page 198).

Hard discs can 'crash' (but not as often now as they used to) and your computer could be stolen, or lost in a fire or flood. Any of these events would cause a serious data loss, particularly to businesses, unless you had backed it all up, and stored it somewhere safely, preferably away from the vicinity of your PC.

Making a Back-up

We will step through the procedure of backing up, and then restoring, a selection of files. You should then be happy to carry on by yourself. Clicking the **Back up your data** link under the **Pick a task** entry in Fig. 12.9 (page 198), starts the Backup or Restore Wizard, as shown in Fig. 12.19.

Fig. 12.19 The Windows XP Professional Backup Welcome Screen.

Note the **Advance Mode** link pointed to above. Activating this link allows you to schedule backups. We will look at this later.

The back-up procedure can be carried out on a tape, a floppy disc, or a removable disc. In our example, we first chose in the second Wizard screen to 'back up files and settings', then in the third Wizard screen we selected the 'Let me choose what to back up' option. In the fourth Wizard screen, shown in Fig. 12.20 below, we selected the My Documents folder by clicking the + sign to open its structure in the left-hand pane, then double-clicking the My Pictures folder to check it.

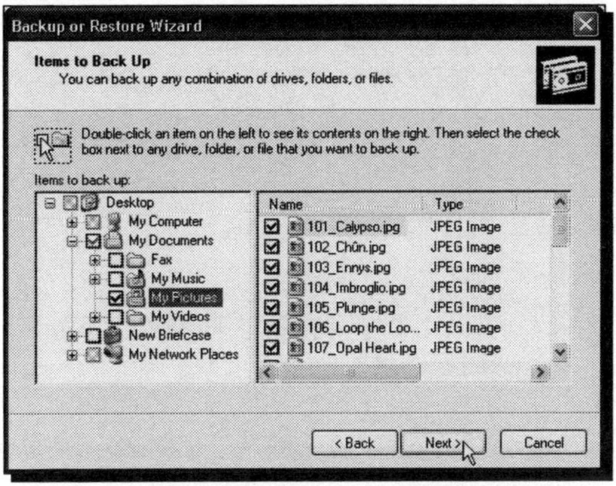

Fig. 12.20 Selecting items to Back Up.

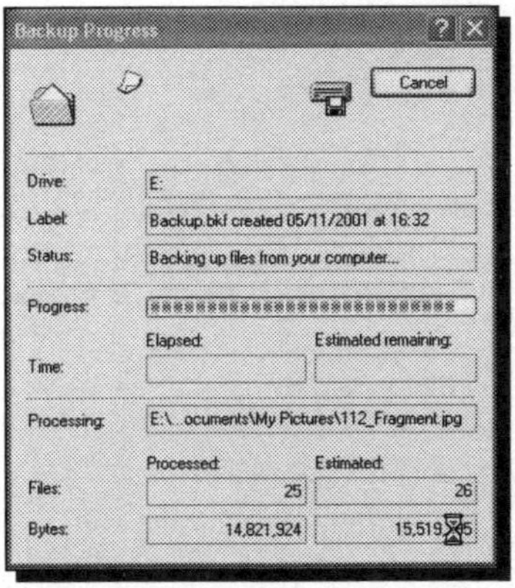

Fig. 12.21 Backing Up Process.

To select, or deselect, individual files, tick in their boxes in the right-hand pane, as shown above, and press the **Next** button. The Backup Wizard asks you to select what and where to back up, give a name to your back-up file that means something to you in the future, gives you a summary of what is intended, and lets you start the process. The window shown in Fig. 12.21, keeps you informed during the backing up process.

Backup Types

By default, during our demonstration, we have created a 'Normal' backup of the selected files. To see what other types of backup exist, first return to the opening screen of the Backup or Restore Wizard, then click the **Advance Mode** link to display the screen in Fig. 12.22.

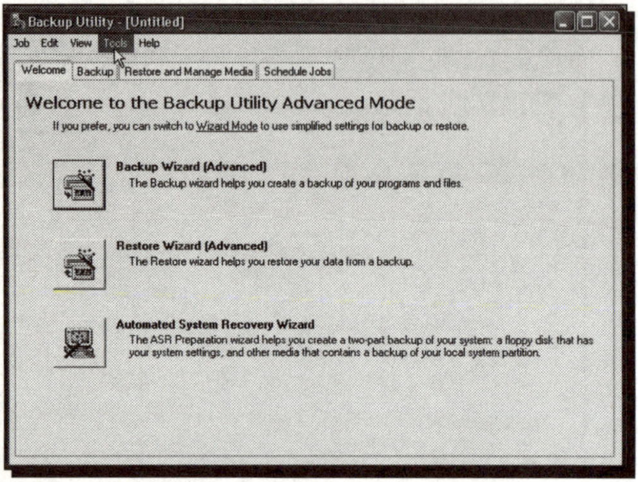

Fig. 12.22 The Advanced Backup Utility.

Next, use the **Tools, Options** command to open the Options dialogue box shown in Fig. 12.23.

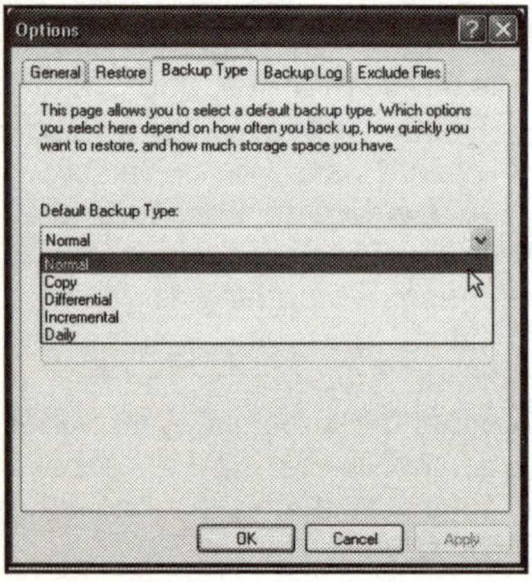

The Backup utility supports five methods of backing up data on your computer or network. These are listed on the next page.

Fig. 12.23 Selecting the Backup Type.

Normal Backup	Copies all selected files and marks them as having been backed up. With normal backups, you need only the most recent copy of the backup file or tape to restore all of the files. A normal backup is usually performed the first time you create a backup set.
Copy Backup	Copies all selected files but does not mark them as having been backed up. Copying is useful if you want to back up files between normal and incremental backups because it does not affect these other backup operations.
Differential Backup	Copies files created or changed since the last normal or incremental backup. It does not mark files as having been backed up. If you are performing a combination of normal and differential backups, restoring files and folders requires that you have the last normal as well as the last differential backup.
Incremental Backup	Backs up only those files created or changed since the last normal or incremental backup. It marks files as having been backed up. If you use a combination of normal and incremental backups, you will need to have the last normal backup set as well as all incremental backup sets in order to restore your data.
Daily Backup	Copies all selected files that have been modified the day the daily backup is performed. The backed-up files are not marked as having been backed up.

If the data files you are backing up are not very large in size, then using a normal backup is the easiest method. The backup set is stored on one disc or tape and restoring data from it is very easy.

If the amount of your storage space is limited, then back up your data using a combination of normal and incremental backups; it is the quickest method. However, recovering files can be time-consuming and difficult because the backup set can be stored on several discs or tapes.

Finally, backing up your data using a combination of normal and differential backups is more time-consuming, especially if your data changes frequently, but it is easier to restore the data because the backup set is usually stored on only a few discs or tapes.

Restoring your Files

To restore files that have been previously backed up, place the first disc of the set in the disc drive, activate the Backup or Restore Wizard and on the second Wizard screen click the Restore radio button followed by **Next**. Again, click the + sign to open the file structure in the left-hand pane of the Restore window, as shown in Fig. 12.24.

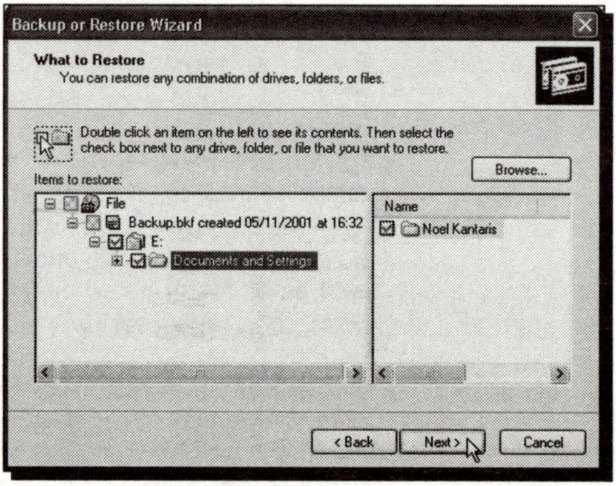

Fig. 12.24 Selecting the Backup Set to Restore.

Pressing the **Next** button, displays a Summary screen of the restore procedure. Clicking the **Advanced** button on this Summary screen, gives you a choice on where to restore the selected items, then what to do when restoring files that already exist, as shown in Fig. 12.25.

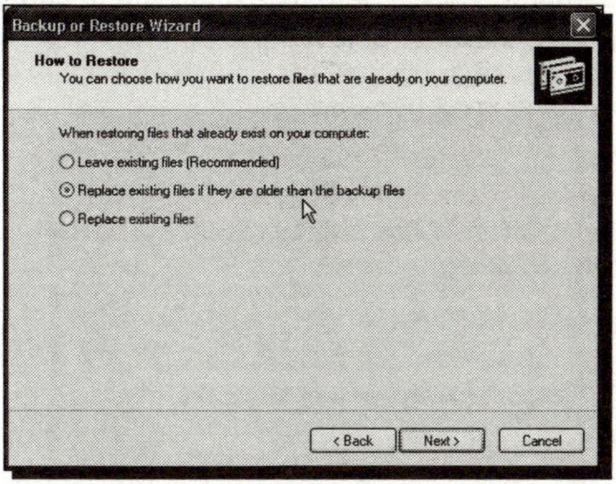

Fig. 12.25 Selecting How to Restore.

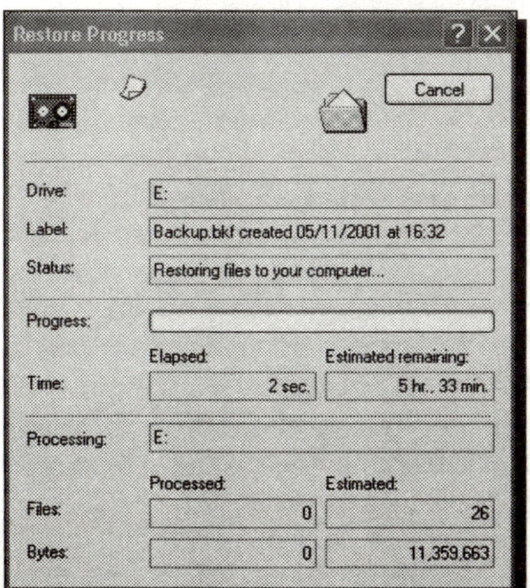

Fig. 12.26 The Restore Progress Screen.

A good choice would be to select the option to 'Replace the file on disk only if it is older than the backup copy'. After making an appropriate selection on file replacement and file security, pressing the **Finish** button causes the Wizard to start the restore process, as shown in Fig. 12.26.

Hopefully you should by now be completely sold on the Backup utility.

Scanning a Hard Disc for Errors

Windows XP incorporates a utility that can check the integrity of your hard disc, and if it finds any errors, it can attempt to repair them. To start this utility, click **My Computer** then in the displayed screen right-click the drive you want to check, select **Properties** from the drop-down menu and click the **Tools** tab to display the screen in Fig. 12.27.

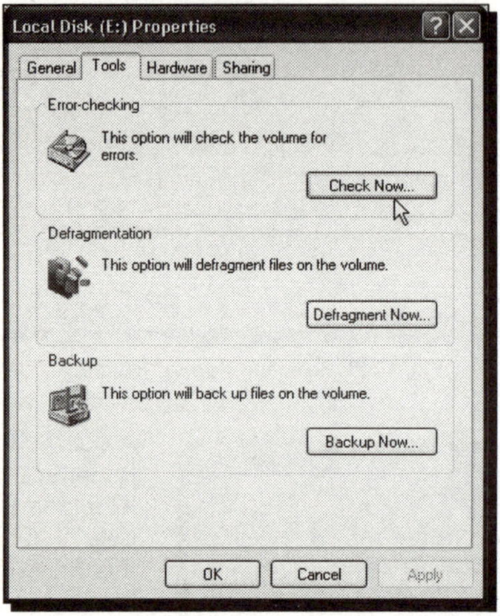

Fig. 12.27 The Disk Properties Screen.

As you can see, you have three choices; **Check Now** for disc errors, **Defragment Now**, or **Backup Now**. The last option is not available in the Windows XP Home edition.

Before you can start scanning your selected drive for errors, all running programs and applications on that drive must be closed. If you start this utility while a program on that drive is running, you will be informed of the fact in a warning box. If your disc or disc partition is formatted as NTFS (see next section), Windows automatically logs all file transactions, replaces bad clusters, and stores copies of key information for all files on the NTFS disc or disc partition.

Drive Conversion to NTFS

If you did not choose to convert your Windows XP drive from the FAT file system to the NTFS file system during installation, you can do so at any time. However, before doing so, you must consider the various advantages and disadvantages associated with such a conversion.

- Do not convert your Windows XP drive to the NTFS file system if you intend to retain your Windows 95/98/Me installation, and you want to exchange document files between the two systems (in both directions).
- Convert to NTFS if you want to get better file security, including the Encrypting File System (EFS) which protects data on your hard drive by encrypting each file with a randomly generated key.
- Convert to NTFS if you want better disc compression and better support for large hard discs.
- Convert to NTFS if you have a large hard drive and don't want its performance to degrade as it does with the FAT or FAT32 system.

Finally, from an NTFS partition you can browse, read and write to files on the FAT or FAT32 partitions, but Windows 95/98/Me cannot detect the NTFS partition, so it cannot interfere with its settings. However, the conversion to NTFS is one-way, therefore, you will not be able to convert back to FAT or FAT32.

To convert your Windows XP FAT or FAT32 drive to NTFS, click on **Start** then select **All Programs, Accessories, Command Prompt** option, then type the following commands in two lines, pressing the <Enter> key at the end of each line, as shown in Fig. 12.28 below.

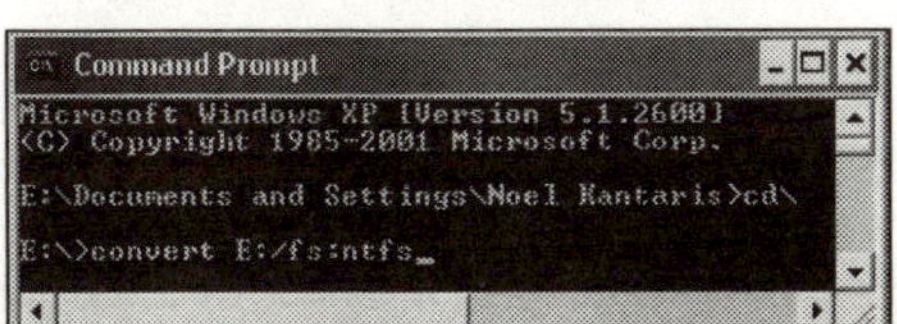

cd\
Convert E:/fs:ntfs

Fig. 12.28 Command Prompt.

System Properties

Clicking the **System** link pointed to in Fig. 12.29, displays the System Properties dialogue box shown in Fig. 12.30 on the next page.

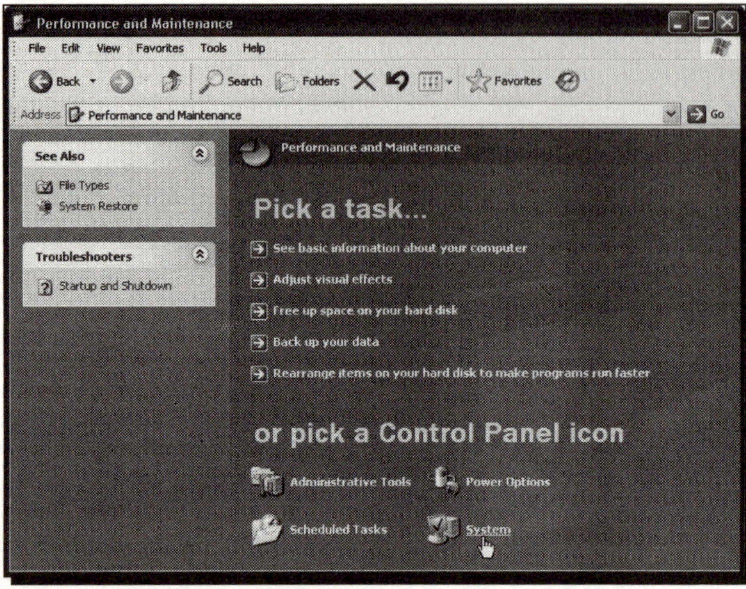

Fig. 12.29 The Performance and Maintenance Screen.

The System Properties multi-tab dialogue box provides you with basic information about your computer, its operating software, and its peripheral drivers. Some, but by no means all, of this information you can change. Below we give a short description of each tab sheet.

General Information

The General sheet of the System Properties screen, displays which version of Windows is installed on your PC, as shown in Fig. 12.30 on the next page. It also specifies registration information for your copy of Windows, and specifies the type of processor and the total physical memory of your PC.

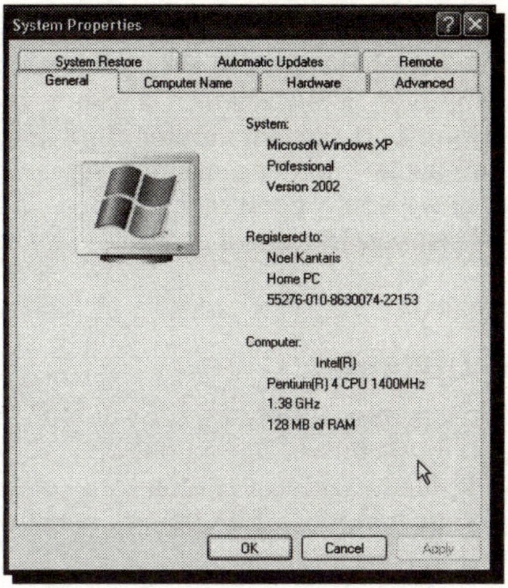

Fig. 12.30 The System Properties Dialogue Box.

Computer Name

The Computer Name sheet of the System Properties screen, provides a space for you to type a descriptive name for your PC. It also identifies the group to which it belongs and provides you with the means to change it.

Hardware

The Hardware sheet of the System Properties screen, allows you to use the Hardware Wizard to detect new hardware and change device properties. You can also use the Device Manager to change the properties and resource settings of hardware devices, and to copy or rename a hardware profile.

Advanced

The Advanced sheet of the System Properties screen, allows you to change settings for program resources, visual effects, and memory usage. You can also change the default operating system that starts when you turn on your computer.

Remote

The Remote sheet of the System Properties screen, allows you to activate remote assistance which allows a friend in another location to connect to your computer from another computer running a compatible operating system. After connection, your friend can view your computer screen and, with your permission, assist you to correct a problem by taking control of your PC.

Automatic Updates

The Automatic Updates sheet of the System Properties screen, allows you to choose one of three possible settings on how you want to be notified when updates are available for your computer, as shown in Fig. 12.31 below.

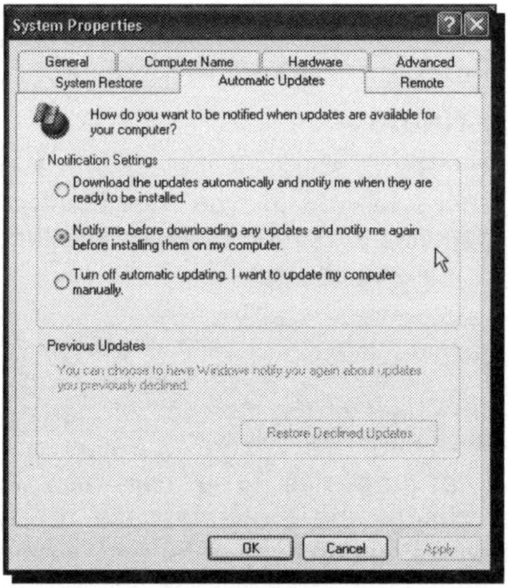

Fig. 12.31 The Automatic Updates Sheet of System Properties Dialogue Box.

If you select the middle option under **Notification Settings**, as shown in Fig. 12.31, and while you are connected to the Internet, you might get the warning message on the right of the Taskbar, as shown in Fig. 12.32 below.

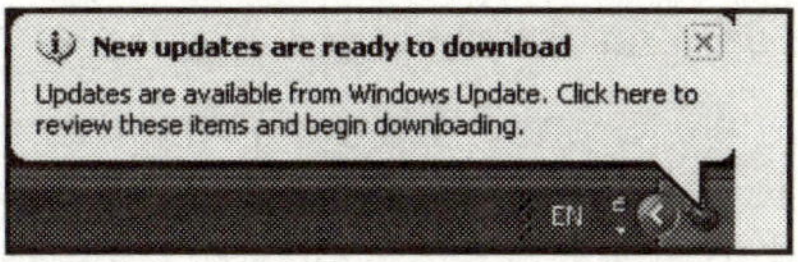

Fig. 12.32 The New Updates Warning Message.

Clicking the Windows Update icon on the Taskbar opens the Automatic Updates window shown in Fig. 12.33 below.

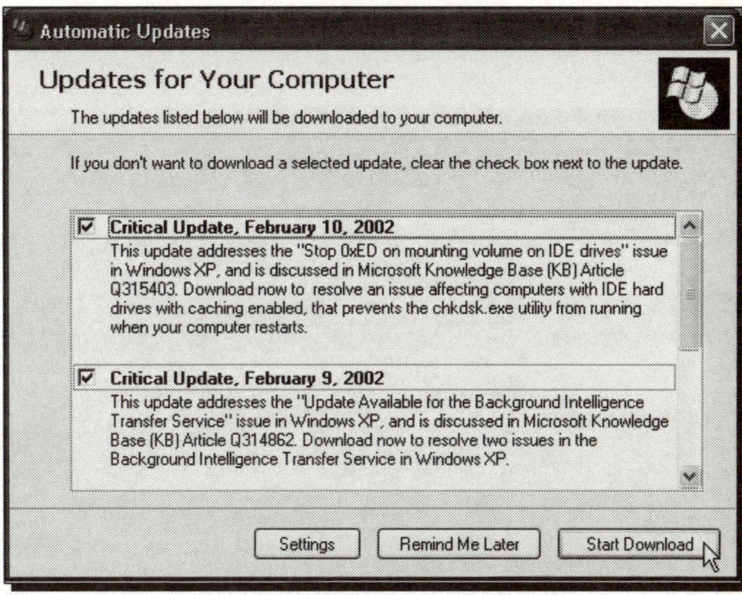

Fig. 12.33 The Automatic Updates Window.

If it is inconvenient to download these updates right now, click the **Remind Me Later** button, otherwise click the **Start Download** button.

From now on the system behaves exactly as if you had initiated a Manual Windows Update (see page 154).

System Restore

The System Restore sheet of the System Properties screen, allows you to turn off System Restore (not advisable) or change the drive settings or the amount of disc space available to System Restore on a selected drive.

If things go really wrong, System Restore can be used to return your PC to the last date it was working properly. Every time you start to install a new program, Windows XP takes a snapshot of your system prior to starting the new installation. Alternatively, you can force Windows to take a snapshot any time you choose.

To examine the System Restore utility, click the **System Restore** link (pointed to) under **See Also** on the left panel of the Performance and Maintenance screen shown in Fig. 12.34.

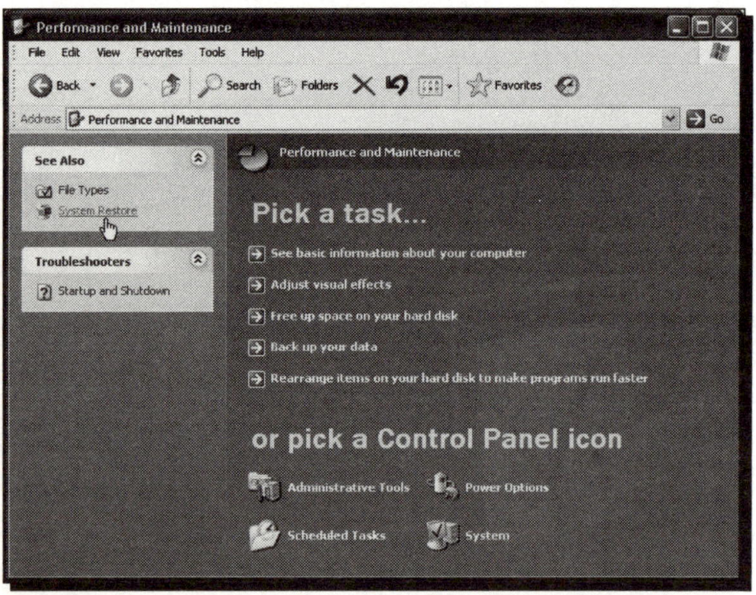

Fig. 12.34. The Performance and Maintenance Screen.

This opens the Welcome to System Restore screen shown in Fig. 12.35 on the next page.

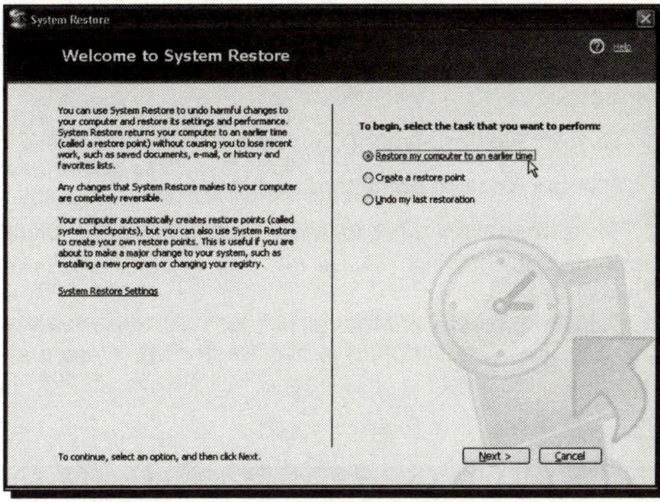

Fig. 12.35 The Welcome to System Restore Screen.

As you can see, you can select to Restore your computer to an earlier time, or create a Restore point. As an example, we chose the **Restore my computer to an earlier time** option, then clicked the **Next** button. This displays a further screen, as shown in Fig. 12.36 below.

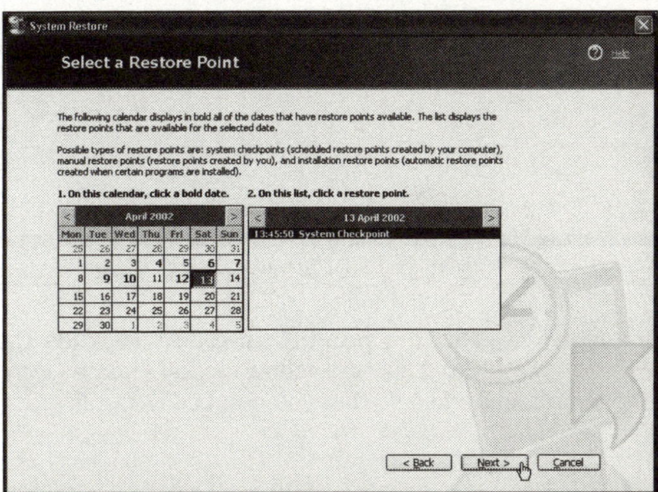

Fig. 12.36 Selecting a System Restore Point.

The dates shown in bold in the calendar are Restore points created by Windows XP. The three possible types of Restore points are:

- System Restore points created by your computer
- Manual Restore points created by you
- Restore points automatically created prior to installing certain programs.

If you select to create a Manual Restore point, Windows XP asks you to give a description of this Restore point so that you can identify it easily at a later stage, as shown in Fig. 12.37 below.

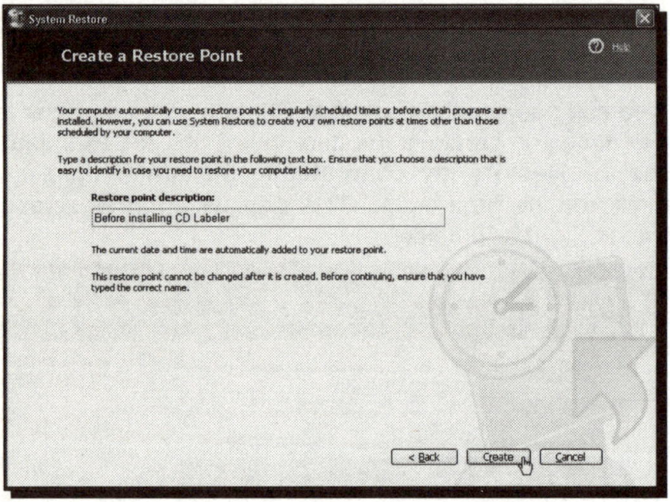

Fig. 12.37 A Manual Restore Point.

Having typed in a **Restore point description**, click the **Create** button to create it. This will show today's date with the description attached to it so that you can easily identify it.

13

Glossary of Terms

Access control	A security mechanism that determines which operations a user is authorised to perform on a PC, a file, a printer, etc.
Active	Describes the folder, window or icon that you are currently using or that is currently selected.
Active partition	A partition from which an x86-based computer starts up. The active partition must be a primary partition on a basic disc.
ActiveX	A set of technologies that enables software components to interact with one another in a networked environment, regardless of the language in which the components were created.
Add-in	A mini-program which runs in conjunction with another and enhances its functionality.
Address	A unique number or name that identifies a specific computer or user on a network.
Administrator	For Windows XP Professional, a person responsible for setting up and managing local computers, their user and group accounts, and assigning passwords and permissions.

Anonymous FTP	Anonymous FTP allows you to connect to a remote computer and transfer public files back to your local computer without the need to have a user ID and password.
ANSI	American National Standards Institute. A US government organisation responsible for improving communication standards.
Applet	A program that can be downloaded over a network and launched on the user's computer.
Application	Software (program) designed to carry out certain activity, such as word processing, or data management.
Archie	Archie is an Internet service that allows you to locate files that can be downloaded via FTP.
ASCII	A binary code representation of a character set. The name stands for 'American Standard Code for Information Interchange'.
ASP	Active Server Page. File format used for dynamic Web pages that get their data from a server based database.
Association	An identification of a filename extension to a program. This lets Windows open the program when its files are selected.
Attachment	A file that is added to an e-mail message for transmission.
Audio input device	A device that records music and voice input into your computer, such as a microphone or a CD-ROM player.
Authoring	The process of creating web documents or software.

AVI	Audio Video Interleaved. A Windows multimedia file format for sound and moving pictures.
Backbone	The main transmission lines of the Internet, running at over 45Mbps (million bits per second).
Background	An image, colour or texture which forms the background of a Web page or document.
Backup	To make a back-up copy of a file or a disc for safekeeping.
Bandwidth	The range of transmission frequencies a network can use. The greater the bandwidth the more information that can be transferred over a network.
Banner	An advertising graphic shown on a Web page.
BASIC	Beginner's All-purpose Symbolic Instruction Code - a high-level programming language.
Basic volume	A primary partition or logical drive that resides on a basic disc.
Batch file	A file that contains commands which are automatically executed when the file is run.
Baud rate	The speed at which a modem communicates.
BBS	Bulletin Board System, a computer equipped with software and telecoms links that allow it to act as an information host for remote computer systems.

Beta test	A test of software that is still under development, by people actually using the software.
Binary	A base-2 number system in which values are expressed as combinations of two digits, 0 and 1.
BinHex	A file conversion format that converts binary files to ASCII text files.
BIOS	On x86-based computers, the set of software routines that test hardware at startup, start the operating system, and support the transfer of data among hardware devices.
Bit	The smallest unit of information handled by a computer.
Bitmap	A technique for managing the image displayed on a computer screen.
Bookmark	A marker inserted at a specific point in a document. Used as a target for a hypertext link, or to enable a user to return for later reference.
Boot partition	The partition on a hard disc that contains the operating system and its support files.
Boot up	To start your computer by switching it on, which initiates a self test of its Random Access Memory (RAM), then loads the necessary system files.
Bound control	A control on a database form, report or data access page that is tied to a field in an underlying table or query.
Broadband	A communications systems in which the medium of transmission (such as a wire or fibre-optic cable) carries multiple messages at a time.

Broadcast	An address that is destined for all hosts on a particular network segment.
Browse	A button in some Windows dialogue boxes that lets you view a list of files and folders before you make a selection. Also to view a Web page.
Browser	A program, like the Internet Explorer, that lets you view Web pages.
Bug	An error in coding or logic that causes a program to malfunction.
Bus	A communication line used for data transfer among the components of a computer system.
Button	A graphic element or icon in a dialogue box or toolbar that performs a specified function.
Bytes	A unit of data that holds a single character, such as a letter, a digit.
Cable modem	A device that enables a broadband connection to the Internet by using cable television infrastructure.
Cache	An area of memory, or disc space, reserved for data, which speeds up downloading.
Card	A removable printed-circuit board that is plugged into a computer expansion slot.
CD-R	Recordable compact disc.
CD-ROM	Compact Disc - Read Only Memory; an optical disc which information may be read from but not written to.
CD-RW	Rewritable compact disc. Data can be copied to the CD on more than one occasion and can be erased.

CGI	Common Gateway Interface - a convention for servers to communicate with local applications and allow users to provide information to scripts attached to web pages, usually through forms.
Cgi-bin	The most common name of a directory on a web server in which CGI programs are stored.
Chart	A graphical view of data that is used to visually display trends, patterns, and comparisons.
Click	To press and release a mouse button once without moving the mouse.
Client	A computer that has access to services over a computer network. The computer providing the services is a server.
Client application	A Windows application that can accept linked, or embedded, objects.
Clipboard	A temporary storage area of memory, where text and graphics are stored with the cut and copy actions. The Office XP clipboard can store up to 24 items.
Command	An instruction given to a computer to carry out a particular action.
Command prompt	A window used to interface with the MS-DOS operating system.
Compressed file	One that is compacted to save server space and reduce transfer times. Typical file extensions for compressed files include .zip (DOS/Windows) and .tar (UNIX).
Configuration	A general purpose term referring to the way you have your computer set up.

Context menu	A menu that opens when you right-click the mouse button on a feature.
Controls	Objects on a form, report, or data access page that display data, perform actions, or are used for decoration.
Cookies	Files stored on your hard drive by your Web browser that hold information for it to use.
CPU	The Central Processing Unit; the main chip that executes all instructions entered into a computer.
Cyberspace	Originated by William Gibson in his novel 'Neuromancer', now used to describe the Internet and the other computer networks.
Data access page	A Web page, created by Access, that has a connection to a database; you can view, add, edit, and manipulate the data in this page.
Data packet	A unit of information transmitted as a whole from one device to another on a network.
Database	A collection of data related to a particular topic or purpose.
DBMS	Database management system - A software interface between the database and the user.
Default	The command, device or option automatically chosen.
Defragmentation	The process of rewriting parts of a file to contiguous sectors on a hard disc to increase the speed of access and retrieval.

Desktop	The Windows screen working background.
Device driver	A special file that must be loaded into memory for Windows to be able to address a specific procedure or hardware device.
Device name	A logical name used by an operating system to identify a device, such as LPT1 or COM1 for the parallel or serial printer.
Dial-up Connection	A popular form of Net connection for the home user, over standard telephone lines.
Dialogue box	A window displayed on the screen to allow the user to enter information.
Digital signature	A means for originators of a message, file, or other digitally encoded information to bind their identity to the information.
Direct Connection	A permanent connection between your computer system and the Internet.
Directory	An area on disc where information relating to a group of files is kept. Also known as a folder.
Disc	A device on which you can store programs and data.
Disconnect	To detach a drive, port or computer from a shared device, or to break an Internet connection.
Display adapter	An expansion board that plugs into a PC to give it display capabilities.

DLL	Dynamic Link Library; An OS feature that allows files with the .dll extensions to be loaded only when needed by the program.
Document	A file produced by an application program. When used in reference to the Web, a document is any file containing text, media or hyperlinks that can be transferred from an HTTP server to a browser.
Domain	A group of devices, servers and computers on a network.
Domain Name	The name of an Internet site, for example www.kantaris.com, which allows you to reference Internet sites without knowing their true numerical address.
DOS	Disc Operating System. A collection of small specialised programs that allow interaction between user and computer.
Double-click	To quickly press and release a mouse button twice.
Download	To transfer to your computer a file, or data, from another computer.
DPI	Dots Per Inch - a resolution standard for laser printers.
Drag	To move an object on the screen by pressing and holding down the left mouse button while moving the mouse.
Drive name	The letter followed by a colon which identifies a floppy or hard disc drive.
Drop-down list	A menu item that can be clicked to open extra items that can be selected.

DSL	Digital Subscriber Line - a broad-band connection to the Internet through existing copper telephone wires.
Dual boot	A PC configuration that can start two different operating systems.
DVD	Digital Video Disc; a type of optical disc technology. It looks like a CD but can store greater amounts of data.
E-mail	Electronic Mail - A system that allows computer users to send and receive messages electronically.
EISA	Extended Industry Standard Architecture, for construction of PCs with the Intel 32-bit micro-processor.
Embedded object	Information in a document that is 'copied' from its source application. Selecting the object opens the creating application from within the document.
Encrypted password	A password that is scrambled.
Engine	Software used by search services.
Ethernet	A very common method of networking computers in a LAN.
Expansion slot	A socket in a computer, designed to hold expansion boards and connect them to the system bus.
Extract a file	Create an uncompressed copy of the file in a folder you specify.
FAQ	Frequently Asked Questions - A common feature on the Internet, FAQs are files of answers to commonly asked questions.
FAT	The File Allocation Table. An area on disc where information is kept on which part of the disc a file is located.

File extension	The suffix following the period in a filename. Windows uses this to identify the source application program. For example **.mdb** indicates a Microsoft Access file.
Filename	The name given to a file. In Windows 95 and above this can be up to 256 characters long.
Filter	A set of criteria that is applied to data to show a subset of the data.
Firewall	Security measures designed to protect a networked system from unauthorised access.
Floppy disc	A removable disc on which information can be stored magnetically.
Folder	An area used to store a group of files, usually with a common link.
Font	A graphic design representing a set of characters, numbers and symbols.
Format	The structure of a file that defines the way it is stored and laid out on the screen or in print.
Fragmentation	The scattering of parts of the same file over different areas of the disc.
Free space	Available disc space that can be used to create logical drives within an extended partition.
Freeware	Software that is available for downloading and unlimited use without charge.
FTP	File Transfer Protocol. The procedure for connecting to a remote computer and transferring files.

Function key	One of the series of 10 or 12 keys marked with the letter F and a numeral, used for specific operations.
Gateway	A computer system that allows otherwise incompatible networks to communicate with each other.
GIF	Graphics Interchange Format, a common standard for images on the Web.
Gigabyte	(GB); 1,024 megabytes. Usually thought of as one billion bytes.
Graphic	A picture or illustration, also called an image. Formats include GIF, JPEG, BMP, PCX, and TIFF.
Graphics card	A device that controls the display on the monitor and other allied functions.
Group	A collection of users, computers, contacts, and other groups.
GUI	A Graphic User Interface, such as Windows 98, the software front-end meant to provide an attractive and easy to use interface.
Handshaking	A series of signals acknowledging that communication can take place between computers or other devices.
Hard copy	Output on paper.
Hard disc	A device built into the computer for holding programs and data.
Hardware	The equipment that makes up a computer system, excluding the programs or software.
Help	A Windows system that gives you instructions and additional information on using a program.

Helper application	A program allowing you to view multimedia files that your web browser cannot handle internally.
Hibernation	A state in which your computer shuts down after saving everything in memory on your hard disc.
Hit	A single request from a web browser for a single item from a web server.
Home page	The document displayed when you first open your Web browser, or the first document you come to at a Web site.
Host	Computer connected directly to the Internet that provides services to other local and/or remote computers.
Hotlist	A list of frequently used Web locations and URL addresses.
HTML	HyperText Markup Language, the format used in documents on the Web.
HTML editor	Authoring tool which assists with the creation of HTML pages.
HTTP	HyperText Transport Protocol, the system used to link and transfer hypertext documents on the Web.
Hub	A common connection point for devices in a network.
Hyperlink	A segment of text, or an image, that refers to another document on the Web, an Intranet or your PC.
Hypermedia	Hypertext extended to include linked multimedia.
Hypertext	A system that allows documents to be cross-linked so that the reader can explore related links, or documents, by clicking on a highlighted symbol.

Icon	A small graphic image, or button, that represents a function or object. Clicking on an icon produces an action.
ICS	Internet Connection Sharing.
Image	See graphic.
IMEs	Input Method Editors for entering East Asian language characters.
Insertion point	A flashing bar that shows where typed text will be entered into a document.
Interface	A device that allows you to connect a computer to its peripherals.
Internet	The global system of computer networks.
Intranet	A private network inside an organisation using the same kind of software as the Internet.
IP	Internet Protocol - The rules that provide basic Internet functions.
IP Address	Internet Protocol Address - every computer on the Internet has a unique identifying number.
ISA	Industry Standard Architecture; a standard for internal connections in PCs.
ISDN	Integrated Services Digital Network, a telecom standard using digital transmission technology to support voice, video and data communications applications over regular telephone lines.
ISP	Internet Service Provider - A company that offers access to the Internet.

Java	An object-oriented programming language created by Sun Microsystems for developing applications and applets that are capable of running on any computer, regardless of the operating system.
JPEG/JPG	Joint Photographic Experts Group, a popular cross-platform format for image files. JPEG is best suited for true colour original images.
Kernel	The core of layered architecture that manages the most basic operations of the operating system and the computer's processor.
Kilobyte	(KB); 1024 bytes of information or storage space.
LAN	Local Area Network - High-speed, privately-owned network covering a limited geographical area, such as an office or a building.
Laptop	A portable computer small enough to sit on your lap.
LCD	Liquid Crystal Display.
Linked object	An object that is inserted into a document but still exists in the source file. Changing the original object automatically updates it within the linked document.
Links	The hypertext connections between Web pages.
Linux	A version of the UNIX operating system for PCs which incorporates a Graphical User Interface (GUI) similar to that of Microsoft Windows.

Local	A resource that is located on your computer, not linked to it over a network.
Location	An Internet address.
Log on	To gain access to a network.
MBR	The first sector on a hard disc, which starts the process of booting the computer.
MCI	Media Control Interface - a standard for files and multimedia devices.
Megabyte	(MB); 1024 kilobytes of information or storage space.
Megahertz	(MHz); Speed of processor in millions of cycles per second.
Memory	Part of computer consisting of storage elements organised into addressable locations that can hold data and instructions.
Menu	A list of available options in an application.
Menu bar	The horizontal bar that lists the names of menus.
MIDI	Musical Instrument Digital Interface - enables devices to transmit and receive sound and music messages.
MIME	Multipurpose Internet Mail Extensions, a messaging standard that allows Internet users to exchange e-mail messages enhanced with graphics, video and voice.
MIPS	Million Instructions Per Second; measures speed of a system.

Modem	Short for Modulator-demodulator devices. An electronic device that lets computers communicate electronically.
Monitor	The display device connected to your PC, also called a screen.
Mouse	A device used to manipulate a pointer around your display and activate processes by pressing buttons.
MPEG	Motion Picture Experts Group - a video file format offering excellent quality in a relatively small file.
MS-DOS	Microsoft's implementation of the Disc Operating System for PCs.
Multimedia	The use of photographs, music and sound and movie images in a presentation.
Multitasking	Performing more than one operation at the same time.
My Documents	A folder that provides a convenient place to store documents, graphics, or other files you want to access quickly.
Network	Two or more computers connected together to share resources.
Network adapter	A device that connects your computer to a network.
Network server	Central computer which stores files for several linked computers.
Node	Any single computer connected to a network.
NTFS file system	An advanced file system that provides performance, security, reliability, and advanced features that are not found in any version of FAT.

ODBC	Open DataBase Connectivity - A standard protocol for accessing information in a SQL database server.
OLE	Object Linking and Embedding - A technology for transferring and sharing information among software applications.
Online	Having access to the Internet.
Online Service	Services such as America On-line and CompuServe that provide content to subscribers and usually connections to the Internet.
Operating system	Software that runs a computer.
Page	An HTML document, or Web site.
Parallel port	The input/output connector for a parallel interface device. Printers are generally plugged into a parallel port.
Partition	A portion of a physical disc that functions as though it were a physically separate disc.
Password	A unique character string used to gain access to a network, program, or mailbox.
PATH	The location of a file in the directory tree.
PCI	Peripheral Component Interconnect - a type of slot in your computer which accepts similar type peripheral cards.
Peripheral	Any device attached to a PC.
Perl	A popular language for programming CGI applications.

PIF file	Program information file - gives information to Windows about an MS-DOS application.
Pixel	A picture element on screen; the smallest element that can be independently assigned colour and intensity.
Plug-and-play	Hardware which can be plugged into a PC and be used immediately without configuration.
POP3	Post Office Protocol - a method of storing and returning e-mail.
Port	The place where information goes into or out of a computer, e.g. a modem might be connected to the serial port.
Posix	The specification for a look-alike UNIX operating system drawn up by the American National Standards Institute (ANSI). Linux is an independent Posix implementation.
PostScript	A page-description language (PDL), developed by Adobe Systems for printing on laser printers.
PPP	Point-to-Point Protocol - One of two methods (see SLIP) for using special software to establish a temporary direct connection to the Internet over regular phone lines.
Print queue	A list of print jobs waiting to be sent to a printer.
Program	A set of instructions which cause a computer to perform tasks.
Protocol	A set of rules or standards that define how computers communicate with each other.

Query	The set of keywords and operators sent by a user to a search engine, or a database search request.
Queue	A list of e-mail messages waiting to be sent over the Internet.
RAM	Random Access Memory. The computer's volatile memory. Data held in it is lost when power is switched off.
Real mode	MS-DOS mode, typically used to run programs, such as MS-DOS games, that will not run under Windows.
Refresh	To update displayed information with current data.
Registered file type	File types that are tracked by the system registry and are recognised by the programs you have installed on your computer.
Registry	A database where information about a computer's configuration is deposited. The registry contains information that Windows continually references during its operation.
Remote computer	A computer that you can access only by using a communications line or a communications device, such as a network card or a modem.
Resource	A directory, or printer, that can be shared over a network.
Right-click	To click the right mouse button once.
Robot	A Web agent that visits sites, by requesting documents from them, for the purposes of indexing for search engines. Also known as Wanderers, Crawlers, or Spiders.

ROM	Read Only Memory. A PC's non-volatile memory. Data is written into this memory at manufacture and is not affected by power loss.
Root	The highest or uppermost level in a hierarchically organised disc directory.
RTF	Rich Text Format. An enhanced form of text that includes basic formatting and is used for transferring data between applications, or in e-mail messages.
Screen saver	A moving picture or pattern that appears on your screen when you have not used the mouse or keyboard for a specified period of time.
Script	A type of program consisting of a set of instructions to an application or tool program.
Scroll bar	A bar that appears at the right side or bottom edge of a window.
Search	Submit a query to a search engine.
Search engine	A program that helps users find information across the Internet.
Serial interface	An interface that transfers data as individual bits.
Server	A computer system that manages and delivers information for client computers.
Shared resource	Any device, program or file that is available to network users.
Shareware	Software that is available on public networks and bulletin boards. Users are expected to pay a nominal amount to the software developer.

Shortcut	A link to any item accessible on your computer or on a network, such as a program, file, folder, disc drive, Web page, printer, or another computer.
Signature file	An ASCII text file, maintained within e-mail programs, that contains text for your signature.
Site	A place on the Internet. Every Web page has a location where it resides which is called its site.
SLIP	Serial Line Internet Protocol, a method of Internet connection that enables computers to use phone lines via a modem to connect to the Internet.
Smart tag	New to Office XP. A button that when clicked, opens a shortcut menu to give fast access to other features or Office applications.
SMTP	Simple Mail Transfer Protocol - a protocol dictating how e-mail messages are exchanged over the Internet.
Socket	An endpoint for sending and receiving data between computers.
Software	The programs and instructions that control your PC.
Spamming	Sending the same message to a large number of mailing lists or newsgroups. Also to overload a Web page with excessive keywords in an attempt to get a better search ranking.
Spider	See robot.
Spooler	Software which handles transfer of information to a store to be used by a peripheral device.

SQL	Structured Query Language, used with relational databases.
SSL	Secure Sockets Layer, the standard transmission security protocol developed by Netscape, which has been put into the public domain.
Standby	A state in which your computer consumes less power when it is idle, but remains available for immediate use.
Subscribe	To become a member of.
Surfing	The process of looking around the Internet.
SVGA	Super Video Graphics Array; it has all the VGA modes but with 256, or more, colours.
Swap file	An area of your hard disc used to store temporary operating files, also known as virtual memory.
Sysop	System Operator - A person responsible for the physical operations of a computer system or network resource.
System disc	A disc containing files to enable a PC to start up.
System files	Files used by Windows to load, configure, and run the operating system.
Task bar	The bar that by default is located at the bottom of your screen whenever Windows is running. It contains the Start button, buttons for all the applications that are open, and icons for other applications.

Task Manager	A utility that provides information about programs and processes running on the computer. Using Task Manager, you can end or run programs and end processes, and display a dynamic overview of your computer's performance.
Task Pane	A pane or sub-window that gives a range of options pertaining to the task currently being performed. New to Office XP applications.
TCP/IP	Transmission Control Protocol/ Internet Protocol, combined protocols that perform the transfer of data between two computers. TCP monitors and ensures the correct transfer of data. IP receives the data, breaks it up into packets, and sends it to a network within the Internet.
Telnet	A program which allows people to remotely use computers across networks.
Text file	An unformatted file of text characters saved in ASCII format.
Thread	An ongoing message-based conversation on a single subject.
Thumbnail	A small graphic image.
TIFF	Tag Image File Format - a popular graphic image file format.
Toggle	To turn an action on and off with the same switch.
Tool	Software program used to support Web site creation and management.
Toolbar	A bar containing buttons or icons giving quick access to commands.

TrueType fonts	Fonts that can be scaled to any size and print as they show on the screen.
UNC	Universal Naming Convention - A convention for files that provides a machine independent means of locating the file that is particularly useful in Web based applications.
Unicode encoding	A character encoding standard developed by the Unicode Consortium that represents almost all of the written languages of the world.
Uninstall	When referring to software, the act of removing program files and folders from your hard disc and removing related data from your registry so the software is no longer available.
UNIX	Multitasking, multi-user computer operating system that is run by many computers that are connected to the Internet. Linux is a version of Unix.
Upload/Download	The process of transferring files between computers. Files are uploaded from your computer to another and downloaded from another computer to your own.
URL	Uniform Resource Locator, the addressing system used on the Web, containing information about the method of access, the server to be accessed and the path of the file to be accessed.
USB	Universal Serial Bus - an external bus standard that enables data transfer rates of 12 Mbps.

Usenet	Informal network of computers that allow the posting and reading of messages in newsgroups that focus on specific topics.
User ID	The unique identifier, usually used in conjunction with a password, which identifies you on a computer.
Virtual Reality	Simulations of real or imaginary worlds, rendered on a flat two-dimensional screen but appearing three-dimensional.
Virus	A malicious program, downloaded from a web site or disc, designed to wipe out information on your computer.
Volume	An area of storage on a hard disc. A volume is formatted by using a file system, such as FAT or NTFS, and has a drive letter assigned to it.
W3C	The World Wide Web Consortium that is steering standards development for the Web.
WAIS	Wide Area Information Server, a Net-wide system for looking up specific information in Internet databases.
WAN	A communications network connecting geographically separated computers, printers, and other devices.
Watermark	Toned down image or text that appears in the background of a printed page.
WAV	Waveform Audio (**.wav**) - a common audio file format for DOS/Windows computers.

Web	A network of hypertext-based multimedia information servers. Browsers are used to view any information on the Web.
Web Page	An HTML document that is accessible on the Web.
Webmaster	One whose job it is to manage a web site.
WINSOCK	A Microsoft Windows file that provides the interface to TCP/IP services.
Wizard	A Microsoft tool that shows how to perform certain operations, or asks you questions and then creates an object depending on your answers.

Index